All is True

All is True

The Claims and Strategies of Realist Fiction

Lilian R. Furst

Duke University Press

Durham and London

1995

© 1995 Duke University Press
All rights reserved
Printed in the United States of America
on acid-free paper ∞
Designed by Cherie Holma Westmoreland
Typeset in Joanna with Helvetica Condensed display
by Keystone Typesetting, Inc.

Library of Congress Cataloging-in-Publication Data

Furst, Lilian R.
All is true : the claims and strategies of realist fiction
/ Lilian R. Furst.
p. cm.
Includes bibliographical references and index.
ISBN 0-8223-1632-3 (cloth). —
ISBN 0-8223-1646-3 (paper)
1. Criticism. 2. Realism in literature. 3. Fiction—
19th century—History and criticism. I. Title.
PN98.R4F87 1995
809.3'912—dc20   95-13072   CIP

Contents

ॐ

Preface

ॐ

This book has been long in the making. Its origins lie over ten years back when I was a fellow at the Stanford Humanities Center, then under the direction of Ian Watt. Rereading his *Rise of the Novel*, I noted the three features that he identifies as the hallmarks of realism: particularity of time, of place, and of characterization. It struck me that of the three, particularity of place had received relatively little critical attention. Most studies are either phenomenological, in the wake of Gaston Bachelard's *Poétique de l'espace*, or sociohistorical, concerned with reconstructing Balzac's or Zola's Paris, the London of Dickens, Thomas Mann's Lübeck, and so on. While such approaches often produce interesting findings, they do not really deal with the literary and rhetorical dimensions of place.

The topic intrigued me increasingly as I saw American students, most of whom had caught only fleeting glimpses of European land- and cityscapes in films and pictures, very well able to develop a distinct sense of the location of a fictive action solely from reading the text. I also became aware of the vividness of my perception (derived from Steinbeck's *Grapes of Wrath*) of the desert on old Route 66 when I was hesitant to drive through it during a notorious heat wave even in an air-conditioned car and on a modern interstate highway, patrolled, as I discovered, by helicopters and lined with barrels of water. The Joads' experience of that stretch of road had evidently strongly impressed itself on my mind. So the issues addressed in this book came to be formulated: How does a text create a sense of place for readers? What literary strategies are brought into play? By what means are readers persuaded to believe in the authenticity of the illusion?

The larger problem underlying these specific questions has been very succinctly summarized by the French novelist and critic, Michel Butor, who asks in his meditation on the poetry of narrative: "D'où vient ce singulier pouvoir, rendre présents les objets absents, cette 'hantise', comment la chambre imaginaire peut-elle s'imposer à ce point?"[1] ("From where does this strange power come, of making absent objects present, this 'haunting,' how can the imaginary room impress itself to this degree?"). This comes very close to the heart of the matter that puzzled me. By his invocation of "haunting," Butor seems to suggest an almost supernatural procedure, yet he concedes that in the last resort "ces objets sont à leur tour des 'mots'" ("these objects are in their turn 'words'"). The places of realist fiction can be conveyed only in words and are therefore ultimately the product of an illusion: "un stable fantasme" ("a stable illusion"), as Butor calls it. This essentially illusory nature of art, however realistic it may strive to appear, was already fully recognized in the later half of the nineteenth century, although it was neither widely voiced nor acknowledged. In a letter to Louise Colet of 16 September 1853, Flaubert proclaims: "La première qualité de l'Art et son but est l'illusion"[2] ("The primary quality of art and its aim is illusion"). Nietzsche, in 1880, puts it more tersely and violently: "Der Realismus in der Kunst Täuschung"[3] ("Realism in art, deception").

To unmask realism as illusion or deception—or, more broadly, as a literary artifact—does not detract from, much less explain, its capacity to haunt readers through its strange power of making absent objects not only present but credible. On the contrary, when its intrinsic masquerade is accepted, the mystery of how it attains its effects is heightened. If realist fiction is an illusion (or a deception), what disposes readers to pretend to believe in its semblance of veracity? The answer is hinted at in Butor's comment that the objects are in turn "words." "Lire, en effet, est un travail de langage"[4] ("To read is, in fact, a labor of language"), Barthes reminds us at the beginning of S/Z. For the presentation of place, that "labor of language" would likely reside primarily in the analysis of description. I assumed initially, as most critics have done, that description was realism's major tactic. The lengthy expositions of the Vauquer boardinghouse in the opening pages of Balzac's Le Père Goriot and of the house in his Eugénie Grandet remain in readers' memory, not least for the irritation provoked by these overdetermined, obsessive inventories of every detail that seem to delay the beginning of the action proper—until we come to understand, on rereading, that description of environment is already action in Balzac.

But this tendency to an automatic association of place with description is disproved by many major nineteenth-century texts. George Eliot's Middlemarch, beyond doubt the foremost English novel of the period, and one, moreover, that derives its very title from its location, is wholly devoid of any description of the town of the kind that Balzac would have delighted in for page after page. The television Masterpiece Theater adaptation of Middlemarch opened each episode with the same panoramic glimpse of street scenes—an appropriate and ingenious indication to viewers of the centrality of this place in the narrative—yet the scenes were all added, freshly invented material, for description of Middlemarch is remarkable for its absence in Eliot's text. A similar scantiness of description is characteristic of Thomas Mann's Buddenbrooks and of the novels of Henry James, in which place is pivotal to behavior and hence to plot, yet is not shown in descriptive passages.

So I came to two allied realizations. First, the creation of a sense of place for readers devolves from many narrative strategies beyond overt description. It depends closely on the establishment of a sound, trusting relationship between narrating voice and readers, a secure narrative contract that disposes readers to persuasion by the rhetoric. The words printed on the page are designed to act on readers in certain ways: to encourage belief in the illusion by fostering a shared angle of vision with the narrator and, at times, with the protagonists and by implicating place causally in the action. The role and creation of place turns out to be far more complex in realist narrative, as well as more vitally encoded, than I had anticipated.

This in turn led to my second realization: that the presentation of place cannot simply be separated out as a single strand of realism. As the scene and not infrequently the partial motivation of the action, place has a crucial function in the whole enterprise of making believable the world inhabited by the characters. Place not only intersects with time, but also figures quite prominently in the protagonists' minds, conditioning and often limiting their possibilities. It is a product of a multiplicity of narrative strategies and, as such, fundamentally grounded in the aesthetics of realism. For this reason, the horizon of my study necessarily expanded from an examination of place into a wider consideration of the ways in which realism conceptualized itself and how it has been perceived by subsequent generations of critics and readers. In so doing, I aim not to add yet another theory to the plethora of theories of realism but rather, by means of a constellated series of arguments about its key, contested features, to evolve a mode of reading that reconciles starkly antithetical views without canceling any out. Referentiality and textuality—that is, the belief, on the one hand, that realism's portrayal of life is directly based on an extraneous model, and, on the other, that it is a purely verbal product—are not mutually exclusive, as is generally supposed. I seek in this book to probe and map where and how they interact in the creation of place and, beyond that, in the fashioning of the realist text.

My method is reader-oriented. I distinguish this approach from a reader response one, which is subjective, while the reader-oriented method is concerned with the cognitive process whereby readers construct the text. The choice of texts was perplexing. I faced an immense wealth of potential material and a variety of options. I rejected any attempt at encyclopedic coverage, because I am not composing a complete account, let alone a history of realism. I was equally averse to concentrating on only one or two authors, because I am a comparatist by inclination and because I sought a reasonably representative sample. I decided, therefore, to focus the study on third-person narration, since this is the dominant mode of realist fiction, and on a few major, paradigmatic works: Balzac's *Eugénie Grandet*, Flaubert's *Madame Bovary*, George Eliot's *Middlemarch*, Zola's *L'Assommoir*, *The Bostonians* by Henry James, and Thomas Mann's *Buddenbrooks*, invoking other novels as the occasion warranted. Ideally I would have liked to range more widely over Italian, Spanish, Russian, Scandinavian, East European, and non-European writings, but I refrained from such expansion because of my growing conviction as the study progressed that rereading realism is indeed literally "a labor of language," the prerequisite for which is immediate contact with the original language and awareness of all its resonances. However, it is my hope that readers with expertise in other areas will be able to explore the aptness of my approach for their particular fields.

The translation of citations is mine unless otherwise stated, and the italics or emphases are the authors', again unless otherwise noted. Sources are given briefly in notes at the end of the text, all keyed to a full bibliography. I use the pronoun "his" generically, as it were, and without sexism so as to avoid the awkwardness of his/hers in each instance.

I have, over the years, been given generous support. I want to record my thanks to the Stanford Humanities Center, where the project was started and whose facilities I was graciously permitted to use again in the final stages. The work of one of my fellow fellows in 1982, Kendall L. Walton, provided an important impetus to the development of my thinking. I am also grateful to the National Humanities Center for a National Endowment for the Humanities Fellowship in 1988–89, which gave me the luxury of time to read, reflect, and experiment as the project began to take shape, and to the Institute for the Arts and Humanities at the University of North Carolina at Chapel Hill for a first summer session fellowship in 1990 to complete a draft of the opening chapter. I thank Patricia Merivale for her searching and stimulating questions at the International Comparative Literature Association meeting in Munich in August 1988 in response to a paper that was to become the nucleus of chapter 5. The late Raymond A. Prier gave me invaluable support, not only by reading each chapter hot off the printer, but above all by believing that I should and could write this book. I am indebted to Véronique Machelidon, Sasha Strelka, and Ian Wilson, for their competence and cheerful willingness to do library work for me. Reynolds Smith, executive editor at Duke University Press, has generously and patiently given me the benefit of his expertise, especially in the choice of a title, while the two very perceptive readers of the manuscript rekindled my enthusiasm by offering constructive suggestions. Finally, I would like to express my gratitude to those students who took my course on realism and to the members of my 1992 National Endowment for the Humanities Summer Seminar for College Teachers who thought this a good way to set about rereading realism.

Chapel Hill/Stanford, June 1994

1

Truth to Tell

৯৭

That book was made by Mr. Mark Twain, and he told the truth mainly.
There were things which he stretched, but mainly
he told the truth.—Mark Twain

"All is true," the narrator declares at the opening of *Le Père Goriot* before launching into the description of the Vauquer boardinghouse and its inhabitants in 1819.[1] The phrase makes an immediate impact on readers through both its appearance in a foreign language and its typographical presentation in italics. It functions as a prefatory frame to the "drama" about to be narrated. In explicitly emphasizing that "ce drame n'est ni une fiction ni un roman" (2:848; "this drama is neither a fiction nor a novel"), Balzac is subscribing to the categories of "the true" and "the fictitious" instituted in the eighteenth century. What is more, he is very firmly placing his own novel under the former heading. In his preface to *La Comédie humaine* he repeatedly underscores the need for rigorous adherence to the truth if the writer aspires to become "un peintre plus ou moins fidèle" (1:7; "a more or less faithful painter") of humanity. Yet at the same time he distinguishes between history, which is or should be exactly as it was, and the novel, which tends toward "le monde meilleur" and "le beau idéal" (1:11; "the better world" and "ideal beauty"). Indeed, he goes so far as to refer to the novel as "cet auguste mensonge" (1:11; "this august lie") that would be as nought were it not "vrai dans les détails" (1:11; "true in its details").

Openly to confront and to take into account this paradox between the sonorous proclamation "*All is true*" and the hushed admission that it is an illusion suggests a new approach to realist fiction: that its strength lies precisely in its readiness to use contradiction as its pivot instead of denying and bypassing it, as critics have tended to do by envisaging the realist novel *either* as a faithful portrayal of a social situation at a particular *time* in a particular place *or* as a textual web of discourse. Both these conceptions are valid, but each is partial in more than one sense, not least because of its exclusion of the other. Taken together, Balzac's statements offer a basis for a binary reading that does not eliminate or minimize the dissonances in favor of one or the other alternative. On the contrary, it is in the very precariousness of its endeavor that the ultimate attraction of the realist novel resides: in its risky attempt to create truth and/in illusion.

This duality is already implicit in that "*All is true*." On the one hand, it represents an aggressive effort to program readers to take the narrative as an authentic transcription of actuality: "[I]l est si véritable," the narrating voice argues, "que chacun peut en reconnaître les éléments chez soi" (2:849; "It is so true to life that everyone can recognize its elements in their own surroundings"). This injunction to gauge the events of the fiction against the matrix of personal experience is an open exhortation to a referential reading. But many readers will see Old Goriot as an archetypal figure too, strongly reminiscent of King Lear. This second, intertextual source of Balzac's novel is also, albeit indirectly, hinted at in "*All is true*," for it carries an allusion to Shakespeare. *Henry VIII*, on its first production, was subtitled *All Is True*, a fact revealed in the *Revue de Paris* of 10 August 1831 in an important article by Philarète Chasles, a leading literary figure of the day.[2] Some contemporary readers of *Le Père Goriot* would have caught the covert signal alongside the overt message. Certainly to readers in our age of suspicion, the crosscurrents are apparent and have been underscored by Brombert: "The extreme signal of realism (*all is true*) thus places the elaborate opening disclaimer of literarity under the sign of literature" (21). Brombert puts forward the provocative suggestion "In the particular case of Balzac, the analysis lends support to the hypothesis that so-called 'realistic' texts call for an ironic reading of the message of realism" (22). "Ironic" is not the most appropriate word in this context, because it normally denotes a certain intentionality of reversal. A more neutral term such as "binary" or "dialogic" (with its echoes of Bakhtin's *Dialogic Imagination*) would be preferable. The double import of "*All is true*" points to the urgency of questioning and reassessing such dicta in order to understand the underlying complexities of the realist enterprise, that daring interface of referentiality and illusion, to which only a dualistic reading can hope to do fuller justice.

The claim *"All is true"* is a good starting point for a reconsideration of realist fiction, because it implicitly raises the essential critical issues. Are readers still willing to accept the postulate that the realist novel gives a true and faithful account of a preexistent, stable, knowable reality? If truth to life is to be the predominant criterion, what sort of truth or life is it to be? Is the literalism of *Tristram Shandy* or of Arno Holz's *Papa Hamlet* in their minute recording of sensory impressions to be taken as the consummate form of realism? If such literalism is not to be equated with realism, what is the nature of the relationship between the aesthetic artifact and the world in which it is embedded? Can the objects of that world be translated into and conveyed by words, and if so, by what means? What is the role and function of readers in such a process? Because these questions resist conclusive answers, the debate about realism will continue as long as there are readers and critics. To prepare the ground for renewed discussion, we need to recall how the realists themselves and their successors have envisioned the problem.

Pronouncements about the realist novel's truthfulness are legion and invariably raise more difficulties than they allay. Most of the major realists have expressed their views on this issue, which was a basic tenet of their program, yet the statements all have the same curious tendency to limit or undercut their own contentions, as Balzac's assertion does. *"All is true"* is paradigmatic both in its boldness and its self-subversiveness.

No one wrestles the problem with as much searching honesty as George Eliot at the opening of chapter 17 of *Adam Bede*. Rejecting the idealism of "things as they never have been and never will be" and avoiding any "arbitrary picture," the narrator sets out to "give a faithful account of men and things as they have mirrored themselves in my mind."[3] More directly than Balzac, George Eliot avows the obstacles and flaws inherent in her creed, even while ardently continuing to defend its intrinsic integrity:

The mirror is doubtless defective, the outlines will sometimes be disturbed, the reflection faint or confused; but I feel as much bound to tell you as precisely as I can what that reflection is, as if I were in the witness-box narrating my experience on oath. (171)

Eliot does not attempt to conceal the subjectivity of her vision, nor does she underestimate the difficulties of "truth" in contrast to the relative ease of "falsehood" which she dreads and shuns. But the vivid example she chooses to illustrate her contentions is perplexing:

The pencil is conscious of a delightful facility in drawing a griffin—the longer the claws, and the larger the wings, the better; but that marvellous facility which we mistook for genius is apt to forsake us when we want to draw a real unexaggerated lion. (173)

The griffin stands for the fabulous, while the lion belongs to the domain of the actual, though not quite to "the dusty streets and the common green fields," the everyday world "in which we get up in the morning to do our daily work" (172). More telling, however, than the ontological status of the object is the method of portrayal: "the longer the claws, and the larger the wings" adumbrates the grotesque stylization of caricature, but what are the proper proportions for "a real unexaggerated lion"? The dearth of established literary conventions for the middle-of-the-road sobriety of realism was a grave handicap to the realists, who sought to overcome the problem with an appeal to truth. But the truthfulness of the portrait of the lion is dependent on the artist's perception, which will vary according to circumstances, such as the size of the lion in relation to that of the beholder, its distance from the artist, the feelings aroused by it, and so on. Once the presence of the artist's eye and mind as reflecting intermediaries is admitted, the notion of truth as an absolute has to be abandoned. The filter of the perceiver necessarily entails a significant modification of the implied ideal of a faithful representation of an independently existent actuality, that is, the lion. Eliot's "quality of truthfulness," described by her as "rare" and "precious," proves extraordinarily slippery as a doctrine. The unquestionable sincerity of her quest cannot compensate for the fragility of the argument.

Despite their groping and tentative tone, Eliot's theories show greater discernment than George Lewes's simplistic and dogmatic declaration:

Art always aims at the representation of Reality, i.e. of Truth; and no departure from truth is permissible, except such as inevitably lies in the nature of the medium itself. Realism is thus the basis of all Art, and its antithesis is not Idealism, but Falsism.[4]

The authoritarianism of the capital letters (Reality, Truth, Art, Idealism, Falsism) smacks of sententiousness. Nevertheless, Lewes makes an important contribution to the debate in his interpolated phrase "except such as inevitably lies in the nature of the medium itself." This concession is crucial insofar as it recognizes, at least by implication, the essential difference between reality and a representation. The "nature of the medium itself" requires that the artist be granted the right to select, to combine, to shape the material, in short, to create rather than to copy. Although Lewes himself was certainly unaware of the implications of his modifying phrase, it can be connected to George Eliot's quandary: how "to draw a real unexaggerated lion." It was obviously far easier for the realists to define in general terms what they wanted to achieve than to figure out the specifics of how to do so. For this reason, quite early already in the unfolding of realism the spotlight began to move from its matter ("truth") to the question of the most appropriate manner.

No one was more obsessively conscious of the centrality of manner than Flaubert. In his letters to Louise Colet during the composition of *Madame Bovary*, he repeatedly laments the near impossibility of writing, to his own satisfaction, about the mediocre personalities and environment he has deliberately chosen for his novel as a kind of challenge to his artistic ability. "*J'ai été cinq jours à faire une page!*"[5] ("I have taken *five days to do one page!*"); in mid-September 1853 he scrapped all he had done the previous week in order to remodel the phrases (429); often he was exasperated, despondent, oppressed by the task he had set himself. From his struggles one paramount insight emerged: that the subject matter is more or less incidental: "[I]l n'y a pas en littérature de beaux sujets d'art, et . . . Yvetot vaut donc Constantinople, et . . . en conséquence l'on peut écrire n'importe quoi aussi bien que quoi que ce soit" (362; "There are no beautiful subjects in literature, and . . . Yvetot is as good as Constantinople, and . . . consequently one can write just as well about one thing as about any other"). It is solely the artistic virtuosity of the writing that counts in the shaping of the aesthetic artifact: "Je suis convaincu d'ailleurs que tout est affaire de style, ou plutôt de tournure, d'aspect" (238; "I am convinced, besides, that it is all a matter of style, or rather of turn of phrase, of perspective"). Flaubert endows realism with an aesthetic considerably more subtle than Balzac's. However, even in the process of delineating it, he offers a supreme example of its refractory nature.

Attempts to work round the dilemma of how "to draw a real unexaggerated lion" are manifest in the palpable shift of emphasis that occurs in the later years of the century: from Balzac's blunt and literalistic "*All is true*" to the more evasive tenet that it is the impression of truth that matters. This finds its most cogent expression in Henry James's often cited phrase, "the air of reality."[6] For James it is the semblance of truth that is the supreme virtue of a novel, although, like Balzac, he sees it as most likely to be attained by "solidity of specification." While asserting that "the only reason for the existence of a novel is that it does attempt to represent life" (5), James not only stubbornly resists rigid rules, but also admits that what is produced in the novel is "the illusion of life" (12). This significant modification of realism's position is reiterated in the 1888 preface to *Pierre et Jean*, where Maupassant reassesses the creed of "Rien que la vérité, et toute la vérité"[7] ("The whole truth and nothing but the truth") and replaces it with the Jamesian concept of verisimilitude through illusion. "Les Réalistes de talent," Maupassant concludes, "devraient s'appeler plutôt des Illusionistes" (16; "Talented realists ought rather to call themselves Illusionists"). Such a perception may offer the only valid answer on how "to draw a real unexaggerated lion."

To accept such propositions is to acknowledge the innate paradoxicality of the realist novel. It stakes its claim to special authenticity by accenting its primary allegiance to experience over art, thus purporting to capture truth. In keeping with this view, the role played by observation in the realist novel is proportionately greater than that of artistic convention. This ordering of priorities has to be seen in the context of the growing interest in documentary as a genre, which followed the debut of photography in 1839 with the daguerreotype. The pressure on writing to mimic and compete with this new form is evident in the program outlined by Duranty in the first issue of the short-lived journal *Réalisme* (1856–57): art should give a truthful representation of the real world by studying contemporary life and manners through meticulous observation, and it should do so dispassionately, impersonally, and objectively. These prescriptions are predicated on two fundamental assumptions: the intelligibility of the universe and the capacity of the individual eye "to see things clearly, as they *really* were, and to draw appropriate conclusions from this clear apprehension of reality."[8] Much of the authority that the notion of realism commanded derived from widespread acquiescence in these postulates.

Yet the very reproducibility of that representation was bound to reduce its worth. Together with photography, the rapidly advancing technology of printing (in which Balzac took a personal interest) facilitated procedures of reproduction. As Ann Jefferson has pointed out, the key words in the rhetoric of realism, 'copy,' 'imitate,' and 'reproduce' are all double-edged, in having the simultaneous sense of faithful representation and plagiarized repetition.[9] The implications of "*All is true*" could thus be derogatory to the artist, if his powers of accurate observation and representation were now to take precedence over the traditionally prized skills of manipulating readerly sensibilities. The image of itself that realism nurtured thus turns out to be strangely self-defeating. Its basic aesthetic position is logically untenable; moreover, it undermines its own prestige as an imaginative artifact by deliberately setting itself on a par with reproductive technologies. It seeks thereby, no doubt, to heighten its appeal to audiences of the period, captivated by the mode for the documentary, but as a corollary, ironically, it weakens its standing as art.

This thrust on the part of the realist novel toward documentary status can be understood better within the larger frame of the evolution of prose narrative. Through much of the eighteenth century, the newly emerging form of the novel was still regarded as "a transgressive genre,"[10] operating in the space between romance and history. The latter half of the eighteenth century, however, witnessed the elaboration of a theory of the arts that "ignores the communication between appearance and what appears, setting up the work of art as a self-sufficient replica."[11] This meant a substantial change in the relationship of art to appearance as the earlier ideal of *aletheia* gave way to the new one of *adequatio*. *Aletheia* maintains the awareness of the illusion as an integral part of the audience's imaginative involvement with the aesthetic artifact, which is acknowledged as being bimodal in partaking simultaneously of both illusion and imitation. *Adequatio*, on the other hand, makes a separation between the two; it is bipolar in creating a distinctive consciousness of the work of art as a stabilized, self-contained illusion imitative of but not corresponding identically to an existent actuality. In other words, the nascent realist novel declares its independence in terms of *adequatio* as a self-sustaining reproduction of actuality while at the same time insisting on its dependence on that actuality as a true eyewitness account.

This emendation of the novel's self-image coincided with a radical transformation in the individual's understanding of the relationship between the self and the universe, which came in the wake of the revolution wrought in philosophy by Kant. A growing skepticism about our ability to grasp an external reality with any degree of assurance spurred writers to assert the contrary, that "*All is true.*" Once the very possibility of such faithfulness to actuality had been thrown open to question, the historicist and documentary facets of fiction were increasingly publicized. The emphatic tone of the realists' rhetoric suggests that it comes in response to a threatening, though repressed, challenge.

One important aspect of that challenge was to convert illusion into truth. In the French classical seventeenth-century theater, illusion, denoting magical enchantment and the marvellous, had been opposed to *vraisemblance*, that is, to what is plausible and appears true. Illusion or truth, on the stage, hinges, however, on a quite different set of physical conditions from truth on the printed page. So the rising novel of the eighteenth century approached the dilemma of illusion and truth under new conditions; it was no longer obliged to conceive them as opposites and could aim instead to fuse them. *Tristram Shandy* and, to a lesser extent, *Clarissa* are experiments in bridging the gap between illusion and truth through a literalistic realism that follows the flow of consciousness minutely and records it in such typographical figures as dashes, exclamation marks, pauses, and the like. The nineteenth-century realists largely abandoned such stylistic devices. They could dispense with them because they laid claim to an overarching truth value for the illusion they created. Instead of trying to legitimate the veracity of the illusion piecemeal and literally, they wanted readers to accept it wholesale as both metonymically and figuratively true. Illusion is invested with truth through belief in the power of representation, which was thought to reside in the referential force of the word; hence the recourse to "solidity of specification" as the way to attain an "air of reality." The earlier distinction between illusion and *vraisemblance* has vanished. Illusion, the appearance of reality, and truth are collapsed into a single coterminous entity, whose authenticity is guaranteed by the factuality of the documentation. It is only when these slippages inherent in the formation of realist theory are recognized that its basic contradictions can begin to be exposed. The announcement *"All is true"* marks a determined effort to paper over the cracks with an apparently simple and encompassing formula.

The cracks continue to show, nevertheless. They surface, for instance, in the image of the mirror, so strongly favored by the realists as a cipher for the relationship between world and word. George Eliot uses it in her phrase "a faithful account of men and things as they have mirrored themselves in my mind." Dickens, in the second chapter of *Our Mutual Friend*, invokes "the great looking-glass,"[12] a highly effective invitation to readers to contemplate the realm of the fiction and nicely equivocal about the degree of reflection or transparency implied. Stendhal concocts the ideal realist summation of the novel as "un miroir qu'on promène le long d'un chemin" ("a mirror that is walked along a road") and, with his usual love of disguises, ascribes it in the epigraph to chapter 13 of *Le Rouge et le noir* to a seventeenth-century French historian, Saint-Réal (that is, the saint of the real). The appeal to the mirror seeks to attenuate the fictive status of the fiction, to mask its existence as a verbal system, and so to deny the discrepancy between language and actuality. Yet it is laden with ambiguities. Because of its potential for distortion, the mirror is a most dubious emblem with which to validate this concept of the novel as a human document, based on observation and verifiable data, in which "*all is true.*" A mirror image has its parts reversed by an intervening axis or plane. "Mirror" is also etymologically connected to "mirage," through their common derivation from the Latin *mirare*, which means "to wonder" at as well as "to look at." So the word may connote an optical illusion rather than the true picture that the realists claimed in their usage. Their attraction to this image serves to bring out their con-fusion of illusion and truth, their desire to pass illusion off as truth.

In its very deceptiveness, the mirror assumes a new significance—as the symbol of realism and, simultaneously, as the incarnation of the pretense that it tries to maintain. Far from the anonymous, unbiased, scientific instrument that it was meant to be, the mirror acts as a prism in its passage through the artist's evaluating mind. It offers, therefore, not a faithful, objective replica of actuality as it "really" is, but a subjective interpretation of things as they seem through the refraction of the perceiving mind. Often allied to the image of the mirror is the image of the eye, as in Zola's "un coin de la nature vu à travers un tempérament"[13] ("a corner of nature seen through a temperament"). This phrase reiterates the fallacies embedded in the mirror analogy by portraying the artist's eye as a passively registering camera. The "ocular metaphor," as a recent critic observes, can imply "the notion of language either as 'mirror' or as 'window', as that which 'reflects' or that which is 'transparent.'"[14] In attributing to both mirror and eye the capacity for faithful representation, the realists wanted to have it both ways, by ascribing transparency to the reflection and so inscribing it with truthfulness. Their wish scenario suppressed the distinction between mirrors and works of art that has been so clearly articulated by Gombrich: "Works of art are not mirrors, but they share with mirrors that elusive magic of transformation which is so hard to put into words."[15] By eliminating the "magic of transformation," the realists strove to assimilate the novel to documentary. Whether such an ideal is worth pursuing and what sort of narrative it produces is a separate question.[16] The realists' insistence on equating truth with illusion means that they could achieve their aims only on the level of pretense, by prevailing upon their readers to accept the validity of their contentions and to believe without reservation in the reality of the fictive worlds they created. They were remarkably successful in doing so because they were able largely to conceal the literariness of their practices. In a sense, therefore, the realist novel can be seen as a prodigious cover-up. Translated into more affirmative terms, the realist endeavor can be taken as an ambitious exercise in bringing the novel to terms or at least to a truce with the essential artificiality of art, through an act of repudiation that takes the form of the defiant assertion "*All is true.*"

The greatest difficulty in grappling with this claim is to find the right degree of compromise. It is far easier to dismiss theoretical programs that are fundamentally flawed, such as the proposition by the German naturalist, Arno Holz, that art equals nature minus x; x here stands for the deficiency in the artist's capacity to reproduce nature with such accuracy that a fly would alight on a still-life of food, mistaking it for the actual thing. This is a reductio ad absurdum of "*All is true*," a literalism run amok, into which the realists were never drawn. Their "*All is true*" is canceled out by the counterargument that *all is fiction*. What immediately vitiates the issue, however, is that fiction is by no means antagonistic to truth, although some critics, including Käthe Hamburger,[17] have concluded that the notion of truth cannot be applied to aesthetic works because they are open to plural interpretations, whereas truth is nonrelative and nonsubjective. But, as Inge Crosman Wimmers has recently reminded us, Western literature has for centuries been grounded in the notion of sincerity, in short, on "true" discourse. And she adds the important rider: "Nor can we ignore it if the quest for truth has been built into the text we are reading,"[18] as is patently the case with the realist novel.

The third element, allied to truth and fictionality, that complicates any consideration of realism is factuality. "Fact, not truth, is the opposite of fiction,"[19] Harry Levin maintains in *The Gates of Horn*, in which he argues that the term *roman réaliste* is an oxymoron:

[O]ur highest recommendation for a work of fiction is that it be as unlike fiction as possible. Hence realistic fiction, which goes out of its way to avoid the appearance of the fictitious, is bound to involve a contradiction in terms, which comes out most clearly in the French *roman réaliste*. (25)

For Levin it is the fabulous (implicit in *roman*) that is at odds with the attachment to truth (implied in *réaliste*). This is a reprise of George Eliot's contrast between the griffin and the lion. But the French term "*roman*," which was originally synonymous with "romance," has modulated in meaning to denote the same as "novel," which is no longer bound to the fabulous. On the contrary, the modern novel, as Ian Watt has shown,[20] is distinguished precisely by its particularity of time, place, and characterization. Often that particularity is attained by the skillful incorporation of fact into the fiction, which has the effect of enhancing its truth quotient. Indeed, the introduction of factual elements into realist fiction is one of its primary devices to buttress its authenticity as "truth."

Ultimately, none of the sweeping generalizations commonly made in the past about realist fiction can be upheld. It is not "all true" in the strict sense, because it is a construct of words selectively shaped by the artist's creative mind. On the other hand, it is evidentially not all false or invented, because it has a more or less strong factual strand as well as a dimension of psychological truth in its portrayal of archetypal patterns of human behavior. In confronting this quandary, Marthe Robert has formulated some pertinent questions:

Et que signifie "feint" ou "vrai" dans un domaine où même les données de la réalité empirique sont interpretées dès l'instant qu'elles ne sont plus vécues, mais écrites? Entre le "vrai romanesque" et le "vrai réel", y a-t-il identité, ressemblance naturelle ou seulement analogie?[21]

(What do "truth" and "fiction" signify in a sphere where even empirical data are not experienced but written and therefore interpreted? Is "novelistic truth" identical, similar, or simply analogous to "real truth"?)

By separating "novelistic truth" from "real truth" she is projecting two distinct entities that may stand in varying relation to each other ("identical, similar, or simply analogous"). Balzac would no doubt have opted for the first alternative, "identical," since he saw himself as secretary to the nineteenth century, recording in narrative form what happens in real life. He came so to believe in the actuality of his fictional world that on his deathbed he called for Dr. Bianchon, a recurrent figure in La Comédie humaine. Robert's "similar, or simply analogous" leave more leeway for the artist's act of creation and also, in "analogous," hint at metaphoricity.

But in the last resort, one has to conclude that there is no wholly satisfactory reply to the realist narrator's generic claim of truthfulness. Faced with the kinds of assertions I have cited, we as readers have a number of options. We may choose to enter into a collusive complicity with the narrator, willingly suspending disbelief, and agreeing to accept the narrative as a paradigmatic sample of what occurs in the real world. On the other hand, we may adopt a posture of detachment and maintain our skepticism vis-à-vis an artifact of the imagination, a fiction contained within the pages of a concrete object, a book. The most precarious but most scrupulous route is to steer as best we can between these extremes, recognizing simultaneously the basic enframing artifice of the narrational situation while acknowledging the potential for an analogous, exemplary kind of truthfulness in the fictive representation. Such a conception of the realist novel rejects the customary antithesis between fact and fiction to dwell instead on the fruitful interplay between the two. It is the sustained dialogue between reference to actuality and the textual creation of a fabricated realm that is the distinctive hallmark of the realist novel. Through its incessant oscillation between reference to an actual world and the imagined realm of the fiction, it manages to merge them so seamlessly that readers are persuaded to take illusion for truth. The truth of the actually existent is interwoven into the illusion of the fiction in such a way that by a metonymic extension all indeed seems as if it might be true. That, of course, is the ulterior aim of the realist novel. Its hyperbolic motto "*All is true*" is a literalistic and wishful expression of what it hopes will happen in the reading process. The literary intertext of that motto concedes that a text can but evoke an illusion; yet that illusion can be presented in a manner designed to elicit belief in its truthfulness.

⁂

"*All is true*" and its analogues, though lately and rightly branded as "philosophically naive,"[22] were remarkably successful in their own time in attaining their primary goal: to program readers to perceive the text not as an aesthetic artifact but as a record of the vicissitudes of human existence under the given circumstances of a particular place at a particular time. They encouraged a referential reading of the fiction as a replica or an extension of readers' own experiences. The realists' deliberate choice of commonplace lives in everyday surroundings as their subject matter was more than a mere reaction against the strange happenings, often in exotic environments, preferred by the romantics. The temporal and spatial closeness of the realist novel's scenario to the reader's own world was conducive to the sort of referential reading projected in the theoretical declarations.

What is more, these theoretical declarations were frequently incorporated into the actual texts of the narratives themselves, for instance by Balzac and

George Eliot, so that they were bound to be noticed by readers. Zola expounded his views in succinct prefaces (e.g., to *Thérèse Raquin* and *L'Assommoir*) in response to or in anticipation of adverserial criticism. So the realist narrative contained "within itself directions for its own consumption."[23] Only late in the nineteenth century, with Henry James's *The Art of Fiction* of 1884, did criticism of the novel emerge as an independent genre. Throughout the nineteenth century, novelists were taken as authoritative spokesmen of narrative theory. Apart from Flaubert, whose comments are scattered in his private correspondence, James was the first to dignify the novel with serious critical analysis. The other pioneering theoretical critic of the novel, E. M. Forster, was likewise a practicing novelist. His *Aspects of the Novel* (1927), originally the Clark lectures at Trinity College, Cambridge, conceals under its unassuming title the beginnings of the systematic study of narration.

For a surprisingly long time, indeed into the middle of the twentieth century, the majority of critics were guided in their approach to realist fiction by the reading instructions enunciated by the novelists themselves. By underscoring the affinities between the fiction and everyday life, they were implicitly subscribing to referentiality as the appropriate mode of reading. If the realist novel was for over a century the victim of simplistic readings, it was because critics took it at its face value, accepting the self-image that the realists actively propagated of themselves as artless chroniclers of their day.

So in critical usage, "realist" was normally employed descriptively as meaning "true to the facts," a faithful account or reflection of the events presented. Commonly definitions of realism dwelled on a small group of often repeated and singularly elusive terms such as "truth," "reality," "accuracy," and "objectivity." One of the first to realize the dangers of these vague, unexamined usages was Roman Jakobson, who protested in an article of 1921 against the slippages he perceived in the diverse senses attributed to the term.[24] But his warning that these senses were not interchangeable and that the concept of realism was extremely relative went unheeded. The title of Auerbach's monumental study, *Mimesis* (1946), reinforced the association of realism with mimesis. For all his subtlety as a critic, Auerbach still regarded mimesis and representation as intrinsically nonproblematical, assuming the conceptual foundation stone to be intact. His book carries the subtitle *Dargestellte Wirklichkeit in der abendländischen Literatur* (*Represented Reality in Western Literature*). The translator, Willard Trask, introduced a slight but significant change in rendering it as: *The Representation of Reality in Western*

Literature, thereby placing greater emphasis than Auerbach did on the act of representation. The specter of mimesis stalks even so new and imaginative a collection of essays as *The Monster in the Mirror* in its assertion that "the Realists can be viewed collectively by virtue of the profound mimetic urge which underlies and determines much of their literary practice."[25]

By and large, the older views of realism, in seeking to capture its essence in explanatory phrases, favored an exclusively bipolar method in attempting to define realism in contrast to an other. For instance, in *Realism and Truth* Devitt cites the "traditional doctrine" of realism from the 1967 *Encyclopedia of Philosophy*:

The view that material objects exist externally to us and independently of our sense experience. Realism is thus opposed to idealism, which holds that no such material objects or external realities exist apart from our knowledge or consciousness of them, the whole universe thus being dependent on the mind or in some sense mental.[26]

Such a definition is predicated on the presumed opposition between an external realm and an inner consciousness, between the existent on the one hand, and the mentally or linguistically created on the other. Once, however, these two poles are envisaged as complementary and interdependent, the possibility of a more differentiated approach to the question of realism is opened up.

The insistence on dichotomies usually takes the form, in literary criticism, of a distinction between realism and romanticism. Wellek is typical of the many who consider "subjective symbolic art" as the other pole to realism. He develops a concept of realism in antithesis to its antecedents: "[R]ealism definitely breaks with the romantic exaltation of the ego, with the emphasis on imagination, the symbolic method, the concern for myth, the romantic concept of animated nature."[27] Proceeding by inversion, Wellek selects objectivity, *impassibilité*, as "certainly the main watchword of realism" (246–47), adding: "The author must not comment, must not erect sign-posts telling us how we are to feel about his characters and events" (249). Such a view runs counter to current theories of the reading process, which pivot on the collaboration between the narrating voice and readers in the construction of the text. In fairness to Wellek, despite his emphasis on the absence of the author as an indispensable criterion of realism, he does express some hesitation on the matter of objectivity and eventually concludes: "The theory of realism is ultimately bad aesthetics because all art is 'making' and is in a world in itself of illusion and symbolic forms" (255).

A similar unease about realism's avowed program can be sensed in several other critics, who have suggested a variety of modifications. Egon Schwarz, for example, though clinging to the tenets of exact observation and descriptive reproduction, acknowledges the incommensurability of art and life, and accordingly takes a stand against the idea of a direct transference from the empirical world into that of the fiction.[28] Erich Heller, under the promising title "The Realistic Fallacy,"[29] argues for two distinct realisms: that of the great nineteenth-century novel, which has a Hegelian quality, and another kind that begins with Flaubert, is manifest in Baudelaire, Mallarmé, Rimbaud, Valéry, Rilke, Joyce, and Döblin, and joins the streams of realism and romanticism. Heller's hypothesis stems from a conflation of the transcendental reality that was the concern of Rilke, Mallarmé, and Valéry with the concrete substantiality of appearances that fills the nineteenth-century novel. A more far-reaching and compelling reassessment is made in Richard Brinkmann's *Wirklichkeit und Illusion* (1957); while still resorting to the stereotyped categories of "subjective" and "objective," Brinkmann turns them upside down by positing the subjective as the sole reality.

Nevertheless, the perception of realism as essentially referential persisted with astonishing tenacity. It was central to Marxist readings of realist fiction, which sprang from the underlying postulate that literary texts are reflections of a political reality whose phenomena serve as a prototype for the work of art. The realist novel is cast by Lukács and his followers as "the privileged instrument in the analysis of reality"[30] because it is taken as presenting preformed material for ready scrutiny. Again and again throughout his writings, Lukács asserts that the realist gives a complete, meticulous, and correct picture of an observed social reality. This belief is most directly expressed in his two essays on Balzac's *Illusions perdues* and *Les Paysans* in *Studies in European Realism*, which are seen as offering "a terrifyingly accurate and typical picture of the social reality of capitalist society."[31] Precisely those works and those novelists that have been able to reflect social reality in its concrete historicity are lauded as the supreme exemplars of realism: "What makes Balzac a great man is the inexorable veracity with which he depicted reality even if that reality ran counter to his personal opinions, hopes and wishes" (22). This amounts to an endorsement of Balzac's own claim that "*all is true.*" In keeping with this emphatically referential perception of the realist novel, Lukács repeatedly invokes that favorite nineteenth-century metaphor of the mirror. Admittedly, the artist's receptive stance, which forms the basis for his capacity to reflect social reality, does not for Lukács entail either passivity or "trivial photographic realism" (42). On the contrary, the great realist must be actively engaged in the ideological causes of his own time, just as he must be able to see beyond the average social appearance in order to show the driving forces of history and to articulate the principles motivating social processes. The mirroring of reality is no more than a preliminary stage in the obligation incumbent on the realist to penetrate further into the modalities of sociohistorical evolution.

Among the later generation of Marxist critics, the most interesting is Pierre Macherey, who developed an alternative model in *Pour une théorie de la production littéraire* (1966) by regarding literature as a form of productive labor. In his analysis of Balzac's *Les Paysans*, Macherey conceives the realm of the fiction as both a reflection of a prevailing social reality and as constituting an internal system of its own.[32] The text thereby becomes "disparate," that is, open to a double reading. In underlining the dualism of Balzac's novel, Macherey abandons the perception of realist fiction as simple and unified, without, however, jettisoning the reflectionist view integral to Marxist approaches.

Referentiality has been taken to extremes by those critics who have endorsed recognition as a main element in the process of reading realist fiction. Recognition is, in effect, a transferential attribution to readers of those powers of observation deemed necessary for the writer. But it is also directly connected to belief in the truthfulness of the fiction in the literal sense, of a "close correspondence with reality".[33] The Balzacian scholar who espoused that position went to Tours, looked up the street names in the city archives, did a careful topographical and archeological survey of the site, and concluded that Balzac in *Le Curé de Tours* had got it wrong. Such rabid empiricism is a gross inversion of reading priorities that makes the text subservient to an extraneous model.

Clearly, a distinction has to be drawn between recognition in a purely personal, literal sense or in a wider quasi-metaphorical connotation. Only the latter is of importance in the reading of realist fiction.

The quasi-metaphorical dimension has been well described by Northrop Frye as "the continuous recognition of credibility, . . . not so much lifelikeness as life-liveliness."[34] In contrast to recognition stemming from prior acquaintance, the recognition of credibility hinges on the persuasive powers of the created illusion. It is, therefore, independent of individual readers' horizons of experience and devolves from overt (e.g., "*All is true*") and covert signals emitted by the text and construed by competent readers. Such a focus on the credibility of the illusion conjured up in the realist text by its verbal and narrational strategies, that is, as life-liveliness, manages to extricate realism from the quagmire of mimesis.

Its truth is that of the illusion, not of imitation, whatever its self-advertisement as a reproduction of reality. For this reason its ideal readers are Flaubert's Bouvard and Pécuchet: "Sans connaître les modèles, ils trouvaient ces peintures ressemblantes, et l'illusion était complète"[35] ("Without knowing the models, they found these pictures true to life, and the illusion was complete"). The order could well be inverted here into the causal argument that it is the completeness of the illusion that makes the pictures in realist fiction appear true to life.

To shift attention from the realist novel's faithfulness to some putative reality onto the authenticity of its illusion is to obviate at least some of the difficulties encountered by those critics who accept the realists' program at face value. One of these difficulties is the embarrassing quandary "that Realism should be seen as a misguided direction which happens to connote one of the great areas of world literature."[36] This substantive critique of the prescription encapsulated in "*All is true*" illustrates the folly of ignoring the quintessentially fictional nature of realist narrative. It is, moreover, the acceptance of "*All is true*" that has fostered the tendency to conflate mimesis with representation, because the realists themselves seemed to endorse such a merger as part of their endeavor to nurture belief in the faithfulness of their representations. This is one of the misreadings that has for long vitiated criticism of realism and has recently been the object of a vigorous rebuttal:

The source of the misconception lies in the loose use of words, so that the aim of referring to, reporting on, doing justice to, celebrating, analysing, and being constrained by reality shifts to that of replicating, mirroring, reproducing or copying it. Certain intermediate terms—mimesis, for example—thicken the confusion.[37]

The habit of freely interchanging "mimesis" and "representation" has also been attacked by Wolfgang Iser. He sponsors the adoption of representation in the German sense of *Darstellung*, a term far less imbued with the mimetic connotations that have been absorbed into its English equivalent.[38] Iser bases his objections to mimesis on its concealment of the performative aspects of representation, which "brings about something that hitherto did not exist as a given object" (217). In other words, it brings into being an illusion of truth, whose authenticity is vouchsafed by the credibility that the text is able to evoke in readers. If "the good ship Realism," that is, the notion of "*All is true*" with its freight of accuracy, objectivity, and so on, is indeed "wrecked," as has lately been lamented,[39] the best way to "gather together enough floating planks to make a

tiality are particularly momentous for realist fiction insofar as their inversion contravenes the reading directions written into the novels. The structuralists oust the sociohistorical model, sponsored by the earlier empiricist critics, in favor of a dissection of the text solely as discourse. This is best exemplified in Barthes's highly original handling of Balzac's story *Sarrasine* in S/Z (1970). Admitting that he is proceeding "à la façon d'un menu séisme (20; "in the manner of a minor earthquake" [13]), Barthes divides the short narrative diachronically into 561 fragments called "lexias" and synchronically into five major voices or codes. This transforms the text into a choral network with a succession of entrances and exits and thereby thwarts readers' desire to seize it as an ordered flow of meaning. The impact of this strategy is to disrupt the natural reading process, in which large blocks of material are assimilated sequentially. As a result, the locus of interest is displaced from the product of reading, the signification of the text through the retrieval of meaning, onto the process itself. The verb "to read," like the verb "to write," becomes an intransitive form, designating an activity in pursuit of the text's figuration and structuration. The crux of such open-ended reading is to show that there is none of that singularity of denotation on which conventional interpretations had rested. Barthes's revolutionary method of analyzing *Sarrasine* is at the same time a meditation on the bases and procedures of reading realist fiction. Eccentric or bizarre though it may initially seem, it is a landmark work in its determination to dislodge the old bugbear of mimesis from the discussion of realism.

S/Z represents the swing of the pendulum from the tradition of referentiality. Yet its methodology, for all its seductive brilliance, raises its own set of problems. The resolute dissociation of the fiction from any link to an extratextual dimension gives rise to a peculiar quandary. For the ostensible autonomy of the text that "se raconte" (219; "tells itself" [213]) is undermined by the necessity for readers whose presence alone can actualize the text. Although the author with his craft, not to mention his intentions, is expendable in the structuralist system, readers certainly are not. Barthes himself admits "la voix du lecteur" (157; "the voice of the reader" [151]) as a factor in the reading process, maintaining that "dans le texte, seul parle le lecteur" (157; "in the text, only the reader speaks" [151]). Intransitively and reflexively the narrative may tell itself; but only transitively, through its production by active readers outside its parameters can it be actualized. The various codes for reading have their source in the reader's well-stocked and agile mind. In producing the text, readers are also, perhaps involuntarily, constructing a meaning. What is new in Barthes's S/Z is not the abolition of interpretation but the relocation of the explanatory act out of an extraneous "reality" and into the activity of readers.[48]

This trend is developed and elaborated by Michael Riffaterre in *Fictional Truth*. He espouses a position even more extremely antireferential than that of his predecessors. To him the text is "self-sufficient" and "exclusively linguistic" (7–8) so that "narrative truth is a linguistic phenomenon . . . experienced through enactment by reading" (xiv). Accordingly, a "narrative must contain features that are self-verifiable and . . . resistant to the vagaries of reference" (10). But while spurning or at least redefining referentiality, Riffaterre himself does not hesitate to invoke such factors as "a commonsense template" (37), "a commonplace" (66), and frequently the notion of a sociolect, although these project the presupposition of an extratextual dimension. Riffaterre openly acknowledges that fictional truth is a paradoxical concept (xii) and tries to explain the paradox by interjecting the idea of verisimilitude; however, contrary to normative usage, he conceives verisimilitude as a stance that "tends to flaunt rather than mask its fictitious nature" (21). The upshot of this approach is to supplant mimesis with semiosis, to the point of repudiating the validity of any relationship between text and world for the sake of an unbounded investment in the rhetorical and associative powers of words.

Despite their alleged lack of interest in realism, the structuralists and their successors have significantly modified critical readings by centering on such elements as the verbal texture, the narrative contract with readers, and their active role in the construction of meanings. But, like the Marxists, the structuralists read in the mirror of their own ideology, and for all its modern and sophisticated shape this mirror is no less liable to distortions than that held by the nineteenth-century realists.[49]

ॐ

In the wake of this problematization of realism, now that it "has entered the age of suspicion,"[50] the prevailing modes of reading all appear to some degree wanting or biased: the older, "true-to-life" view not only downplays and neglects the verbal texture of the fiction but also runs into the slough of mimesis, while the newer, linguistically based approaches tend to turn the work of art into a concatenation of devices calculated to evoke certain responses in readers, yet are curiously devoid of human content. How then does one set about beginning to tell some truth about realist fiction? In more specific terms, how can one steer between the extremes of materialism, on the one hand, and formalism, on the other, between the Scylla of the referential fallacy that the realist novel is simply a faithful mirror to everyday life and the Charybdis of the linguistic fallacy that it is simply a web of words? A first step is to remove the qualifier "simply" in order to acknowledge that reading realist fiction is by no means either as simple or as easy a task as used to be assumed. After long being treated as a sort of kindergarten genre, in which a benign narrator naively spins an engrossing yarn to a cozy circle of assenting readers, realism has at last come to be recognized as an art form far more intensely crafted than meets the casual eye. The very "disingenuousness of realist writing" is deceptive; "reading Stendhal seriously as a realist," Jefferson discovers, "may mean ending up by seeing realism as a more self-conscious and sophisticated phenomenon than it has hitherto been conceived as being."[51]

A similar insight emerges from S/Z, too. It demonstrates in detail the "writerly" qualities inherent in a seemingly "readerly" text. However, Barthes's antithesis between, on the one hand, the "readerly" text (whose writing is transitive, acts as a vehicle for an ulterior purpose, and uses language referentially) and, on the other, the "writerly" one (whose writing is intransitive as an end in itself, draws attention to itself, and uses language aesthetically) proves in practice too crass. For the archetypally "readerly" text of a realist novel always turns out, on analysis, to possess more "writerly" elements than are immediately apparent, largely because it lacks the manifest playfulness of the self-conscious narrative. What has so far been largely overlooked is the care with which the realist novel conceals its writerly inner organization beneath a surface readerliness. As David Lodge, himself a novelist, has so aptly commented, "realistic writing . . . tends to disguise itself as nonliterary writing."[52] For this reason, he adds, the realist novel has set peculiar problems for criticism because it has denied its own conventionality (17). Ironically, its success in covering its own tracks and concealing its artifices has led to its being mistaken for an artless form.[53]

To envisage the reading of realist fiction as an either/or option between referentiality and textuality, the "readerly" or the "writerly," is a fundamental misconception. These antipodal alternatives, developed by successive generations of literary critics, have become so ingrained as to form a daunting obstacle to more open readings. The tensions inherent to realism cannot — and should not—be minimized, but it is unproductive to reduce them into the contrarieties

generally advanced by critics: fact or fiction, romantic or realistic, Marxist referentiality or structuralist textuality, reading as recognition or as construction. The
dichotomies are nowhere as clear-cut nor the patterns as neat as our desire for a
convenient understanding would have us wish. To take the most common opposite pairs: the factual melds into the fictitious in the now popular genre of the
documentary narrative (or, more contentiously, in the recent attempts of television news programs to reconstruct actual happenings partly by evidence and
partly by guesswork). The historical novel is compounded of a similar fusion of
romance with verifiable elements taken from actuality, such as names or dates.
The distinction between Marxists and structuralists is a simplification, too, since
many structuralists, including Barthes, had decided Marxist sympathies without,
however, embracing the Marxist vision of literature. The entrenched habit of
thinking about realism in oppositional terms has to be relinquished because it is
misleading and therefore fails to do justice to a form of writing considerably
more complex than it wishes to appear.

Various attempts have been made to work round or through this dilemma.
The most frequent tactic has been to emphasize the status of realism as "a mode
of writing"[54] differing from but on an equal footing with fantasy, romance, or
symbolism. Seen from this ideologically neutral angle, realism is invested with
its own aesthetic and stylistic conventions: these comprise not only chronology,
particularity of circumstance, everyday subject matter, and the ontological restriction to kinds of beings belonging to the actual world, but also the shaping
and patterning of these materials through webs of analogies and contrasts designed to reveal the significance of the experiences portrayed. To recognize
realism as a set of literary conventions, like those of any other way of writing, is
to liberate it from the crushing burden of mimesis. For mimesis then assumes its
rightful place as merely one of the normative conventions of realism, not its
mainspring. But this is exactly the type of reading that the program of realism
resists in its stubborn refusal to admit that it is governed by artistic conventions
rather than by the truthfulness it claims. Readers are deliberately manipulated to
fall for its propaganda and therefore face the task of having to get beyond a
calculated and pervasive camouflage. Thus, even the process of subsuming realism into conventions of discourse reveals once more its peculiar recalcitrance to
assimilation into literary practices. Through its arrogation of truthfulness, it
attempts in effect to remove itself into a privileged category, exempt from the
scrutiny to which literary artifacts are subjected. This is another instance of the

insidious nature of the self-image it so assiduously cultivates and of the circularity in which it enmeshes critics.

An effort to break out of that circle has been made by Marshall Brown, who endeavors to move away from a futile striving for any unitary conception of realism by arguing, "If realism is an effect, then it is a complex one, achievable in a variety of ways and identifiable with no single device."[55] He discriminates between the "comic" realism of details, the "tragic" realism of causal forces, and the "melodramatic" realism of typological destinies (237), but eventually he, too, heads toward a new level of unity, which he sees as residing essentially in the dissonances of realism, particularly in a technique he denotes as "silhouetting," whereby "the dramatic action emerges from a static background that gives it context and representative significance" (231). Yet at the same time Brown continues to insist on the dualities of realism "constantly tending in two directions at once" (232).

The simultaneity of these two directions must be acknowledged if the approach to realist fiction is to transcend the impasse of the critical antitheses in which it has remained locked. Just as unitary conceptions and myths of simplicity have to be shed as inadequate, so too must the polarities that have led to some challenging but invariably partial (i.e., incomplete and biased) readings. The realist novel must be taken at one and the same time as a record (more or less faithful, as the case may be) of a past social situation *and* as a texture made of verbal signs. Far from canceling each other out, the two overlap in an inescapable and reciprocally sustaining tension that forms the core of realism's precarious enterprise.

The topos of place is a good arena to explore these tensions, since particularity of place is one of the cardinal conventions of the realist novel. Its circumstantiality is a valuable device for the storyteller, who can at will invent character, personality, mode of speech, face, habit of movement, and the like:

He dresses him in clothes of a certain style and installs him in a certain kind of house. But where is that house to be situated?—in St. Paul's Crescent, Camden Town, London, or the High Street, Anytown? It is with this decision that the novelist commits himself, or can seem to commit himself, to make-believe or to actuality.[56]

The crucial phrase comes toward the end: "the novelist commits himself, or *can seem* to commit himself, to make-believe or to actuality" (emphasis mine). This implies that place can be taken either literally, as a way to endow the fiction with the stamp of truth, or more obliquely, as part of a complex scenario in which it still plays a vital role—not as a direct replica but rather as a prop in the animation of a pretense. In both cases, place is central to the plausibility of the fiction. If poetry, according to Marianne Moore's famous dictum, "can present/for inspection 'imaginary gardens with real toads in them,' "[57] realist fiction does the opposite, showing imaginary people in places that at least purport or aspire to be perceived as "real." For, as Ralph Freedman has so shrewdly pointed out,

the metaphor for the novel, more than for any other genre, is spatial, because its action unfolds literally in places, i.e., in a world where our selves move and experience one another. Moreover, its illusion depends on the suggestion that the places are real, even if they be symbolical or fantastic.[58]

It is an illusion that is created for readers through the use of verbal and narrational strategies designed to draw readers into belief in its authenticity. But it is essential to realize that the appearance of truthfulness inherent in the illusion must necessarily (because a novel is by nature a construct made up of words) derive primarily from the effect of the words printed on the page, even while they seem to refer to an external world. That referentiality is, ultimately, a facet of the overall illusion.

This incorporation of the semblance of reference into the illusion-making process is a distinctive hallmark of realist narrative. It is this procedure that invalidates the customary contraposition of fact and fiction, as well as the equation of fiction with lying, put forward by George Levine in his article, "Realism, or in Praise of Lying: Some Nineteenth Century Novels." That the realist novel masquerades as truth does not warrant the conclusion that it is a lie, for a lie is a deliberate untruth, whereas the realist novel is a pretense of truth. There is a major difference between these two propositions. Nor should realism be impugned as a form of bad faith on the grounds that it pretends to be what it is not.[59] The realists write in good faith because they sincerely believe in their own creed and wrestle with its problems. It is not bad faith or lying that makes realism so difficult to grapple with, but precisely its slippery, ill-definable, uncomfortable middle situation: not wholly fact, or lie, or truth, or even fiction, and drawing on a spectrum of modes including reference, the simulation of reference, and invention, yet not explicable in terms of any one of them exclusively.[60] The dubiousness of realism, as seen nowadays, has been encapsulated in a brilliant image that amends the realists' self-image: "The mirror that guarantees the representational authenticity of nineteenth-century realism can now only be conceived as a fairground contraption that makes reality an effect that's all mirrors."[61] The challenge therefore becomes, for writers as for painters, that "of conjuring up a convincing image despite the fact that not one individual shade corresponds to what we call 'reality.' "[62]

Gombrich's adjective "convincing" suggests the need for a change of perspective too. The "conviction," the appearance of truth projected by the artifact resides not in its relationship to an anterior model but in the response it evokes, through its artifice, in viewers/readers. So, in order to explore how realist fiction achieves its "air of reality," the focus of analysis must be shifted from the author to the readers, from the novel's origins to its reception, from the putative sources onto the text itself. For to read a realist narrative is to submit to an act of persuasion, the aim of which is to convert readers to the belief that "*all is true.*" Thus, the key question is, What is it in the text that makes us as readers perceive the narration as "real/true" and/or fictive?

These two alternatives are not mutually exclusive, as has often been supposed. Although some fictions choose constantly to underscore their own fictionality (e.g., *Tristram Shandy*, Diderot's *Jacques le fataliste et son maître*) and some assume the contrary posture by accentuating verisimilitude (as does the realist novel), all of them partake of both fictionality and verisimilitude, the difference lying only in proportion and emphasis. The lines of demarcation may be relatively clear if the narrator deliberately breaks the illusion to step forward and comment on the act of writing. Or they may be quite blurred if the primary tactic is to lure readers into the realm of the fiction and to maintain credence in the illusion. The latter obviously corresponds to the desire of the realist novel. For this reason it does its utmost to cover the transition from the real world, in which the writing and reading of the text are located, to the fictive world of the characters and their actions.

These two worlds are contiguous, and at times they overlap, so much so indeed that it is often hard to tell where the real melds into the fictive. The difficulty of disentangling them must, however, be taken as a mark of realism's success in fashioning a fictive realm so plausible as to be barely distinguishable from the actual, except for "the nature of the medium itself," that is, the dependence of the fiction on words for its very existence.

The most provocative and potentially fruitful approach to realism is to focus precisely on this porous interface between the two, particularly on the crossovers from the one to the other, the covert points of transition where the real turns into the fictive, and the fictive takes on the appearance of the real. This is to concentrate on the margins, the slippages, the tensions, the crossings, probing the processes whereby the fiction seeks to validate its claim that *"all is true."* What are the means used to achieve this effect? How is readers' complicity instigated? What are the rhetorical strategies that project an "air of reality"? What are the mechanisms and the psychological ploys that enable the realist novel to solicit readers' belief in the fiction? If "fiction is determinate illusion, and the essence of the literary text is to establish these determinations,"[63] then the essence of literary criticism is to discern and elucidate them.

2

Let's Pretend . . .

ॐ

I hope you have not been leading a double life, pretending to be wicked
and being really good all the time.—Oscar Wilde

ॐ "Let's pretend" is a phrase familiar to all of us since childhood. We pretended to be fairies, or monsters, or doctors and patients, or mothers and
children, depending on our age and gender. Nowadays it is probably astronauts
and space explorers. What is remarkable about these play habits is that mostly
they require no props; just to say "let's pretend" suffices as an invocation to turn
any old stick into a gun, or a space probe, or a magic wand. There is indeed a sort
of magic in these childhood games, the magic of the imagination, to which
children are able to give free rein with genuine spontaneity and unwavering
conviction.

As we grow up and become increasingly self-conscious, pretense is regarded
with a certain amount of suspicion as a perhaps dubious mode of behavior. "Let's
pretend to be robbers" is the only "innocent sense" of "pretend" given by the
Oxford English Dictionary, and it is the last of three senses cited. More commonly,
"pretend" is defined first as "to put forward, assert, allege, as excuse or pretext";
and secondly, as "to feign, profess falsely, to assume, put on a false appearance of
being." The notion of falsehood is central to three of the *Oxford English Dictionary*'s
four meanings of "pretence." The only neutral one is "a claim, pretension to";

all the others carry negative connotations: "a false, feigned assumption of character; simulation; a hypocritical show"; "act of pretending; thing done with intent to deceive or defraud; acts of misrepresentation"; and, finally, "fraud, sham, make-believe." The same aura of disapprobation surrounds the word "illusion," all of whose significations are directly related to misapprehensions: "sensuous perception which conveys an impression other than true of what is perceived; as when a number of lines of equal length are so arranged as to convey the impression that they are of varying length"; "loosely, any visual image, or other sensuous impression which misleads; deceptive appearance e.g. distant view of water which travellers in the desert fancy they see when there is none"; "belief not in accordance with actual facts; baseless opinion held about anything; state of mind in which one is deceived; delusion."

"Delusion," "fraud," "sham," and kindred terms of disparagement have to be cast aside when dealing with the "determinate illusion"[1] of fiction. It is "determinate" insofar as it is a deliberately sought artistic effect designed not for any concrete purpose of self-advantage (as in the hypocrite's fraudulent deception), but with a purely ludic motive. It calls upon the same imaginative capacity exercised in so high a degree by children. Even as adults we retain something of that capacity, at least under certain circumstances. For instance, we tacitly accept the custom that in opera the protagonists discourse in song, and that in romance things turn out well in the end. In so doing, we subscribe to conventions, projecting horizons of expectation to which we have been culturally conditioned.

One of these established artistic conventions was designated by Coleridge as the necessity for "a willing suspension of disbelief for the moment"[2] as we read a poem. This injunction is clearly fundamental to the reading of such works as his "Rime of the Ancient Mariner" and "Kubla Khan," which require readers to take a leap of faith into a supernatural world. However, "a willing suspension of disbelief for the moment" is not nearly so germane to the reading of realist fiction that remains, by programmatic choice, close to ordinary experience. For this reason, Kendall L. Walton has suggested an amendment of the appropriate stance to one of "pretending belief."[3] Readers of fiction, Walton argues, "do not believe in the existence of fictional characters. Appreciation involves playing games of make-believe, and as part of these games appreciators *pretend* to believe in characters" (2). To postulate an unvoiced "let's pretend" as standing at the portals of realist fiction corresponds to the "*Esto (Soit, Admettons)*" ("*It shall be* [Let it *be, Let us admit]*"), the word that Barthes sees as "sous-entendu au seuil de tout discours classique"[4] ("implicitly understood at the threshold of every classical discourse").

The need for that *Esto*, like the need for "a willing suspension of disbelief for the moment" is grounded in the distance separating classical and romantic discourse from the everyday. In entering fictions in those modes, readers are embracing a range of experience and of language beyond the ordinary. This is not the case with realism which, by contrast, always remains within the compass of possibility, centered on the familiar and commonplace, recorded largely in language consistent with that of ordinary people, eschewing flights of fancy or of rhetoric. The possible, to cite the *Oxford English Dictionary* again, denotes "capable of happening or existing; not contrary to nature, or the laws of thought, or to experience." This readiness to submit to the limitations of possibility has been posited as a major yardstick of realism:

Pour autant qu'un pareil écrivain s'engage à restituer à ses simulacres des proportions justes et des traits ressemblants,—ce qui n'implique pas qu'il fabrique une parcelle de réalité de plus, mais que malgré toute volonté secrète de destruction, il rend hommage aux choses telles qu'elles sont—, il se rattache aux motivations nuancées de réalisme.[5]

Insofar as a writer undertakes to maintain his inventions within the bounds of probability and verisimilitude—which does not imply that he constructs a new fraction of reality, but only that, notwithstanding his suppressed deconstructiveness, he pays homage to things as they are—he submits to the subtle motivations of realism.

By substituting "probability" for "possibility," Robert sharpens the issue, but the basic criterion is unchanged. Thomas Pavel, too, insists on this same idea, linking it also to the demand for truthfulness:

[R]ealism is not merely a set of stylistic and narrative conventions, but a fundamental attitude toward the relationship between the actual world and the truth of literary texts. In a realist perspective, the criterion of the truth and falsity of a literary text and of its details is based upon the notion of possibility . . .with respect to the actual world.[6]

Pavel goes on to suggest that "nineteenth century realist novels may have aimed at constructing genuine possible alternatives to the real world, as fostered through the modern scientific episteme" (50).

The relative proximity of realism's fictional worlds to our own encourages in readers certain attitudes that would be highly unlikely to occur in the situation whose prerequisite is "a willing suspension of disbelief." Because it is so easy to (pretend to) believe in the worlds portrayed in realist fiction, "we have a strong tendency to regard them as part of our reality, despite our knowledge that they are not."[7] This "strangely persistent inclination to think of fictions as sharing reality with us"[8] is striking evidence of the porosity between the contiguous spheres of the actual world, in which we read the text, and that created in the text. This accounts for "our habit of playing along with fictions, of fictionally asserting, pretending to assert, what we know to be only fictionally the case."[9] The modest distance between the readers' realm and that of realist fiction facilitates the crucial transition into belief that is made as we accede to the invitation to invest credence in the fiction through our readiness to pretend.

To move from pretending to believe in a fiction to empowering it with any kind of truth is a larger step. But just as fact and fictionality are by no means incompatible, as I argued in the previous chapter, so also fictionality and truth are not the polar opposites for which they are often taken. Admittedly, certain reservations have to be interjected here. These have been very carefully formulated by Walton in his proposition that "representational works of art and games of make-believe . . . *generate* fictional truths."[10] The alternative possible world, embodied in the fiction, institutes truths that hold for the fiction and that may or may not coincide with actual truths. Walton gives as an example that "it is Tom Sawyer-fictional, and true as well, that the Mississippi river runs alongside the state of Missouri."[11] It is, incidentally, significant that *place* is here invoked to illustrate the coincidence of truth within and outside the fiction; this points to the vital role of place as one of the primary crossovers from the actual to the fictional.

In order to accommodate this dual and ambivalent type of truth, Walton posits the introduction of a distinctive category: "fictional truth." "The work generates, in the first place," he maintains, "the fictional truth that the narrator utters (or writes) certain words, viz., the words contained in the text, and this implies all the other fictional truths which the work generates."[12] Thus, to be perfectly accurate, in speaking or writing of fictions, we should say: "In the novel Crusoe survived," or "Emma Bovary poisoned herself with arsenic," or "Eugénie Grandet got married but had no children." By skipping the introductory phrase, "in the novel (or play)" or "it is fictional that," which should logically enframe any comment made on a fiction, we are, without consciously realizing it, engaging in the pretense that underlies our readings. By speaking or writing as we would in referring to a real person, we are de facto subscribing to the (relative and fictional) truth of the fiction. Hence the importance of Walton's theorem for an understanding of the processes of reading realist fiction:

Propositions which are "true in a novel," "true in (the world of) a picture," etc. are "fictionally true." A novel or picture determines what is fictionally true; it *generates* fictional truths. . . . Roughly, a fictional world consists of the fictional truths generated by a single work.[13]

Such fictional truths may vary in force, some needing emphasis for the sake of the plot dynamics, while others may remain in the background because they have less direct relevance to the action. What matters is not the extent of their role in the fiction, but their ontological status as fictional truths, equivalent to, though not necessarily coincident with actual truths.

Through its projection of fictional truths, the realist novel creates "a relational model"[14] to reality. Such a "relational model," however faithful it may appear to be, is not to be confused with a mimetic copy. The relational model, while faithful in its overall proportions, retains the freedom to invent at will, provided it observes the bounds of possibility. Simulation and illusion, as Alexander Gelley contends, "do not cancel one another out but are essentially imbricated and reinforcing."[15] "Imbrication" is an evocative term for describing the relation of the actual and the fictive in realism because of its etymology: it refers to an overlapping arrangement of tiles. In some instances, the illusion on which the relational model rests may be unmasked as a mere "charade." That is the word used by Raymond Tallis in his discussion of the television serial, *Dallas*. After commenting on the intense speculation that occurred throughout one summer on who shot J. R. Ewing, Tallis says that viewers were "at liberty to dismount from the charade."[16] *Dallas* is here dismissed as no more than a "charade" on account of its sustained preference for exaggeration and its cult of the melodramatic, in short, its shrill sensationalism, which strains viewers' credulity. It is less likely that readers will "dismount" from, say, *Middlemarch*, *Buddenbrooks*, or *L'Assommoir*, because they are not only more plausible, being altogether in a lower key, which rings truer, but also more densely and subtly crafted. The question of aesthetic quality is crucial in the animation of the illusion, since it is the imagination animating the work of art that can in turn inspire an equally imaginative response from viewers / readers.

This imaginative response is a performance, an implementation of the assent to pretense. As such it is indispensable to the reading of realist fiction, insofar as it forms the basis for the organization of readers' perceptions. The construction of the text by readers who proceed as if they believed in it leads to the actualization of that text as realistic. This idea is encapsulated in Pavel's observation that "fiction is when world versions find secondary users."[17] The "secondary users" are those who follow the fiction's implicit command, whether it be "*Esto,*" or "a willing suspension of disbelief for the moment," or pretending belief, as befits the mode. And it is "shared pretense" that "enables us to talk about anything at all; . . . such pretenses proliferate and make the world."[18] Certainly "shared pretense" makes us as readers and as literary critics speak and write about fictional characters and events as if they were real, as in the examples I just cited about Tom Sawyer, Emma Bovary, and Eugénie Grandet. Our confidence in the fiction also allows us to overcome another problem innate to realist constructions, namely that of incompleteness. Even in so grandiose and meticulously detailed a cycle as Zola's twenty-volume *Les Rougon-Macquart,* readers cannot know everything about the figures. But our faith in the fiction's essential viability permits us to accept the gaps because we have made a fundamental commitment to pretend to believe in the entire fiction. The affirmation of pretense thus also induces acts of supposition.

The act of supposition involved in "Let's pretend" raises both epistemological and ontological questions about the nature of fiction and its relationship to reality. Pavel has identified three kinds of question that can legitimately be addressed to fictional worlds:[19] those that are metaphysical in thrust, that is, concerned with fictional beings and truth, and surfacing in regard to realist fiction as epistemological inquiries into the basis and methods of readers' knowledge; those that are demarcational, that is, that examine the possibility of establishing clear boundaries between fiction and nonfiction in both theory and practical criticism, and on which the present analysis will concentrate; and those that are institutional, that is, related to the place and importance of fiction as a cultural institution, a category that lies beyond the scope of this study.

Not surprisingly, in both the epistemological and the ontological domain, disputes are rife as to the status of fictional truth. Radically opposed views have been put forward. Christopher Prendergast, for instance, envisages realism as "epistemologically naïve," and elaborates on the consequences of this trait:

As with all epistemologically naïve positions, naïvety is purchased at a price, which is precisely what, in order to proffer itself as "naïve", it is compelled to mask; it rests on

Let's Pretend

making tacit what, if brought out into the open and critically examined, might cause the whole theoretical edifice to collapse.[20]

That edifice does not in fact collapse because the alleged naïveté on the part of the fiction is neutralized by readers' semblance of belief in its posture as if it were real. Such a disposition to pretend to believe may denote an equal naïveté on the part of readers, though not necessarily so. To Walton the dilemma is far more complex:

"What readers know" is ambiguous, . . . between what they "know" qua participants in their games of make-believe and what they know qua observers of a fictional world (the work world or the world of our games), between what it is fictional that they know and what they know to be fictional.[21]

Thus, even while at one level pretending to believe, readers maintain an awareness, on another level, that they are engaging in a pretense of belief. Like simulation and illusion, these two positions are not mutually exclusive. To make his point, Walton introduces the figure of Charles, who goes to see a horror movie, and whose heart rate and blood pressure rise as he watches the green slime ooze out toward him, threatening to engulf him. Charles " 'loses hold of reality' and momentarily takes the slime to be real and really fears it,"[22] even though he knows perfectly well that he is sitting in a movie theater (and has paid five dollars for admission!). His fear, as his physiological reactions reveal, is no less genuine for being the product of pretending to belief. At most, Charles can be seen as the dupe of his own capacity for entering believingly into the fiction. In this sense, "the central metaphysical problem concerning fiction is . . . mirrored in the very experience of appreciation."[23]

The differences of opinion surface most acutely in the controversies between the "segregationists" and the "integrationists," that is, between, at one end of the spectrum, those who perceive fictional texts as purely imaginative inventions, devoid of any truth value and, at the other end, those who refuse to admit that there are any ontological differences separating reality and fiction. Exemplary of the former is Käthe Hamburger, who declares that "in fiction . . . even a well-known real locality is divested of any question as to its reality."[24] The here and now, she continues, "no longer possess any character of 'reality,' even though the field of fiction may exhibit some constituents that originate in a more or less familiar realm of reality." Hamburger here espouses an extreme non-, or rather, antireferential position, and again, significantly, it is locality that she chooses to illustrate her hypothesis. Locality, or place, as I call it, is inevitably one of the areas most hotly contested by segregationists and integrationists, because it is most likely to appear referential through its naming of knowable landmarks, yet it functions in the text in ways far more devious than direct reference, as will be shown in chapter 5.

An equally ardent segregationism is expounded by Barbara Herrnstein Smith, who draws a radical distinction between a natural and a fictive utterance. The former is a linguistic event that occurs in a historical context: "someone's saying something, sometime, somewhere,"[25] whereas the latter is an ahistorical, non-contextual linguistic structure. The one is actual, "real" (25), the other possible, that is, feigning to be real. Hence for Herrnstein Smith the essential hallmark of literary artworks is a fictiveness that lies not in the unreality of the characters, objects, events alluded to, "but in the unreality of the *alludings* themselves. In other words, in a novel or tale, it is the *act* of reporting events, the *act* of describing persons and referring to places, that is fictive. The novel *represents* the verbal action of a man reporting, describing, referring" (29). While the soundness of such assertions is beyond question, there is a further dimension of fictive narration that Herrnstein Smith excludes and that functions as a partial rebuttal, or at least as a counterposition to such a sharp division of actual and fictive speech acts and worlds: namely that the person reporting, describing, and referring is, in so doing, adopting a stance of belief in the reports, descriptions, and references. Readers are invited and expected to respond to this stance in the same manner by pretending on their part to believe in what is being reported, described, and referred to.

The segregationists' notion of an unbridgeable gulf between fictional worlds and the real world can neatly be vindicated, but the very neatness of the vindication renders it suspect as concealing a more enigmatic situation. The fluctuations in the borders, paralleling the relativity of fictional truth, are now widely acknowledged, however unsettling such a concession may be to the resulting picture. Fiction is bordered not only by actuality, but also by myth (including other fictions), as well as by the space dividing/linking it to its readers. Rather than a gulf, it is a continuous slippage that occurs between real and fictional worlds, although some of these slippages may be less apparent than others. These fluctuating "levels of reality" in fictions have been explored with remarkable subtlety by Italo Calvino in his essay "I Livelli della realtà"[26] in which he suggests the possibility of an ever changing kaleidoscope of relationships instead of a single stable situation. Likewise, Pavel is concerned in reading *Don Quixote* with "the delicate problem of *gradual* adhesion to an internal model or another, perhaps even of the gradual validity of such a model."[27]

In this context, in the discussion of such a shift, the theoretical framework outlined by Benjamin Harshav (Hrushovski) in "Fictionality and Fields of Reference" is particularly useful. Harshav posits the coexistence of "external" and "internal fields of reference." The former are defined as

outside of a given text: the real world in time and space, history, a philosophy; ideologies, views of human nature, other texts. A literary text may either refer directly to or invoke referents from such External Fields of Reference. This category includes not only such obvious external referents as names of places and streets, historical events and dates or actual historical figures, but also various statements about human nature, society, technology, national character, psychology, religion, etc.[28]

Complementary to these are the "Internal Fields of Reference":

a whole network of interrelated referents of various kinds: characters, events, situations, ideas, dialogues, etc. The language of the text contributes to the establishment of this Internal Field and refers to it at the same time. (230)

The attractiveness of Harshav's model lies in the compromise it affords by admitting the simultaneous input of external and internal information. In this scenario, a fiction can have a referential grounding, as realist fiction certainly does, within and upon which it builds its own world.

Harshav is the most discriminating of the integrationists in conceding the separateness of the two adjacent domains while nevertheless insisting on their interdependence. The use of external information in the ways that he delineates heightens the porosity of the text. The realists are, indeed, conspicuous for holding their texts open to outside data, appropriating them in order to make close connections between the real and the fictional domains. For instance, at the beginning of *Eugénie Grandet*, Grandet's wealth is fastidiously accounted for, as his monetary operations are related directly to the economic upheavals following the French Revolution and the opportunities afforded by the ensuing social and financial reorganization for amassing riches through cleverly calculated speculative ventures. To grasp this freedom of travel between the real and the fictional spheres is to begin to understand how realist fiction works, how it validates its claim to truthfulness, and how it encourages readers to pretend belief. Of salient importance in this process are what Pavel denotes as "points of articulation" where "the two worlds meet in what can be called a series of *ontological fusions*."[29] As examples of such points he cites holy mountains or sites of worship. Once again, it is place that is prominently featured in the crossover as the external field of reference is assimilated and then converted into the internal field of reference.

The invocation of dual fields of reference as twin buttresses of realist fiction indicates its doubled structure. The role of "the act of combination" has recently been emphasized by Wolfgang Iser in the crossing of intratextual boundaries "ranging from lexical meanings to the constellation of characters."[30] Such acts of combination can equally well take place intertextually and also between the real and the fictive realm. Iser develops his hypothesis in a phenomenological context:

Every word becomes dialogic, and every semantic field is doubled by another. Through this double-voiced discourse every utterance carries something else in its wake, so that the act of combination gives rise to a duplication of what is present by that which is absent—a process that often results in the balance being reversed and the present serving only to spotlight the absent. Thus what is said ceases to mean itself, but instead enables what is not said to become present. (220)

In the realist text, the absent duplicated in the present is the silhouette of the real world; it becomes manifest in the interpellation of data from the external field of reference, which then becomes intrinsic to the fictional world. Perhaps this is not quite the interpretation that Iser has in mind, yet his comments lend themselves to such a reading. And, despite the fact that he regards "the world of the text as being bracketed off from the world it represents" (220), he sanctions "a continual oscillation between the bracketed world and that from which it has been separated" (220–21), and even speaks of "the interplay between them" (221). Iser's somewhat contradictory position is, at least to some extent, resolved by his final dyadic affirmation of performance *and* semblance:

Representation is therefore both performance and semblance. It conjures up an image of the unseeable, but being a semblance, it also denies it the status of a copy of reality. The aesthetic semblance can only take on its form by way of the recipient's ideational, performative activity, and so representation can only come to full fruition in the recipient's imagination; it is the recipient's performance that endows the semblance with its sense of reality. And so representation causes the recipient to repeat the very same performance out of which it arose, and it is the repeat of this performance that initiates and ensures the transfer from text to reader of that which is to be represented. (226)

Iser's rather grandiloquent terms, "the recipient's ideational, performative activity," allude to what can be otherwise formulated as readers' compliance with the realist text's implicit exhortation to pretend belief.

☙

"Let's pretend" and its concomitant category of "fictional truth" enable readers to approach realist fiction from a new angle. Objections can and have been raised against such a displacement of the discussion of realism from the traditional opposition between an external reality and the subjective consciousness of it onto the question of "meaning and truth conditions."[31] Such a stricture, because it would dissociate realism from any semantic doctrine, is unacceptable to literary critics who conceive texts as a tissue of words, to which questions of language, including semantics, are integral. Clearly, no consideration of realism as a literary phenomenon can afford to ignore its linguistic nature, for what is at stake is the "reality effect" created singularly by words printed on a page.

A more pressing issue is that of the truth potential of nonexistent objects. How much sense does it make to say that Emma Bovary poisoned herself with arsenic, or that Eugénie Grandet got married but had no children, knowing full well, as we do at some level, that these are not real people who have lived in the past, but fictional constructs? It can be argued that Emma and Eugénie are types, representative of the women of their time, wrought out of observation, and therefore not purely inventions of the imagination. Flaubert did indeed maintain that Emmas were weeping in villages throughout France, and he may have been right, given the limitations imposed on women in the mid-nineteenth century. This is the argument put forward by Barbara Herrnstein Smith when she asserts that "representation . . . does not constitute the imitation or reproduction of existing objects or events, but rather the fabrication of fictive objects and events of which there are existing or possible instances or types."[32] The danger underlying such an approach is that it tends to steer realism back toward a referential reading, measuring its truth quotient against a putative extraneous model.

One way out of this impasse is to resort to Alexis Meinong's theories of the logic of existence, which do leave space for fictional truths. Meinong's system rests on the principle of the radical independence of the *Sein* properties of an object, that is, its existence or nonexistence, from its *Sosein* properties, that is, its quality of being golden, being a mountain. For him "both being and non-being are equally external to an Object"[33] so that "in the *Sosein* of each Object, knowledge already finds a field of activity to which it may have access without first answering the question concerning being or non-being, or without answering this question affirmatively" (86). This view parallels and corroborates Walton's proposition about fictional truth insofar as, in Meinong's terms, "the *Sosein* of an Object is not affected by its *Nichtsein* (non-existence)" (86). This amounts in practice to differentiating between the actual existence of certain kinds of entities and the capacity to acquire knowledge of their qualities. As readers of texts we can acquire the latter, especially if we pretend to believe in the fiction, without necessarily having to be concerned about the former. "Fiction is fiction is fiction," George Levine has reminded us.[34] Hence "there is not the slightest doubt that what is supposed to be the Object of knowledge need not exist at all."[35]

Meinong's stipulative posture works better in some instances than in others. It is most efficacious when the distinction between the *Sein* and the *Sosein* properties is most clear-cut. An example would be the statement, "Mrs. Gamp is fat," where Mrs. Gamp is recognized as a fictional persona in a novel by Dickens, who has chosen to ascribe to her the property of fatness, although the only property she herself can possess is a literary one, such as being introduced in chapter 3. However, the situation is often much more complicated. The Julius Caesar of Shakespeare's play has a fictional life besides, and probably different from, the literal existence he had in ancient Rome.[36] Even more perplexing is the status of Dickens's London and Balzac's or Zola's Paris. Like Julius Caesar, these cities have had a literal existence, and continue to have it in changing form. Moreover, their fictional existence may seem to correspond so closely to the historical model that it is tempting to assess the accuracy of the representation along referential lines rather than to think in Meinong's separatist categories.

Instead of shunning such contamination as perilous, it is more constructive to see it as yet another example of the porosity of world and text. "The barrier between worlds is not airtight," Walton admits.[37] This can be applied to the barrier between the historical and the fictional as well as between the real and the fictional. All historical images partake of the fictional, as Hayden White has insisted in *Metahistory*. This realization compounds the problem of realism by impugning the stability of the historical model, which in turn intensifies the dubiousness of the fictional portrayal, certainly insofar as it purports to reflect a once existent historical reality. Again, place proves a major locus of seepage between past and present, real and fictional. If we assume "a geological view of texts,"[38] as consisting of amalgamated strata of diverse provenance, we can read place in fiction as made of various layers, some derived from an actuality contemporaneous to the fiction, that is, from external fields of reference, while others are accrued by literary elaboration, that is, from internal fields of reference. Place thus becomes one of the ideal means for "cross-world"[39] transactions, for creating a bridge between the real and the fictional realms. Through the setting of the action, the fictitious can be mounted onto the real so that the two worlds are linked by elision.

"Let's pretend" is also conducive to the metaphorization of place, such as occurs, for instance, with the town, Middlemarch in George Eliot's novel, the Paris of Zola's L'Assommoir, and the Lübeck of Thomas Mann's Buddenbrooks. Metaphorization devolves from the philosophy known as constructivism, which goes back to Kant and Hume, and was significantly advanced by Nelson Goodman in Ways of World Making (1978) and Of Mind and Other Matters (1984). A recent cogent exposition of constructivism is given by Jerome Bruner in Actual Minds, Possible Worlds. Bruner reasons that "what we call world is a product of some mind whose symbolic procedures construct the world."[40] This world making is accomplished by minds with languages or other symbol systems. Consequently no world should be deemed more "real" than others: "none is ontologically privileged as the unique real world" (96). Such a perception has important implications for the conceptualization of the work of art:

The moment one abandons the idea that "the world" is there once and for all and immutably, and substitutes for it the idea that what we take as the world is itself no more nor less than a stipulation couched in a symbol system, then the shape of the discipline alters radically. And we are, at last, in a position to deal with the myriad forms that reality can take—including the realities created by story, as well as those created by science. (105)

Science and art are here regarded as constructing worlds by different methods, but not as fundamentally dichotomized into objective and subjective nor as having disparate worth. Even more important, once the idea of some aboriginal reality is relinquished, the criterion of correspondence is supplanted as the primary way of distinguishing true from false models of the world. Bruner urges the adoption of this "new, more powerful mode of logic," in which "we ask of a proposition not whether it is true or false, but in what kind of possible world it would be true" (45). The ultimate message of constructivism is the need to study *how* worlds are constructed instead of sizing fictional worlds up against some in itself disputable "reality" for their degree of truthfulness or distortion.

Within the parameters of constructivism, Bruner differentiates between the elements of a good story and those of a well-formed argument. Both aim to convince another, although they use divergent means to do so. The argument, in seeking to convince of its truth, "verifies by eventual appeal to procedures for establishing formal and empirical proof" (11); accordingly, it constructs from the top down in a paradigmatic, logicoscientific manner. A good story, on the other hand, wants to convince of its "lifelikeness," and therefore "establishes not truth but verisimilitude," working imaginatively from the bottom up to narrative "believable (though not necessarily 'true') historical accounts of experience located in time and place" (13). This characterization of a "good story" is eminently pertinent to realist narration. Though phrased in the context of constructivism, it is a remarkably close restatement of the tenets of both the later realists, notably James and Maupassant, and of the critic, Northrop Frye. The idea of "lifelikeness" or verisimilitude is in conjunction with the stance of "Let's pretend" through their common emphasis on appearance. In realist fiction, that appearance is, in concrete terms, the text as it invites readers' complicity. As Todorov has so succintly formulated it, "[L]e vraisemblable est le masque dont s'affublent les lois du texte, et que nous sommes censés de prendre pour une relation avec la réalité"[41] ("Verisimilitude is the mask that is assumed by the laws of the text and that we are meant to take for a relation with reality").

A mask is, negatively, a concealment; positively, a pretense. Either way, this imagery derives from the conceptualization of the fiction as an "as-if" structure expounded by Hans Vaihinger in his *Die Philosophie als-ob*[42] (*Philosophy of the As-If*). As such, fiction can be "neither true nor false but simply fictional."[43] "Simply" is possibly misleading, for the as-if structure can take varying forms and is by no means single-dimensional. Two major options are open to narrative in its handling of fictional illusion: it may act as if there were no such thing as an "as-if," in other words, as if the narration were a slice of life; or alternatively, by focusing on the "as-if," it can underline its status as a fiction. The latter is the mode of self-conscious and fantastic narration, while the former is that of the realistic, intent always on covering its tracks. It could be said to masquerade as reality, to return to the image of the mask, which captures its dual proclivity to concealment and pretense. But even though, as a verbal artifact, it purports to do what it cannot (*because* it remains first and last and always a verbal artifact), it is not "a kind of sustained lie."[44] It comprises truth of a psychological as well as factual nature; moreover, its audience is not a passive victim of deceit, as in a lie, but is actively cooperating in a pretense.

Far from being a lie, realist fiction is a construct in its own right: it constructs an alternative, possible world adjacent to the real world. While it is legitimate to declare, "Der Realismus von Literatur und Dichtung enthüllt sich endlich selbst als Fiktion"[45] ("The realism of literature and poetry ultimately reveals itself to be a fiction"), it is just as vital to acknowledge that realist fiction certainly sets greater store in upholding the integrity of the illusion than in betraying its fictive nature. The illusion of reality is created by artistic means, by selection, concentration, ordering, webs of images, metaphorization, repetition, stylization. These have to be combined and presented in such a way as to elicit readers' willingness to believe in the fiction. Ironically, therefore, realism faces the necessity of bringing narrative to grips and to terms with the artificiality of art, as in George Eliot's quandary how to "draw a real unexaggerated lion." Its artifices are in the service of a controlled illusion, concerned not merely with surface appearances but also adumbrating depth and meaning. No wonder that the realists were more easily able to define their program in broad strokes than to specify its methods. These emerge and evolve gradually by experiment through the course of the nineteenth century as writers explore, with increasing virtuosity, the channels whereby the pretense can be authenticated as the semblance of a realm in which readers can be persuaded to pretend to believe.

Among the conditions essential for the creation of illusion, the context of the action is often prominently cited.[46] Setting and place thus play a crucial role in validating a fiction, frequently by reference to knowable entities, such as Paris, London, or Boston. This kind of reference, veering into pseudoreference, is so large a topic that it will form the subject of chapter 5, "The Game of the Name."

Attempts to schematize references to real world objects, figures, and happenings have not been particularly felicitous. At times, it has been taken as a matter of course that readers can instinctively draw the lines of fictionality. "Nous savons bien," Michel Butor assures us, "que le Père Goriot n'a pas existé de la même façon que Napoléon Bonaparte"[47] ("We know full well that Old Goriot did not exist in the same way as Napoleon Bonaparte"). How are we supposed to know this? Besides, as a type of person, Old Goriot very likely could have existed, not to mention his literary antecedent in King Lear. Butor's assumption is facile, and does not stand up to critical scrutiny for it fails to take into account the porosity between various spheres. None too helpful either is Parsons's division into "artificial examples," such as "the king of France," and "more natural cases," such as "Sherlock Holmes."[48] The latter, as "objects of *de re* beliefs," could exist, that is, they have the status of potentiality, which is that of fictionality. Pavel elaborates on Parsons, developing his categories of objects native to a story, immigrant objects, and surrogate objects:

The natives can be extranuclearly described as invented or created by the author of the text, the way Mr. Pickwick was created by Dickens. Immigrants to the text come from elsewhere, either from the real world (St. Martin's-le-Grand and London) or from other texts (Quixote in Avellaneda's plagiarized continuation of Cervantes' novel, Iphigenia in Racine's tragedy, Doctor Faustus in various texts about him). Surrogate objects are fictional counterparts of real objects in those fictional texts that substantially modify their descriptions: it may be argued that Balzac's novels describe a Paris that in a sense is different from the actual city.[49]

Although he expounds on them at some length, Pavel himself is dissatisfied with these categories as being "difficult," and ends up preferring "the Meinongian project" because it "is a unifying one" (30).

Yet Pavel poses some challenging questions:

During the reading of Pickwick Papers does Mr. Pickwick appear less real than the sun over Goswell Street? In War and Peace is Natasha less actual than Napoleon? Fictional texts enjoy a certain discursive unity; for their readers, the worlds they describe are not necessarily fractured along a fictive/actual line. (16)

We could reply that Mr. Pickwick is less real than the sun over Goswell Street because he is overdrawn, larger than life, almost grotesque, certainly not "unexaggerated." Conversely, Natasha appears more real than Napoleon because she is central to War and Peace, foregrounded and a psychologically complex, "round" character, while Napoleon is only glimpsed in the distance and primarily as a symbol. In the last resort, therefore, the questions to be addressed to a realist fiction must focus on the manner and skill of the literary presentation, not on the actual existence of the models. The fracture, as Pavel observes, occurs not "along a fictive/actual line," but in terms of the credibility that the text can provoke.

And that "fracture" is, in any case, in realist narration papered over with the utmost care.

⸎

"Let's pretend" translates, linguistically, into the perception of the verbal artifact as a performance by readers. The command governing their performance would be "imagine" in the case of a poem or a fantastic fiction, "suppose" or "let's pretend" for a realist narrative. The introductory, illocutionary word, though usually not voiced, forms a frame for the fictive discourse. It is this enframing that distinguishes an ordinary declarative sentence making a simple assertion about the real world from fictive discourse that contains as context a "higher" sentence, such as "I imagine (myself in) and invite you to conceive a world in which . . . "[50] As an obvious example, the linguist, Samuel R. Levin adduces the poem by e. e. cummings that opens with "Suppose life is an old man carrying flowers on his head" (117); here the effect of the opening line is comparable to that of a "higher" sentence, except that it is made explicit. In realist fiction, that "higher" enframing sentence is generally not allowed to become visible because the fiction cultivates the pretense of authenticity, and must therefore, perforce, suppress, as far as possible, those elements that would reveal its fictional status. Nonetheless, as with a poem, reading is "a condition of poetic faith,"[51] dependent on readers' willingness to pretend belief.

The discourse of realism is also more complicated than that of poetry precisely because it is not immediately recognizable as "poetic," since it cultivates the appearance of ordinariness. It does not seem to comprise wide-scale deviance from literal discourse into metaphorization, as does, say, allegory. Yet deviant sentences are, in Levin's view, "to be taken literally" (127) with the result that a shift in orientation is required so that

"real" world objects are modulated in their transportation to the world that is imagined. They are no longer defined by space coordinates or the time dimension; rather, they are given an implicit definition by their relation to the other objects and events assigned by the poet to his imagined world. . . . The world of the poem is entirely one of the imagination but some features normally of the real world have been transported into the imaginary world of the poem. (130)

This holds for realist fiction too, though with the crucial difference that readers are not conscious of having been transported into another sphere. The realm of realist fiction maintains the semblance of continuity with the real world. The external field of reference, to revert to Harshav's useful terms, merges seamlessly with the internal one. The conversion that is abrupt in the deviance of the poem is so gradual and gentle in realist fiction as to be virtually imperceptible.

The interaction of the external and the internal fields of reference inaugurates "a dual system of reference."[52] For Levin this is a problem. "Is there," he asks, in poems, "a dual system of reference, one part keyed to the imaginary world for deviant sentences, and the other to the actual world, for nondeviant sentences, particularly those in which real references are made?" (129). The answer for realist fiction is definitely in the affirmative. It makes constant use of a dual system of reference, to the point where its slippery pretenses even blur the distinctions between apparently ordinary sentences and possibly deviant ones. In this "référence dédoublée"[53] ("redoubled reference"), normal reference is not suspended in favor of "une dénotation de second rang" (279; "a second-order denotation"), as Ricoeur suggests. On the contrary, it is the nonsuspension of normal reference and the simultaneity of the twin systems that is the hallmark of realist fiction.

This coexistence of the dual system of reference is at once a consequence, an expression, and a reinforcement of the porosity between the real and the fictional worlds. If "it is by virtue of its enclosure that the poem achieves its amplitude and infinitude,"[54] it is, contrariwise, by virtue of its *openness* that realist fiction attains its amplitude and illusion of authenticity. The continuity of its discourse with readers' own both fosters the enframing "Let's pretend" and covers the transition being enacted.

The duality of its system of reference and the concomitant porosity between the real and the fictional worlds are the paramount features of realism that contradistinguish it from other modes of writing. As Karen Mann has commented, "The most difficult and yet most satisfying aspect of realism is its dual allegiance to two apparently opposed principles: art and life."[55] She goes on to single out "the capacity of [realism's] language to refer to not one but two realms (the realm of the world referred to and the realm of the words themselves)." Other recent critics also show an awareness of realism's duality, although often, like Levin in the domain of metaphor, they see it largely as a difficulty. For instance, William W. Stowe describes Henry James's writing as "both highly referential in its treatment of character and events, and highly literary in its creation of complex textuality."[56] He sets up an antithesis between two views of the work of art: the first is "that literature teaches us how to respond to actual situations by representing such situations in words" (xi). This is the referential, humanistic perception, and it is supported by allusion to George Eliot's theory in chapter 17 of *Adam Bede*. The other position is that

the literary work is primarily an artifact made of language rather than the representation of the world. We do not perceive it in the same way as we perceive the rest of the world, and the process by which we interpret it has very little to do with the process we use to interpret everyday situations. If we learn anything from literature, it is something about what language can do, and how we use it. (xi)

Stowe recognizes that "neither of these approaches suffices"; however, he does not realize the rich potential that is released by ceasing to agonize over the polarity and exploring, instead, the doubleness.

That doubleness has best been understood, significantly, by critics who are themselves also practising novelists. Both David Lodge and Laurence Lerner use the word "continuum" to envisage a spectrum of possible alignments between referentiality and self-reflexivity. Lodge characterizes "language as a continuum, rather than two sharply divided modes,"[57] while Lerner writes of "a continuum between—say—the poles of mathematics and dream."[58] Similarly, Robert grants that the novel "vit tout à la fois aux frais des formes écrites et aux dépens des choses réelles dont il prétend 'rendre' la vérité"[59] ("is naturally compelled to subsist both on the written word and on the material world whose reality it purports to 'reproduce' "). Robert takes the precaution of putting "reproduce" in quotation marks to denote a certain dubiousness surrounding it. There lies the crux of the argument about realism: *how* it sets about fusing its dual systems of reference in so inconspicuous a manner as to be barely detectable. If George Eliot's quandary was how to "draw a real unexaggerated lion," that of readers is to fathom how words are manipulated to convey the impression that they are "reproducing" a real unexaggerated lion in such a way as to seduce us into pretending belief in the verbal construct as if it were a portrait.

The difficulty of attaining a balance between the twofold imperatives of world and word is reflected in the complexity of realism as an art form. In his article, "*Don Quixote, Ulysses*, and the Idea of Realism," Terence Doody subtly encompasses the manifold, conflicting factors subsumed into the idea of realism:

The polarity intrinsic to the idea of realism, the equilibrium that realistic novels try to maintain, is a recognition of the essentially equal but contending claims that issue from, and yet also bind together, the self and the world, the author and his work, one character and another, readers and their experience.[60]

It is in the consensus of these "equal but contending claims" that the essence of the realist novel resides in its endeavor "to acknowledge the world's plurality and to give everything its due" (201). "Consensus" is also the key concept for Elizabeth Deeds Ermarth in *Realism and Consensus in the English Novel*, which, likewise, concentrates on the concurrence of perspectives necessary to bring wholeness to the realist novel without abnegating their very multiplicity.

To read in a binary, dialogic manner is to avow and accept a certain contradictoriness as a central feature of realism. That contradictoriness surfaces at the outset when Balzac proclaims his faith in the realist fiction's absolute truthfulness by citing a phrase from Shakespeare. The paradox of this self-validation must not be forgotten; it represents the crack inherent in the texture of realism which can be overlaid only by readers' allegiance to "Let's pretend."

To explore the hidden doubleness of realist fiction, to elicit the tactics whereby the text induces us to pretend to believe that it is a replica of an actuality is the main purpose of the following five chapters. For in its circumspect concealment of its literary devices, realist fiction stands at the opposite pole to self-conscious narration, which flaunts and revels in its own artifices. Yet, by virtue of its status as a text, a web of words, the realist fiction must perforce also depend for its very existence on narrational strategies, however much it tries to cover them up. It is this paradoxical tension that is the subject of this study. Each of the subsequent chapters will probe one of the distinctive ways whereby realist fiction seeks to fuse its dual system of external and internal reference. In effect, the aim is to pinpoint the cracks in the edifice by lifting the paper that screens them from view. So the next chapter is devoted to an analysis of the various kinds of frames through which readers enter the realm of the fiction. The fourth deals with the function of historical allusion as a code designed to vouchsafe authenticity. The fifth chapter examines the games that are played with names, actual and invented, to provide a geographic grounding. In the sixth, the transfer into the protagonists' consciousness through the use of indirect discourse and the implications for readers of this shift of focalization are discussed, while in the seventh it is the figuration of the language, particularly the slippage from denotative to connotative, from metonymy to metaphor, that is at issue. The conclusion, "The Enactment of Place," summarizes the function of place in the plotting of realist fiction, explaining the role of the rhetoric of locality in the novels' dynamics.

3

Framing the Fiction

སྒྲ

Language is not simply a reporting device for experience but a
defining framework for it.—Benjamin Whorf

སྒྲ In a memorable passage in S/Z, Roland Barthes introduces the image of the
frame as "le cadre vide que l'auteur réaliste transporte toujours avec lui"[1] ("the
empty frame that the realistic author always carries with him"). Barthes suggests
that the frame acts as a means of distancing and of distinguishing what it
contains, that is, the realm of the fiction, from its surroundings. For, he goes on
to argue, "le réalisme (bien mal nommé, en tout cas souvent mal interpreté)
consiste, non à copier le réel, mais à copier une copie (peinte) du réel: ce fameux
réel, comme sous l'effet d'une peur qui interdirait de le toucher directement, est
remis plus loin, différé" (61; "realism [badly named, at any rate often badly inter-
preted] consists not in copying the real but in copying a [depicted] copy of the
real: this famous *reality*, as though suffering from a fearfulness which keeps it
from being touched directly, is *set farther away*, postponed" [55]). The frame
therefore marks both the limits and the threshold of the fiction, the point of
intersection between the real and the fictional worlds; it sets the boundaries of
the created world, while at the same time disposing readers to cross those
boundaries in order to see what is within the frame. Its dual function of contain-
ment and bridging reiterates the central paradoxicality of realist fiction in its

twin thrust toward truth and artifice. In this respect the frame plays an ambivalent role, as Derrida has pointed out: "It is therefore necessary to know . . . how to define the intrinsic, the frame, and what to exclude as frame *and* beyond the frame."[2] In Derrida's usage, "the *parergon* is precisely a detachment which is not easily detached" (22).

The frame is, in a sense, the fundamental fictional truth that the text has to generate. Its function, in linguistic terms, is that of the *Esto*, "I imagine myself," or "Let's pretend" that is understood at the portals of the fiction and that inaugurates the slippage from the real to the fictive. It becomes manifest as the words that the narrator utters or writes, that is, the words that make up the fiction. The extent of the narrator's visible presence is, in this context, unimportant; the mere and essential sound of the voice, even if it chooses to feign absence, as Flaubert's does, is the cornerstone of the entire fictional edifice. The narrator is the "figure with a pair of eyes, or at least a field-glass"[3] that Henry James sees standing at each of the millions of windows of the house of fiction. The image of the window conjures up, first, panes of glass through which the viewer may look into a space, as into the display of a store, or out of, as onto the vista of a street or distant hills from, say, a second-floor room. But a window also has another component, a frame, which generally serves merely as the holder and support of the glass. In the house of fiction, however, because its windows are more often refractive than transparent, the frame comes to have a far greater significance as the underpinning that sustains the entire enterprise. So it is surely no coincidence that "the same public which demanded mimetic art also preferred to set the most minutely detailed of realistic paintings—and even their mirrors and photographs—in the most elaborately ornate frames."[4]

The frame that surrounds a fiction is fashioned cooperatively by the joint venture in pretense on the part of the narrator and readers. The narrator, through suggestive strategies, acts as the instigator of the illusion, the agent of the stance "Let's pretend." In so doing, he functions as one half of the frame. Its complementary other half is provided by the assenting audience through its willingness to enter into that pretense in response to the invitation extended by the narrator. In its readiness to comply with the narrator, the audience is engaging in the game of make-believe that animates realist fiction. The arena of that game is the text within the enclave of the frame that encompasses the fictive realm. The frame is permeable, so certain elements from an extraneous reality, such as historical data or geographic names, can be appropriated into it from an external field of reference. These components are assimilated into the totalizing pretense, so they are naturalized into the fictive realm. The ways in which they form bridges between the worlds, extraneous and internal to the frame will be discussed in the next two chapters. As the scene and plot take shape and the protagonists interact, the fictive realm becomes less and less dependent on the external field of reference, and more and more on its own self-supporting internal field of reference. The worlds that Eugénie Grandet, Emma Bovary, Gervaise Coupeau, Dorothea Brooke, Lydgate, Basil Ransom, Verena Tarrant, and the Buddenbrooks inhabit ultimately acquire a substantiality and a credibility within the peripheries of their respective frames, not because of their connection to recognizable things beyond the frame.

Such a contention must inevitably provoke the question raised by Horst Steinmetz: "[W]ie kommt es, dass einige Werke 'realer' sein sollen als andere, wenn sie doch alle Fiktion und Illusion sind?"[5] ("How come that some works are said to be more 'real' than others when they are all fiction and illusion?"). Steinmetz goes on to ask "ob man es bei sogenannter realisticher Dichtung mit einer besonderen Art von Fiktion und Illusion zu tun habe" ("whether in so-called realistic writing one is dealing with a special kind of fiction and illusion"). These are crucial issues for an understanding of realism. I would argue that realist writing does indeed use some very particular means to create and sustain its fictional illusion, and one of my principal aims is to identify and analyze those means. The idea of the fictional, Martin Price has pointed out, must be "opposed to the literal or to the deceptive and mendacious."[6] Translated into the terms I am using, the "fictional" would correspond to what happens or is said within the parameters of the frame.

What vastly complicates the situation in realist fiction and distinguishes it from other types of narrative is, precisely, its concern to conceal its own devices, including its frame, in its endeavor to pass itself off as "truth." Therein lies a partial answer to Steinmetz's questions. In creating its illusion, it has to eschew such familiar, formulaic phrases as "Once upon a time" that clearly signal to readers both the genre invoked and the entry into a strange world. Similarly, it must recoil from the overt, often multiple enframing artifices favored by self-conscious narratives such as Sterne's *Tristram Shandy* or Diderot's *Jacques le fataliste et son maître*, which constantly remind readers of their ontological status as fictions by their repeated movement between levels of narration and illusion. Such techniques are anathema to realist fiction as contrary to its underlying purpose of validating itself as a true and faithful account of the middle reaches of human existence. The task it sets itself of seducing readers to enter its portals without disclosing their lineaments is thus an extraordinarily tricky one. Yet the realm of the realist novel, although contiguous to the ordinary world and coextensive with it, is nonetheless fictitious. It must somehow deal with the curious combination of its characteristic porosity between real and fictional and its innate inclination to minimize the necessity of the frame as a means of access to the fictional realm.

This problem is confronted in various ways. Some novels have extrinsic frames in that they are part of a more or less cohesive series. The two primary nineteenth-century examples of such enframement are Balzac's *La Comédie humaine* and Zola's *Les Rougon-Macquart*, but there are other instances too, such as Gottfried Keller's *Die Leute von Seldwyla* (*The People of Seldwyla*). Its organizing principle is, significantly, the use of a place, Seldwyla, as the scene for a collection of narratives about the eccentricities of its inhabitants. For *Les Rougon-Macquart* Zola has recourse to a biological schema that traces patterns of heredity in the two branches of one large family: the legitimate, respectable Rougons on one side, the progeny of Adélaïde Fouqué's marriage to Pierre Rougon, and on the other the socially marginal Macquarts, the offspring of her alcoholic lover, Antoine Macquart. Zola drew heavily on the scientific and medical theories of his day in devising this genealogical frame, and he presented it to readers in the form of a family tree that specifies in considerable detail each persona's place in the hereditary process. As a result, the novels that constitute *Les Rougon-Macquart*, though each a complete entity in itself, also possess a wider perspective that lends depth to every single unit as well as unity to the whole. *L'Assommoir* is a clear example of Zola's procedure. Its opening plunges in medias res without any apparent frame by showing Gervaise sitting at the window waiting all night for Lantier's return. Only gradually in the course of the first chapter is the background to her predicament sketched. But as the seventh of the *Rougon-Macquart* series, *L'Assommoir* is embedded in that larger context; the initial novel, *La Fortune des Rougon*, contains Gervaise's prehistory in her abuse by her alcoholic parents and her elopement to Paris with Lantier, so that her appearance at the beginning of *L'Assommoir* is in fact a reappearance, already prepared—and enframed—by what has gone before.

Balzac's overarching framework is both larger and more complex than Zola's, but like Zola, he hit on it midway in his most productive years when he arranged his enormous output under the general heading *La Comédie humaine*, to which he wrote a preface ("Avant-propos") in 1842. Balzac assigned his diverse novels to a number of large subcategories such as *Scènes de la vie privée*, *Scènes de la vie de Province*, *Scènes de la vie Parisienne*, *Scènes de la vie politique*, *Scènes de la vie militaire*, and *Scènes de la vie de campagne*.[7] The quite flexible cohesion given by this design is greatly reinforced by the technique of recurrent figures, some of whom appear in major or minor roles in as many as twenty to thirty discrete novels. Both Balzac's and Zola's practices stem from their vision of the writer as an observing social scientist recording analytically a panorama of contemporary French society. This type of frame therefore serves also to support the fiction's claim to truthfulness.

Besides the totalizing frame of *La Comédie humaine*, each novel has an intrinsic frame too. One of these, the introductory paragraphs to *Le Cabinet des antiques* (1837), is specially interesting for its provocative and equivocal commentary on the ensuing narration in this direct address to readers:

Dans une des moins importantes Préfectures de France, au centre de la ville, au coin d'une rue, est une maison; mais les noms de cette rue et de cette ville doivent être cachés ici. Chacun appréciera les motifs de cette sage retenue exigée par les convenances. Un écrivain touche à bien des plaies en se faisant l'annaliste de son temps! . . . La maison s'appelait l'hôtel d'Esgrignon; mais faites comme si d'Esgrignon était un nom de convention, sans plus de réalité que n'en ont les Belval, les Floricourt, les Derville de la comédie, les Adalbert ou les Mombreuse du roman. Enfin, les noms des principaux personnages sont également changés. Ici l'auteur voudrait rassembler des contradictions, entasser des anachronismes, pour enfouir la vérité sous un tas d'invraisemblances et de choses absurdes; mais, quoi qu'il fasse, elle poindra toujours, comme une vigne mal arrachée repousse en jets vigoureux, à travers un vignoble labouré.[8]

In one of the least important districts in France, in the center of the city, at the corner of a road, stands a house; but the names of this road and this city must here be concealed. Everyone will appreciate this wise suppression, demanded by convention. A writer touches on many a wound when he turns himself into the annalist of his time! . . . The house was called the Esgrignon Mansion, but take Esgrignon to be a conventional name with no greater reality than the Belvals, the Floricourts, the Dervilles in comedy or the Adalberts and the Mombreuses in novels. The names of the main characters have likewise been changed. Here the author wants to pile up contradictions and heap up anachronisms so as to bury the truth under a mass of improbabilities and absurdities; but, do as he will, the truth will always out, like a vine badly torn out, grows again in vigorous spurts across a tilled vineyard.

This frame is striking for its open avowal of the deviousness of the novelist's endeavor. On the one hand, convention is cited as the reason for a kind of anonymity in the suppression of identifiable details. This seems to hark back to the typological locations, often denoted merely by a capital letter and a dash, favored by eighteenth-century fiction. Yet despite this necessity for prudent concealment, the underlying truth will emerge, Balzac insists. The fiction, presented as a fiction, is also to be read as an avatar of reality. This is probably the closest approximation of its own actual practices to be found in the entire corpus of realist fiction.

Another attempt to read the fiction as an avatar of reality and to provide it with an extrinsic frame is represented by the exploration of its links to the author's life and opinions. Such a procedure is especially tempting in novels that lack a readily visible frame but seem to have a close connection to the author's biography. A case in point is *Buddenbrooks*, which starts with vivid dialogic exchange interspersed with brief descriptive passages, and where the internal frame is finely wrought, consisting as it does essentially of the discreetly ironic narratorial voice. This attenuation of the fictional enframement has encouraged the long-standing predilection for siting the novel in relation to the life of Thomas Mann and his family. Such a reading, while undoubtedly defensible at one level, nevertheless violates a text that has a validity extending far beyond the autobiographical.[9] Yet, curiously, the upshot of even these traditionalistic approaches to *Buddenbrooks* is to expose again the fluidity of the categories, the "real" and the "fictional," and readers' instinctive tendency to conflate the two. While this is one of the purposes of realist fiction, it is achieved only reductively and simplistically when the text is envisaged on a personal level by equating Thomas Mann, the scion of a business family, with Thomas Mann, the author / narrator of *Buddenbrooks*.

The difficulties and pitfalls of trying to draw a direct connection between author and narratorial voice have been well defined in regard to Mary Ann Evans, who reinvented herself as George Eliot. Readers of *Adam Bede*, according to J. Hillis Miller, are faced with

the impossibility of deciding whether the "I" who speaks in chapter 17 is Mary Ann Evans talking of the real, historical, autobiographical world of her father, her home county, and her childhood experience, or whether, as it must also be, it is those transposed into the fictive voice of an invented male narrator speaking of fictive events and valuing them in groundless figurative exchanges moving back and forth from love to nature to art to religion. It is both and so neither.[10]

This open-ended and self-negating conclusion ("and so neither"), although the only fair one, perhaps unintentionally suggests the unproductiveness of such efforts. Since the duality of Mary Ann Evans / George Eliot is inescapable, all her / his novels cannot but testify to the same ambivalence. Reference to the authorial persona as frame to the fiction is, at best, an inconsequential mode of reading because it directs attention back onto an anterior reality instead of inwards onto the text.

It is the evidence of the written text that matters ultimately. Thus it is immaterial whether it is Mary Ann Evans and / or George Eliot who is the source of the "Prelude" to *Middlemarch*, where the historical Saint Theresa is invoked as a paradigm of aspiration for the fictive Dorothea Brooke. What counts is the clear delineation of a frame for the plot of the novel in which "a certain spiritual grandeur ill-matched with the meanness of opportunity"[11] is embodied in the male as well as in the female figures. Less conspicuous but equally telling as a frame is the puzzling "Nous" ("we"), the first word of *Madame Bovary*: "Nous étions à l'étude, quand le Proviseur entra, suivi d'un *nouveau*" ("We were in class when the headmaster came in, followed by a *new boy*"). These silent spectators, as I have elaborated elsewhere,[12] ally and bond us, the readers, to the narrator in a unifying gaze that will prevail throughout the action to follow.

The frame of *Middlemarch* and of *Madame Bovary* is intrinsic to the fiction as an element of the narrative, whereas in the cycle format of *La Comédie humaine* or *Les Rougon-Macquart* it is extrinsic to the individual novel. In some instances, as in the case of Balzac, the two types of frame overlap and interact. Whichever the format, realist fiction has to contend with the contradiction between the necessity for a frame to the artistic entity and its innate desire to deemphasize the presence of that frame in order to promote the continuity between the real and the fictive worlds. By incorporating its enframement into the text, realist narrative succeeds in turning its frame into a crossing rather than a dividing device between an external reality and the internally created forum of the fiction.

The frame is incarnated and manifest in the narrative as the narratorial voice, the primary agent for the evocation of the fictional illusion. To buttress his credibility, the narrator must establish his standing as a knowledgeable beholder of the place, even though that knowledge in itself may be fictitious, that is, a part of the overall pretense. It is well to recall at this point that the Latin "narrare" is akin to "gnarus" ("knowing," "acquainted with," "expert in"), both being derivates of the Indo-European root "gna" ("to know") which comes from a family of words related to the Latin "cognoscere," the Greek "gignoskein" ("gnosis") and the Old English "geenawwan."[13] Given this context, it is not surprising that so many of the realists opted to write about places they themselves knew from the inside, as it were: Flaubert's Rouen and Normandy in *Madame Bovary*, Thomas Mann's Lübeck in *Buddenbrooks*, George Eliot's Coventry in *Middlemarch*, Zola's Paris in *L'Assommoir*, and Balzac's Paris and the provinces in *La Comédie humaine*. However, when the narrator just pretends to knowledge, as Balzac did of Douai in Belgium in *La Recherche de l'absolu*, the effect is by no means diminished for what matters is not the narrator's actual knowledge but rather his posture of mastery. "Realistic novels," Douglas Hewitt observes, "do not affect us as being like life: they are like the experience of being told about life by someone whom we trust."[14] The fundamental trust is essential, and the realists, well aware of this, took care to cultivate the image of reliability and stability in their narrators. To support this image, Balzac, Zola, and Mann imply that the narrator can have unhampered access to the systems of knowledge that inform and govern the text. Other narrators, while in command of forward and backward dimensions of knowledge beyond readers' ken, do not lay claim to such omniscience. Indeed, the Jamesian narrator, in *The Bostonians*, for instance, makes repeated confessions of not knowing.[15] The extent of the narrator's knowledge does not compromise its quality. On the contrary, the narrator's readiness openly to admit certain limitations enhances the profile of honesty. This absolute honesty is the fulcrum of the narrative contract in realist fiction:

Fictional truths about narrators' reliability frequently affect what other fictional truths are implied. If it is fictional that the narrator is honest, intelligent, and knowledgeable, that and the fact that fictionally he asserts such and such are likely to imply that fictionally such and such is the case.[16]

Readers' willingness to (pretend to) believe is dependent on the degree of trust that the narrating voice can evince.

It is, therefore, readers' capacity to put credence in the narrator that enables them to believe in the fictional illusion, and with it in the reality of the place. The narrator becomes one of the major cruxes, in the literal sense of crossings, on which readers' sense of place pivots. Just as "the painter can accomplish his task only by giving tactile values to retinal impressions,"[17] so the writer can accomplish his only by means of words. But the web of words must be animated by a belief in their validity as evidence, and hence by faith in the trustworthiness of the narrator. To this extent the act of writing realist fiction is as much an exercise in persuasion as advertising or political rhetoric. Thus the issue of truth or falsehood becomes as pertinent to the maker of a statement as to the statement itself. Often the two are inseparable: the extent of the confidence that the speaker is able to inspire will determine the likelihood of the statement's veracity and hence acceptability. The Balzacian narrator has been characterized as "someone in whom we can put our trust, a 'broker' who will supply the reader with the requisite language and interpretative strategies for understanding the modern world."[18] Such a narrator holds out the promise of "a transformation of the opaque landscape of Paris into an entirely legible surface" (103). This interpretability of the text has been seen as an expression of the narrator's supreme power for he subjugates the "inflow of meaning from a position of despotic transcendence" (228). "Transcendence" seems a dissonant term since this quality is so markedly lacking in Balzac's materialistic world and thought. More disturbing still is the critique of "the mimetic endeavour" that is developed from this concept of power:

[T]he model of the authoritative narrator standing at the apex of the triangle of representation does not adequately explain, or indeed "explain" at all, the success of the mimetic endeavour. The limitation of the model is that it is internally self-confirming, the authority of the narrator ensures mimesis because the narrator is authoritative. (30)

What Prendergast takes to be the "limitation" of realism, namely "that it is internally self-confirming" can, conversely, be read as a source of its strength insofar as it rests solely on its own artfulness. But such an amendment entails a renunciation of the view that realist fiction is a "mimetic endeavour" and the recognition instead that it is a construct of pretense: a pretense of mimesis. This ulterior frame of pretense, as I suggested in the previous chapter, in turn enframes the frame put into place by the narratorial voice.

How then does the narratorial voice function in enframing the narrative? This question, like so many others that have to be addressed to realist fiction, produces a spectrum of sometimes ambivalent answers. For in the process of trying to work out the narrator's tactics, another of realism's paradoxes comes to surface: that it would wish largely to draw a veil over the storytelling and the teller so as to appear to be precisely not a story told but a true and faithful exposé of life. Yet here is realism's predicament again: it can do no more than *pretend* not to be a story. For its very texture of language betrays its nature as a narrative, and a narrative clearly implies a teller with a certain vision and a verbal repertoire. The typical narrative method for the realist novel, as David Lodge reminds us, is the third-person past tense "in which, whether the narrator chooses to intervene rhetorically or not, the grammar is a constant sign of his presence, and hence of some context, some reality larger than that defined by the limits of any character's consciousness."[19]

Only rarely were the realists able to fulfill that desire for a semblance of absence so vividly summarized in Flaubert's oft repeated dictum: "L'artiste doit être comme Dieu dans la Création, invisible et tout-puissant, qu'on le sente partout, mais qu'on ne le voie pas"[20] ("The artist should be like God in Creation, invisible and omnipotent; he should be felt everywhere, but not seen"). How to seem absent though pervasive in the narrative is the realist's foremost challenge. While eighteenth-century narrators were a strong presence within their fictions, addressing readers on numerous occasions, the realist program of a true and faithful copy of reality demands an apparently autonomous action emanating from an impersonal, disembodied, imperceptible voice. The narrator wants to become "a presence that strives to appear solely as an absence."[21] He must disappear into the fictional world, ceasing to be an identifiable personality, becoming instead a "nobody," dematerialized, unindividualized and noncorporeal.[22] This leads to an insistence on "external perspective" as "one of the conventions of 'realism.' " "External perspective" is taken to denote a technique that "reproduces the gradual and fragmentary fashion in which we come to any knowledge of the people we encounter. The writer carefully conceals his own omniscience, releasing information about his characters only a little at a time."[23]

Such an external perspective prevails at the opening of both *Madame Bovary* and *Buddenbrooks*: the characters and the action are presented primarily in scenic, dialogic form so that the narratorial voice recedes, although it can never wholly disappear. For even in those texts where the once popular and now disproven myth of narratorial absence seems to be upheld, there are passages of description whose source can be no other than a narrator in possession of knowledge. That knowledge may be limited largely to what the protagonists are in a position to know; in the description of the "Landschaftszimmer" ("landscape room") on the second page of *Buddenbrooks* the narrator is reportorial rather than evaluative, letting the objects of the decor speak for themselves without openly interpreting their significance as does his Balzacian counterpart. Similarly, in the first two sections of Part 2, selected physical details are mentioned such as the satin eiderdown, the richly embossed wallpaper, and the opulent breakfast, details indicative of the Buddenbrooks' luxurious lifestyle. The descriptions in *Buddenbrooks* are never extensive; generally they are interrupted by dialogue, so that readers acquire information only gradually and piecemeal through a process of learning as the action unfolds. In the long account of Hanno's school day (part 9, chap. 2),[24] the scene is registered in impersonal terms, though it clearly has partly satirical, partly elegiac overtones. The extreme of impersonality is then reached in the following chapter (part 11, chap. 3) in the presentation of the typhoid fever that kills Hanno. Often the narrator pretends to be alongside rather than ahead of readers, assuming a stance of innocence by putting questions such as might come from readers: "Was war es mit dem Direktor Weinschenk?" (540; "What was up with Director Weinschenk?"), or "Wo war Christian?" (547; "Where was Christian?") as if to underscore his detachment from the narration.

But that detachment in *Buddenbrooks*, as in *Madame Bovary*, may be tinged with an irony that breaks out of the posture of absence through the implication of a value judgment. True, the narrator still remains anonymous and uncharacterized as a persona, yet the ironic tone of the narration points to a hidden presence that insinuates a view of things other than that held by the protagonists. Even deliberately impersonal modes of narration can take on an ironic force. So in the later stages of *Buddenbrooks* when the narrator states, "So aber geschah es . . . " (680; "Thus, however, it happened . . . "), or: "Die Dinge lagen so . . . " (718; "Things were such that . . . "), the apparently innocuous turn of phrase has an ironic impact because readers know that these happenings and situations are not mere chance but the result of the Buddenbrooks' declining business acumen. A more overt irony is practiced at the expense of the city's "ersten Familien" ("leading families") through the frequent reiteration of the phrase in connection with pedestrian habits such as summer visits to the resort of Travemünde. In all these instances the narrator remains technically invisible, yet he promulgates a subtext that suggests his latent presence. Flaubert is as adroit as Mann in these manipulations of the narrator / readers relationship. When Charles Bovary, during his days as a medical student, indulges his passion for dominoes, for example, we hear that this "lui semblait un acte précieux de sa liberté, qui le rehaussait d'estime vis-à-vis de lui-même. C'était comme l'initiation au monde"[25] ("seemed to him a precious act of freedom, which raised his self-esteem. It was like an initiation into the world"). While playing dominoes may raise Charles's self-esteem, it lowers readers' esteem of him, especially as this addiction to a game that demands little skill and no intellect contributes to his failing his exams. The irony, while internal to the narrative, simultaneously functions as an enframing device by suggesting the potential for an alternative reading. The narrating voice here, as in *Buddenbrooks*, is at once concealed and palpable. The passage just cited about Charles also reveals the role of interior monologue in evoking the same dualism when an internal perspective counterbalances (and often ironically contravenes) the external one.[26] The predominance of external perspective as one of the conventions of realism proves itself to be a critical convention with no more than a partial validity.

Associated with the external perspective is the image of the realist narrator as a "stage manager."[27] The narrator of *Buddenbrooks*, for instance, has been described as a "Regisseur" ("stage manager") who disappears in favor of the actors.[28] Likewise, Fontane's narrators have been envisaged as observers standing vis-à-vis a landscape or looking at a picture or into a decor that "opens like a stage scenario."[29] The notion of enframement is clearly implicit in these images of the stage manager, the observer of the landscape, or the viewer of a picture. The stage manager's / observer's / viewer's vision projects and encloses the drama / land-scape / picture that is the object of contemplation. The narrator is cast as a controlling persona in possession of ulterior knowledge and therefore able to mastermind the illusion. Equally important, the terminology of stage and of observer / viewer denotes the acceptance of pretense and performance, as an element of narrative as well as of drama. Only in its linguistic form, as a speech act, has this performative aspect of narration been adequately recognized. The affinity with the stage also serves as a link to another cardinal feature noted by Barthes as typical of the realistic novel: "donner à l'imaginaire la caution for-melle du réel, mais laisser à ce signe l'ambiguïté d'un objet double, à la fois vraisemblable et faux"[30] ("it involves giving to the imaginary the formal guaran-tee of the real, but while preserving in the sign the ambiguity of a double object, at once believable and false"). It is "at once believable and false" because it is the product of a staged pretense.

The stage manager, though not visible, can certainly be audible in the direc-tion he gives for the instigation of the performative pretense. This is Balzac's method in many of the novels of the *Comédie humaine*, where the extensive overtures are like prologues or monstrously overgrown stage decors. The narrator himself refers to this enframement, which he calls variously "Ce préambule" (2: 15; "This preamble") in *La Fausse Maîtresse*, "Ce petit préambule" (2: 247; "This little preamble") in *Honorine*, and "Cet immense tableau, . . . poétiquement encadré" (2: 678; "This huge picture, . . . poetically enframed") in *La Femme de Trente Ans*. At the opening of *Eugénie Grandet*, the picture is delineated by an essentially cinematic technique as the camera lens zooms in on the house, the street, the town from an external perspective to be sure, but with an insider's insight into the scene. In the description of the Vauquer boardinghouse in *Le Père Goriot*, such terms as "histoire" (2: 847, 853, 857; "story"), "récit" (2: 854; "narrative"), "spectacle" (2: 854), and "tableau" (2: 856; "picture") all point to the narrator's function as the introducer and mediator of the setting in which the plot is to be enacted. In all these cases the narrator openly presents himself as an authorial figure, positioned close at hand to the scene as an eye-witness with intimate knowledge of the place he is describing: the implication is that he has been there before and speaks from personal experience. This, together with the serious tone of the discourse and the circumstantial detail, authenticates the veracity of the account through the warranty of the narrator's personal familiarity with these locations. The narrator is here playing a dual role of stage manager and initiated spectator. While he does not flaunt his presence, he makes no attempt, either, to conceal it, standing up in front of his audience to recite an exposition. His reiterated direct appeals to readers have the effect of inducing them to share his viewpoint, and thus to close the encircling frame.

So Balzac's lengthy, sometimes seemingly self-indulgent and excessively compendious, cataloguing "bibliographical prefaces,"[31] far from being just preliminaries to the action, are vital components as entrances to the realm of the fiction. They mark what Genette has called the "frontière intérieure du récit"[32] ("internal frontier of the narrative"). That internal frontier is very clearly established in Balzac's *Comédie humaine* so that a line can easily be drawn at the clear-cut transition between the end of the exposition and the beginning of the action: in *Eugénie Grandet* when Nanon lights the fire one evening in November 1819 (3: 1044); in *Le Père Goriot* at the point where the narrator proclaims: "Telle était la situation générale de la pension bourgeoise à la fin du mois de novembre 1819" (2: 878; "Such was the situation in the bourgeois pension at the end of November 1819"); and most categorically in *La Cousine Bette* with: "Ici se termine en quelque sorte l'introduction de cette histoire" (6: 264; "Here ends more or less the introduction to this story"). Now, with the frame firmly in place, the plot can start. If readers feel daunted by the proportions of the frame in the informational overload at the outset, it is because Balzac conceives "the task of the would-be historian of manners [to be] syncretic rather than mimetic."[33] The narrator is highly directive, closely controlling interpretation by glossing the meaning and history of every faded and battered object as a reflection of the status of its owner; this is indeed a "world of hypersignificant signs."[34] The narrating voice summarily and bluntly articulates this interdependence (and hence the import of the description) in the words applied to Madame Vauquer: "[T]oute sa personne explique la pension, comme la pension implique sa personne" (2: 852; "Her entire person explains the pension, just as her person implies the pension"). The resultant text is not only systematically self-interpreting, but also comprises its own frame as an intrinsic part of the narration. The descriptions create what Hamon has called "un effet d'emboîtement—texte dans le texte"[35] ("a box-like effect—a text within the text"), a kind of double enframement. Balzac's procedure corresponds to Sartre's model of the nineteenth-century novel: it is narrated from the viewpoint of wisdom and experience and listened to from a viewpoint of order. The narrator appears as a privileged reporter who has mastered his world, and is consequently able to recount to a civilized company of listeners a series of events which he can compose and name.[36] Sartre's vocabulary of mastery, composing, and naming suggests the intermediacy of a frame between readers and plot through the narrator's grasp of the events that form the fiction.

That frame, formed by the narratorial voice, is most evident in Eliot and James. In Middlemarch the Saint Theresa Prelude shows at the outset this narrator's willingness to be a vocal and quite visible stage manager. Indeed, this narrator's intrusiveness is a source of discomfort to some readers, who balk at the sententiousness of the magisterial pronouncements and at the leisurely philosophical reflections intercalated into the narrative. Eliot makes extensive use not only of the "you," familiar from Balzac, but also of a "we" that embraces readers. Even more outspokenly than Balzac, Eliot invokes readers' active participation in the construction of specific situations:

If you think it incredible that to imagine Lydgate as a man of family could cause thrills of satisfaction which had anything to do with the sense that she was in love with him, I will ask you to use your power of comparison a little more effectively, and consider whether red cloth and epaulets have never had an influence of that sort. Our passions do not live apart in locked chambers, but, dressed in their small wardrobe of notions, bring their provisions to a common table and mess together, feeding out of the common store according to their appetite. (196)

The single case of Lydgate prompts wider consideration of the laws of human behavior. The metaphor in the second sentence is, from the strictly diegetic perspective, digressive, yet it is precisely such cognitive passages that endow *Middlemarch* with its aura of mature wisdom. The narrator's steady flow of language is all the more striking in contrast to the often halting communication between the protagonists. Mr. Brooke is a politician with lapidary views uttered in incomplete sentences; Mr. Casaubon is a scholar who fails to structure and disseminate his ideas, leaving a confused mass (mess?) of notes; Fred Vincy and Mary Garth are slow and diffident in expressing their affection, and Rosamond becomes afraid to talk to her husband. *Middlemarch* shows that "in periods of social disorder and incoherence, language is one of the structures that falters."[37]

Yet order and coherence are instilled into the sprawling organism of *Middlemarch* with its multiple strands and large number of diversified protagonists, in part at least, by the insistent comments of the narratorial voice. Speaking out in the first person, this narrator ponders on the task at hand and considers its place in a bigger historical and literary schema:

But Fielding lived when the days were longer (for time, like money, is measured by our needs), when summer afternoons were spacious, and the clock ticked slowly in the winter evenings. We belated historians must not linger after his example; and if we did so, it is probable that our chat would be thin and eager, as if delivered from a camp-stool in a parrot-house. I at least have so much to do in unravelling certain human lots, and seeing how they were woven and interwoven, that all the light I can command must be concentrated on this particular web and not dispersed over that tempting range of relevancies called the universe. (170)

Thus one of the themes of *Middlemarch* is a concern how best to write the kind of novel that is in the process of being written. The contemplations—and vexations—that Flaubert relegated to his private correspondence while he worked on *Madame Bovary* are included in the text of *Middlemarch*:

And here I am naturally led to reflect on the means of elevating a low subject. Historical parallels are remarkably efficient in this way. The chief objection to them is, that the diligent narrator may lack space, or (what is often the same thing) may not be able to think of them with any degree of particularity, though he may have a philosophical confidence that if known they would be illustrative. It seems an easier and shorter way to dignity, to observe that—since there never was a true story which could not be told in parables where you might put a monkey for a margrave and *vice versa*—whatever has been or is to be narrated by me about low people may be ennobled by being considered a parable. (375)

The problem, namely, "the means of elevating a low subject," parallels the one that so preoccupied Flaubert: how to make the trivial, the commonplace, at times the vulgar artistically viable. Inevitably this is a central dilemma of the realist novelist, a consequence of the choice to record ordinary, unheroic lives. Eliot's solution differs from Flaubert's: the narrator in the passage just cited, as elsewhere in *Middlemarch*, opts to use a system of "parables" and metaphors in comments openly addressed to readers. Flaubert, on the other hand, strenuously eschews direct glosses on his writing and instead resorts to such oblique means as shifting focalization, interior monologue, and irony.

Unlike Flaubert, then, Eliot is ready to make unabashed appearances in the text as "the diligent narrator." The exhortations to readers to "remember" (335), like her interjected asides—"you see" (448), "If you want to know more" (442), "we know" (458), "You may ask why" (462)—have the effect of drawing readers intimately into the business of the storytelling. As the narrator solicits readers to share in both her knowledge and her difficulties, a strong bond develops between storyteller and audience. The figure of the narrator takes on the attributes of a chorus hovering beside and above the narration, discussing the vicissitudes—and the meaning—of the protagonists' lives. This gives to *Middlemarch* a quasi-metafictional dimension. The break between the narrator's and the protagonists' language has been deemed problematic, "an evident failure of continuity between the necessary language of the novelist and the recorded language of many of the characters."[38] Conversely, this discontinuity can be interpreted as the intervention of a powerful voice between the world of readers and that of the fiction. That voice creates a bridge between two, and at the same time a frame for the reading of the text.[39]

Similar strategies are used by Henry James, though in an accentuated form. The narrator of *The Bostonians* is a distinctive persona with certain privileges, such as eavesdropping and voyeuristic insight, as well as certain limitations. He is, for instance, "forbidden to do more than mention"[40] some aspects of Selah Tarrant's interview with Olive Chancellor, and this is by no means the only occasion when he has to confess that his knowledge is circumscribed: "Here again I must plead a certain incompetence to give an answer" (337). He is and is not an omniscient narrator insofar as he can see into characters' minds but does not command a total understanding of all the facts of the fictional world. His speech is less formal than George Eliot's, sometimes verging on the colloquial in his addresses to readers. He adopts a confiding tone when he tells readers what he has chosen to do or not to do, as the case may be: "I have not taken the space to mention certain episodes of the more recent intercourse of these ladies, and must content myself with tracing them, lightly, in their consequences" (132), or: "I despair of presenting it to the reader with the air of reality" (311). Often he allows himself remarks aimed specifically at readers: "It would take some time for me to explain the contradiction to the reader" (203); or: "I shall not attempt a complete description of Ransom's ill-starred views, being convinced that the reader will guess them as he goes, . . . I shall do them sufficient justice by saying . . . I suppose he was very conceited. . . . I know not exactly how these queer heresies had planted themselves. . . . I betray him a little . . . as I have hinted" (154–55). James has a constant awareness of his narrator as "the chronicler" (237), "the historian who has gathered these documents together" (220) that "may be communicated to the reader" (188). The fiction is therefore conceived as a narrative and even so called: "my narrative" (2); "which I mentioned in the first pages of this narrative" (204); "the occasion that we described at the beginning of this history" (148). The frequent use of "we" ("we know" [122, 126, 149]; "as we know" [89, 94, 139]; "we need" and "we meet him" [152], etc.) and the repeated references to Basil Ransom as "our young man" or "our Mississippian" (12, 30, 51, 117, 263, 354, 356) create a sense of collusion between narrator and readers. Initiated readers are encouraged to make judgments (117) and to supplement the narrative in their own imagination (79, 137).

In The Bostonians the enframing telling of the story is an ever present facet through the narrator's interpellation of readers as enterprising agents in the construction of the fiction. Because this narratorial persona tempers authority with a pronounced tentativeness, which increases as the story progresses, he makes greater demands on his readers than his predecessors. The assured certainties of Balzac's recitals of facts yield here to a groping exploration of a puzzling situation. This reflects in practical terms the change from the early realist position that "all is true" to the later modulation to "the air of reality." The

Jamesian, like the Balzacian, narrator fulfills representational and interpretive functions, showing and telling, but the balance changes with the decline in the narrator's absolute suzerainty over the fiction and the concomitant expansion of readers' input. Yet the distinction is a matter of gradation, not of kind. The contours of an intrinsic frame in the contract between narrator and readers are always discernible in the realist novel, although they appear in various guises and with different degrees of definition. The picture is composed within some type of frame, the frame that Barthes conceives as the fundamental tool of the realist's trade, and that is filled with the language that makes up the fiction.

That language is construed by readers, who complete the frame by actualizing the illusion in their minds. Such a conception ascribes to readers a far more active involvement in the institution of criticism than was for long granted to them when they were largely ignored because they were regarded as passive recipients. The recognition of readers' vital role is a substantial contribution of contemporary critical approaches which have given a much needed corrective "to a hermeneutic tradition that has tended to view all literary texts as locutions without interlocutors."[41] The impetus for this corrective has come not only from Bakhtin, whom Koelb cites, but also from a variety of directions such as reader response "affective stylistics" (or, as I prefer, reader-oriented),[42] phenomenology, deconstruction, and communication theory. The underlying model is one of interaction between a text possessing certain qualities and readers possessing certain skills: "Construction is a matter of both structure (in the text) and construing (on the part of the reader)."[43] The very act of speech implies, too, the notion of others as interlocutors. We therefore come to perceive a text "as a piece of fiction, a fiction which requires of us a response that includes an awareness of reading as an imaginative construction, rather than an empirically accurate representation."[44]

Because realist fictions have until quite recently been considered precisely as "an empirically accurate representation," relatively little attention has been devoted to the processes of readerly construing in this mode. In her survey article "The Reader in History: The Changing Shape of Literary Response,"[45] Jane Tompkins leaps from the romantic poets to I. A. Richards and T. S. Eliot as if reader response were either nonexistent or a nonsubject in nineteenth-century realist narratives. Yet the realists were very conscious of their implied readers.

They eschewed the introverted forms of the novel in letters, as a diary, or in the first person in favor of a third-person authorial narration directed outward toward to readers. One of the hallmarks of realist fiction is "consensus:"[46] consensus of vision among the protagonists but also between the narrator and readers. That consensus is best achieved through the conjoint fashioning of the frame.

The precondition for this reformulation, which takes readability and intelligibility as the focus of analysis, is to replace the perception of the realist text as a product of mimesis with an acknowledgement of its status as a structure that operates through verbal means of ordering. It is a *pretense* of mimesis in keeping with "the ur-convention of novelistic discourse . . . that the text will permit the creation of a coherent and human, if hypothetical world."[47] This echoes Culler's position in *Structuralist Poetics*: "[T]he basic convention governing the novel is the expectation that readers will be able to recognize a world which it [the text] produces or to which it refers."[48] So the novel comes to be seen as "a generative narrative"[49] insofar as it stimulates readers to project the realm of the fiction at the promptings of the text. Such an approach is distinct from the " 'psychology' of literature" that Bruner pursues in *Actual Minds, Possible Worlds*, where his aim is to "describe systematically what happens when a reader enters the Dublin of Stephen Dedalus through the text of *A Portrait of the Artist as a Young Man*" (3). What a literary analysis seeks is an understanding not of *what* happens, but of *how* it happens. By what means and through what clues does the text instigate readers' performative activity? The role-playing pretense demanded of readers in the construction of a text is based on an implied communicative situation in which readers respond to signals emitted by the narrator's text. The response is guided and controlled by the kind and amount of information offered (or withheld, in the case of gaps and contradictions) in the text. Here the image introduced by Gombrich is useful: the beholder must be given a "screen"[50] onto which to project the expected image. This screen for the visual picture is the equivalent of the frame for the verbal narrative. If the author, narrator, and text form three sides of that frame, readers form its fourth, completing dimension through their capacity to construe as real the fictional illusion contained within the frame. And one of the most fundamental elements of that construction is the orientation through place in answer to the question "Where?"

Such a metaphor of readers as the fourth dimension of the frame validates the argument that "the audience, too, is a presence within the novel."[51] That contention was put forward in relation to *Middlemarch*, but it holds for all realist fiction. The reiterated "you," "we," "us," and "our" in Eliot and James are clear illustrations of the way in which the audience is fictionalized by being named in the text. In chapter 17 of *Adam Bede*, "In Which the Story Pauses a Little," the narrator even engages in a dialogue with putative readers: "I hear one of my readers exclaim . . . "[52] as objections are imputed to readers as a pretext for the elaboration of narratorial opinions. These readers are invested with opinions of their own (172; "you will say") which may or may not coincide with the narrator's: "you would have liked him no better than you like Mr. Irwin" (171). Eliot's practice, is, commonly, to face the imaginary readers, addressing them as if confidentially in the present tense before turning to the scene about to be dramatized. This concern to draw readers into the fiction in a particular manner has been succinctly elucidated by W. J. Harvey:

Unwilling that the reader should stand outside the fictional world which she has so carefully left open and uninsulated, George Eliot challenges the reader to bring this fictional world into the most inclusive context he is capable of framing; that is, his own deepest sense of the real world in which he lives.[53]

It is interesting that Harvey here actually chooses the word "framing" to denote readers' processes. He adds that far from repelling readers or provoking dissent, such narratorial comments "are one of the bridges between our world and the world of the novel" (81) because "no sharp boundaries are drawn here; the edges are blurred and the author allows easy transition from one world to the other" (71). Instead of representing an obstacle to reading through intrusive breaks in the fictional illusion, the narratorial voice is interpreted as a mediating link between text and audience, facilitating the pretense and encouraging slippages. Eliot's art effectively meets Barthes's stipulation that "l'enjeu du travail littéraire (de la littérature comme travail), c'est de faire du lecteur non plus un consommateur, mais un producteur du texte"[54] ("the goal of literary work [of literature as work] is to make the reader no longer a consumer, but a producer of the text").

Readers are not as immediately obvious producers of the text throughout realist fiction as in Eliot and James. But even those narrators who are audible rather than visible, such as Flaubert, Mann, and Balzac, devise strategies for giving readers a presence in the text. The "nous" ("we") that is the opening word of *Madame Bovary* and that crops up sporadically through the first chapter (4,

6, 9) recurs, significantly, just once near the end, as if to close the frame of "our" gaze: "et le bois du cercueil, heurté par les cailloux, fit ce bruit formidable qui nous semble le retentissement de l'éternité" (358; "and the wood of the coffin, hit by the pebbles, made that dread sound that seems to us the reverberation of eternity"). Flaubert also occasionally uses a technique that becomes a central device for Mann: the impersonal "on"/"man," almost always translated— mistranslated—into English by the third person plural "they." When we read of Emma's and Charles's wedding: "Jusqu'au soir, on mangea. Quand on était trop fatigué d'être assis, on allait se promener dans les cours ou jouer une partie de bouchon dans la grange, puis on revenait à table" (31). De Man translates this as: "Until night they ate. When any of them were too tired of sitting, they went for a stroll in the yard, or for a game of darts in the granary, and then returned to table."[55] Admittedly, "one" would be most awkward English; however, it would better catch the subtlety of Flaubert's narration, which assimilates us as readers to the wedding guests. A parallel usage in *Bouvard et Pécuchet* has elicited this question: "Does the switch to the impersonal pronoun 'one' mark this participation, does it indicate the moment when the reader crosses the paper screen of the book, when he enters the fictional universe—the phenomenon we call 'active reading'?"[56] " 'Active reading' " is fostered by readers' positioning as hypothetical participants. That is the impact of Mann's habitual recourse to this open form: readers are made to sit in the Buddenbrooks' "landscape room," their dining room, their nursery, their courtyard, as the case may be, with the family and its entourage, playing a dual role simultaneously as observers from outside the frame and as a presence within its confines. According to T. J. Reed, that "man" generalizes about the present and suggests that this is the way people lived once so that "we see . . . as though through a kind of historical telescope."[57] The very opposite could be argued: that the "man" makes the past more present by taking us there. The narrator of *Buddenbrooks* also solicits reader input by the frequent interspersal of suspension points, which arouse a continuation of readers' thinking in speculative elaboration of the situation just recounted.

The most complex tactics are those of the Balzacian narrator, who resorts to a variety of means to relate readers to the narration. Strenuous efforts are made in the course of the opening descriptions to situate readers in regard to the narrative, and to convey to them their proper function and posture.[58] The open second-person plural allocution of readers as "vous" ("you"), common near the beginning of many of the novels of *La Comédie humaine*, alternates with the "on" formulation, both occurring especially in connection with terms of entrance and visualization to usher readers into the world of the fiction: "On entre dans cette allée" (2: 849; "One enters this alley"); "où l'on entre par une porte-fenêtre" (2: 850; "which one enters by a window-door"); "on ne voit aucun ensemble" (2: 16; "one sees no unity"); "En entrant, vous trouverez un petit palier" (2: 184; "On entering, you will find a small landing"); "En aucun lieu du monde vous ne recontreriez une demeure à la fois si modeste et si grande" (2: 185; "Nowhere in the world would you come upon a dwelling at once so modest and so large"); "La Loire est à vos pieds. Vous la dominez d'une terrasse" (2: 186; "The Loire is at your feet. You overlook it from a terrace"); "Si vous arrivez à Guérande par le Croisic, . . . vous éprouveriez une vive émotion à la vue de cette immense fortification encore toute neuve" (2: 323; "If you arrive at Guerande via Croisic, . . . you will experience deep emotion at the sight of this immense, still quite new fortification"). Apart from inducting readers physically into the fictional realm in these ways, the Balzacian narrator introduces them metonymically by means of surrogates, with whom readers can identify. These are observers of the scene or action in the text who prefigure readers' expected responses. They appear in sundry guises: as "lecteurs" (2: 15; "readers") in La Fausse Maîtresse; as "un voyageur curieux d'examiner cette ville" (2: 321; "a traveler curious to see this town") and "des archéologues" (2: 329; "archaeologists") in Béatrix; as "l'homme le plus insouciant" (2: 848; "the most carefree person") and "les amateurs de symboles" (2: 850; "lovers of symbols") in Le Père Goriot; as "un étranger" ("a stranger") in the third sentence of Eugénie Grandet; and as "un docteur ès sciences sociales" (6: 88; "a doctor of sociology") in La Cousine Bette. These "hypothetical witnesses"[59] function as bridges between the text and readers, who are, through these proxies, endowed with a double existence as outsiders and insiders, unknowing laypeople and knowing experts. With these shadowy figures, who do and do not partake of the fictional world in their capacity as spectators, the frame becomes permeable, and the crossing is mapped out for readers.

All these strategies to impel readers toward a certain construction of the text can be characterized as those of "engaging" narrators. The nineteenth-century realists have not usually been considered as particularly engaging, partly because of the myth of the narrator's absence, and partly because of the contrast with their eighteenth-century predecessors, who would freely address their audience as "dear readers" or tease them with a choice of alternative endings or lengthy, involuted digressions, and even abdicate responsibility for the narrative's course. The purposes and practices of the nineteenth-century engaging narrator have been cogently delineated by Robyn Warhol:

[the narrator] strives to close the gaps between the narratee, the addressee, and the receiver. Using narrative interventions that are almost always spoken in earnest, such a narrator addresses a "you" that is intended to evoke recognition and identification in the person who holds the book and reads, even if the "you" in the text resembles that person only slightly or not at all.[60]

An engaging narrator thus encourages readers' active participation. And even if the narratorial comments break the fictional illusion, they do so in order to bolster, not to undermine it, again in contradistinction to the eighteenth century:

Like any intervening narrator, the engaging narrator, too, intrudes into the fiction with reminders that the novel is 'only a story.' In doing so, however, engaging narrators differ from distancing narrators in that their purposes are seldom playful: they intrude to remind narratees—who, in their texts, should stand for actual readers—that the fictions reflect real-world conditions for which the readers should take active responsibility after putting aside the book. (815)

So the engaging narrator's gestures toward readers, far from acting as reminders of the characters' fictionality, insist instead that they, their predicaments, and feelings are "real" insofar as they concur with readers' own experience. The emphasis is on the community between the narrator and readers. Such narrators stand among the characters but also alongside readers; they represent an inter-section between their world and ours, where an opening, a window (to revert to James's term) onto the text can be made, through which readers are invited to enter the fictional realm. The frame is more a means of transition than of separation.

The contours of the text remain explicit, yet a (partially) illusory continuum arises as its boundaries are transcended by readers' cognitive mapping. This mapping is supported by the presence in many texts of a so-called *Relevenzfigur*, "a predominant scheme or structural matrix that stands as an equivalent for experi-ence."[61] Such a figure may be intertextual and/or intratextual. Foremost among the intertextualities are the aspirational model of Saint Theresa in *Middlemarch*, the strong echoes of *King Lear* in *Le Père Goriot*, the references to Beethoven's Fifth

Symphony in *César Birotteau*, and the importance of Schopenhauer's *Welt als Wille und Vorstellung* and Wagner's *Tristan und Isolde* in *Buddenbrooks*. The underlying presence of these guest works in their host fictions represents another kind of enframement. This type of frame, since it is literary or broadly artistic in nature, helps readers to construct the text by relating it to an already known context, thus providing an overarching *mythos* to guide and structure interpretation. Such a *mythos* can also arise internally from a pattern of repeated images whose significance gradually becomes apparent to readers through iteration. The most obvious example is the image of the web that recurs throughout *Middlemarch* in varying forms so that readers come to understand it as a symbol for the community portrayed. Frequently in realist fiction it is places that fulfill the function of a *Relevanzfigur*: the dreariness and boredom of the provinces encapsulated in Tostes and Yonville in *Madame Bovary* in contrast to the supposed glamour of Paris; the mixture of opportunity and menace in the Paris of *Le Père Goriot* and *L'Assommoir*; the austerity of the windy, restrictive streets of the city in *Buddenbrooks*. More specifically it can be houses and interiors: the Vauquer boardinghouse in *Le Père Goriot*, the shabby home in *Eugénie Grandet*, the ghastly, engulfing tenement in *L'Assommoir*, the "landscape room" in *Buddenbrooks*, and a whole series of habitations in *Middlemarch* (Casaubon's drab house, Lowick; Mr. Brooke's estate, the Grange; Freshitt, where Sir James and Celia live).[62] Through elaborate, symphonic, suggestive structures, meanings emerge for readers from the structuring of the text itself more than from direct statement. The literary strategies of narration: the orchestral organization of themes, the controlled parallelism and opposition of characters and events, and ironic juxtapositions all contribute to the crystallization of a coherent *Relevanzfigur*. And, as Hamon has emphasized in his analysis of realist discourse, "le *cohérent*" is, above all, what conveys to readers "le *réel*."[63]

The outcome, the novelist's "true end product is not the printed page, but the illusion created in the reader's mind."[64] But this illusion is not suspended in opposition to a reality, but rather melded into it. The frame grows increasingly porous as a result of readers' active implication in the construction of meanings. What is contained within the frame offers an analogy both to readers' experience of what lies outside it and to the processes of learning central to action and interpretation alike. The lessons learned by the interpreters in the text, for instance in *Middlemarch*, *Le Père Goriot*, and *The Bostonians*, parallel those learned by interpreters of the text. In their projections onto the screen evoked by cognitive mapping, details gain credibility by both a metonymic contagion and a metaphoric apperception of the whole.

So the frame proves a vital element in realist fiction as the vehicle for communication between narrator and readers. It produces a concord, a contract, by adumbrating a set of agreements not only about the happenings in the narrative, but also about appropriate modes of interpretation. The "implicit intimacy"[65] that has been underscored by recent critics[66] as a necessary precondition for an understanding of what constitutes a commensurate reading, is decisively shaped by the nature of the frame. Readers' ability to accept certain linguistic structures not as the verbal acts they resemble but as representations of such acts[67] is in fact determined by the contextualizing presence of the frame that enables the pretense. In this scenario, the creativity of the author/narrator is the triggering part of a more extensive process in which readers' imagination is an indispensable agent too. Narration becomes an art of mediation as it strives to bring readers into "the house of fiction." Because readers are essential for the actualization of the fiction, it is the activity of reading rather than mimesis, that forms the link between art and life.

4

Not So Long Ago

ॐ

There is a history in all men's lives.—Shakespeare

ॐ "Long ago and far away," like "once upon a time," is a "phrase that lifts you out of the real world."[1] Familiar to us since childhood, these stock locutions induct us as listeners and fledgling readers to respond with pleasurable excitement to their invitation to enter a world of fiction. "Long ago and far away" ushers us through the gates of ivory into a realm of romance and fantasy. It does so by underscoring remoteness from the present. Its parallel formulae in other languages, "il y a longtemps," "es war einmal," also concentrate on the temporal element to create readers' horizon of expectation. The distancing from the here and now is a central convention of romance to project readers into an alternative universe. "Long ago and far away" functions as an overt signal to readers of the narrative's intention and of its mode, and we immediately recognize it as such because we have been culturally conditioned to these conventions of storytelling. In short, "long ago and far away" is a Bakhtinian "chronotope,"[2] an intersection of time and place where the fictive action can develop.

The paramount importance of this dimension of time in narrative is beyond argument. As Christopher Prendergast has recently restated the issue:

Narratives are not only orderings of time, they are also ordered by time; 'about' time, they are also 'in' time. It is history which determines the conditions for (as well as the checks on) dynamic redescription, productive imagination and productive reference.[3]

The equivalence is here readily established between the role of time in narrative and its presence in the form of history. But the relationship of story to history is a complex one, open to multiple interpretations. Historical and fictional storytelling have generally been taken as standing at opposite poles of narrative practice. This traditional view has its source in Aristotle who draws clear-cut distinctions between the purposes of the poet and those of the historian: "[T]he poet's job is not to report what has happened but what is likely to happen: that is, what is capable of happening according to the rule of probability and necessity."[4] The distinction between the historian and the poet lies not in their mode of utterance in prose and poetry respectively, but "in the fact that the historian speaks of what has happened, the poet of the kind of thing that *can* happen" (32–33). Aristotle thus defines history and poetry, to cite Lionel Gossman's penetrating analysis, "in typically classical manner, antithetically: poetry is unified, intelligible, based on proper subordination of the part to the ends of the whole, whereas history knows only the paratactic organization of contiguity and succession."[5] Aristotle also formulates a hierarchy, placing poetic truth above historical truth because it is more philosophical and therefore more worthy of serious attention.

The Aristotelian dichotomy, albeit in altered form and stripped of its value judgments, surfaces again in Barthes's contrast between historical and literary discourse. The former is seen as essentially determined by reference to the "real," to what happened, so that functionality of detail is limited, while the latter is determined by the limits of intelligibility: "La résistance du réel . . . à la structure est très limitée dans le récit fictif"[6] ("The resistance of the real . . . to the structure is very limited in fictional narrative"). To Barthes it is therefore logical that realism should have coincided with the reign of "objective" history, of photography, the exhibition of ancient artifacts such as those excavated from the tomb of Tutankhamen, tourism to historical sites, and so forth. "*To have been there*" (88 [16]; "*l'avoir été là*") is a sufficient touchstone for the nineteenth-century conceptualization of narrative as reportage. On the other hand, readers of today do not have to "have been there" because we construct from signs on the printed page for "the reality effect." What is more, narrative, historical or fictional, is no longer regarded as primarily reportage.

The deep and continuing changes in the assumptions about the relationship between history and literature have been traced with finesse by Lionel Gossman in his essay "History and Literature: Reproduction or Signification."[7] Gossman shows how history and literature came for a while to strain in opposite directions, particularly in the course of the nineteenth century as historians withdrew more and more to the university, to be followed by historians of literature and literary critics. One curious result of this development has been that "the old common ground of history and literature—the idea of mimesis and the critical importance of rhetoric—has thus been gradually vacated by both" (230–31). So the categories of "historical narrative" and of "fictional narrative" are no longer envisaged as mutually exclusive; on the contrary, the writing of story and that of history have become allied activities. The obverse of this new dynamic interchange is that "neither history nor literature offers a terra firma from which the other can be securely surveyed" (3). The beliefs that underpinned nineteenth-century novelists' appropriation of historicity into fiction no longer hold, certainly not with the same force, for readers today. While writers such as Balzac, Zola, Eliot, and Thomas Mann had recourse to historical allusion as part of their claim to truthfulness, their strategies cannot function in this straightforward way in the late twentieth century because nowadays history is almost as relative as fiction. The slippage had been well summarized by Bruner: "So we embellish our hard-core *annales*, convert them into *chroniques*, and finally into narrative *histoires*."[8] The realists attempted the reverse of this process, giving their *histoires* the appearance of *annales*.

Yet even in this problematic guise, time remains central to realist narration because the fiction unfolds at the crucial intersection of time and place. The latter inevitably comprises the former, since every place is shaped by a temporal dimension: a particular place is locality at a particular moment from which it cannot be divorced. Places possess "toujours une historicité, soit par rapport à l'histoire universelle, soit par rapport à la biographie de l'individu"[9] ("always a historicity, either in relation to universal history or in relation to an individual's biography"). Through this dual charge, historicity can serve as a bridge between the individual life, actual or fictitious, and the situation in which the persona existed and which very likely was one of the major determinants of his or her path through life. As Auerbach has pointed out, not one of the characters of Stendhal's *Le Rouge et le noir* (*The Red and the Black*), which bears the subtitle "Chronique de 1830," is "conceivable outside the particular historical situation of the Restoration period."[10] In this sense—and only in this sense—"fiction attains its ends through the formal organization of what are essentially historical materials."[11]

It is, however, important always to bear in mind that realist fiction is using history in order to attain its own ends. It has its own agenda, which is distinct from that of the nineteenth-century historian. The novel is therefore transgressive in its exploitation of historicity, although it endeavors to conceal this, like much else. The narrator, as statement maker, poses as a reliable source with first-hand knowledge of time and place alike. But barely four pages after announcing himself as "le sécretaire" of nineteenth-century society,[12] Balzac goes on to boast: "J'ai mieux fait que l'historien, je suis plus libre" (1: 11; "I have done better than the historian, I am freer"). For Balzac regarded his "artistic activity as equivalent to an activity of a historical-interpretative and even historical-philosophical nature."[13] He "plunges his heroes far more deeply into time-conditioned dependency" (425), defining them sociologically in conformity with the historical moment, as Stendhal had done. Both Stendhal and Balzac grasped that "the serious realism of modern times cannot represent man otherwise than as embedded in a total reality, political, social, and economic, which is concrete and constantly evolving" (408). Yet despite the omnipresence of the temporal perspective, the novelist's stance as historian is a flexible one, to be assumed, and expanded, at will. The paradoxicality inherent in such an ambivalent posture seems not to have troubled Balzac any more than the contradictions in his assertions about the truthfulness of the novel.

In functioning, or posing, as historians, the realists were also intent on fore-shortening the distance between the time of writing and that of the narrative. The question of distance proves indeed more thorny in practice than that of the factuality of the evidence. For the extent of the distance is often considered a central criterion for the differentiation between romance and novel. Romance is predicated on "a certain set distance"[14] between the time (and, frequently, the locale) of the action and that of readers. Romance occurs, in short, "long ago and far away" or "once upon a time." But those are precisely among the few words that "a novel rules out," as Eudora Welty has argued for "they make a story a fairy tale by the simple sweep of the remove—by abolishing the present and the place where we are instead of conveying them to us."[15] "Fiction," Welty continues, whereby she means realist fiction, "is properly at work on the here and now, or the past made here and now; for in novels we have to be there" (58). When the distance is reduced, though not necessarily minimized, the effort required of readers "to be there" is lessened so that the presence of the alternative realm of the fiction is put within closer reach.

Realist fiction therefore aims, typically, at a time "not long ago." This middle distance in many respects makes its task considerably more complicated than that of romance, which creates a timeless time and an unplaceable place merely through the invocation of familiar semiotic cues. As a mode of narration realism seeks to do the opposite of romance: to make readers believe that the action takes place in a credible and close present. This may, at first sight, seem a less difficult goal to achieve; however, its innate problematics soon become abundantly apparent. For while "long ago and far away" is a sweeping formula that leaves all details to readers' imagination, the here and now has to be evoked in its individual specificity so as to persuade readers that they are indeed "there." Moreover, instead of admitting, as "long ago and far away" does, that the story is just that, a story, a make-believe, the realist novel sponsors, on the contrary, the myth of its authenticity.

The motive underlying realism's self-image that "*all is true*," like its assertions about faithfulness and mirroring qualities, discussed in the opening chapter, is to affirm the proximity of realist fiction to a contemporary actuality close to hand. If the purlieu of romance is the remote, some nebulous merry old England or eerie old Germany or enchanting old France, exotic islands or splendid castles, the "long ago and far away," the realist novel dwells on the here and now of ordinary, even humble existences lived out in a modest, nearly present environment.

ॐ

How then is this preferred time setting not so long ago presented in realist fiction? A luminous answer is offered by George Eliot in *Daniel Deronda*. One of its minor characters, Anna Gascoigne, has an older brother, Rex, who has been crossed in love, and who proposes to go to "the colonies"[16] as an escape. Young Anna wants to go with him, thinking: "I should have done with going out, and gloves, and crinoline, and having to talk when I am taken to dinner—and all that!" (121). Here the narrator intervenes:

I like to mark the time and connect the course of individual lives with the historic stream, for all classes of thinkers. This was the period when the broadening of gauge in crinolines seemed to demand an enlargment of churches, ballrooms, and vehicles. But Anna Gascoigne's figure would only allow the size of skirt manufactured for young ladies of fourteen. (121–22)

Apart from the pleasure afforded by its irony and humor, this is a crystalline statement of the way the realist novelist envisaged the temporal contextualization of the action: "I like to mark the time and connect the course of individual lives with the historic stream."

Daniel Deronda appeared in 1876, but the events of the plot take place a good ten years earlier. Gwendolen Harlech's imperviousness to the momentous happenings of her day is underscored as a way to convey the limitations of her mentality. Again, this is narratorial comment:

Could there be a slenderer, more insignificant thread in human history than this consciousness of a girl busy with her small inferences of the way in which she could make her life pleasant?—in a time, too, when ideas were with fresh vigour making armies of themselves, and the universal kinship was declaring itself fiercely: when women on the other side of the world would not mourn for their husbands and sons who died bravely in a common cause, and men stinted of bread on our side of the world heard of that willing loss and were patient: a time when the soul of man was waking to pulses which had for centuries been beating in him unheard, until their new sun made a life of terror or of joy. (159–60)

As Barbara Hardy points out in her introduction to the novel (22), the references here are "topical": what Gwendolen is unaware of is the suffering caused by the American Civil War and the consequent unemployment and famine among the Lancashire textile workers in 1862–63, when the Northern blockade of the Southern ports stopped the export of raw cotton for processing in the British mills. Slavery, poverty, and even freedom are concepts foreign to the mind of this young English Victorian woman, eager only "to make her life pleasant" by marrying as comfortably as she can. Gwendolen's spectacular failure to achieve that modest aim stems from her misjudgment of her future husband, which is another manifestation of the overall narrowness of her horizon and her obliviousness to human nature and experience. Her lens is so limited in its range of vision that she can see only what is immediately before her.

The temporal disposition of *Daniel Deronda* is characteristic of the usage current in the nineteenth-century realist novel. Its practices depart to some extent from its programmatic announcements of its preference for the commonplace occurrences of everyday life in the present rather than the exotic "long ago and far away" favored by the romantics. But the notion of contemporaneity must not be taken too literally since a certain remove generally intervenes between the time of the action and that of writing. Because dates are almost invariably mentioned with great precision at or near the outset, it is easy enough to measure the length of that interval. Nearly all of Balzac's novels are set several years back from the time of writing, and range even further into the past to give the economic, political, and social background to the figures and happenings. *Eugénie Grandet,* published in 1833, starts its action in November 1819 and moves forward some ten years but also reaches back to 1789 and the economic turmoil in the aftermath of the French Revolution to explain Grandet's rise to fame and fortune. Similarly, *Illusions perdues* (1837; *Lost Illusions*) unfolds between 1819 and 1830, although it also looks back as far as 1793 for the evolution of printing. *César Birotteau* (1837) begins when César is forty in 1816, yet goes back to 1792 for his prehistory. Eliot's *Middlemarch*, which came out in 1872, takes place forty years previously between the end of September 1829 and the end of May 1832 during the campaign for the First Reform Bill. *Adam Bede* (1859) is sited "[s]ixty years ago—it is a long time, so no wonder things have changed."[17] Zola's *L'Assommoir*, which dates from 1877, spans the nineteen years from 1850 to 1869 in Gervaise's life, from the moment she comes to Paris until her death. The greatest interspace occurs in Thomas Mann's *Buddenbrooks*, whose date of publication is 1900, but whose time of action extends over the forty years from 1835 to 1875, the period leading up to the unification of Germany under Bismarck.

In many realist novels a precise date for the action is included. Generally this appears right near the beginning when at least a decade, sometimes a month, and occasionally a specific day is named. Many of Balzac's novels follow this pattern: *Le Père Goriot* (1835) refers on its first page to 1819 as "l'époque à laquelle ce drame commence" ("the time when this drama begins"); *La Cousine Bette* (1846) starts with the words: "Vers le milieu du mois de juillet de l'année 1838" ("Toward the middle of July in the year 1838"), while the action of *Ilusions perdues* (1837) is located "[e]n 1821, dans les premiers jours de mai"[18] ("in 1821, in the early days of May"). This habit of overt time markers is continued by other novelists: the second chapter of *Pickwick Papers* (1837) locates its happenings exactly "on the morning of the thirteenth of May, one thousand eight hundred and twenty seven." The initial phrase of Flaubert's *L'Education sentimentale* (1869; *Sentimental Education*) is a categoric date: "Le 15 septembre 1840" ("On the fifteenth of September 1840), just as George Eliot's *Felix Holt* (1866) begins with "On the 1st of September, in the memorable year 1832, some one was expected at Transome Court." The first paragraph of Henry James's *The Europeans* (1878) denotes "a certain 12th of May, upwards of thirty years since" as the time of the events portrayed.[19]

Such dates function, as Käthe Hamburger has pointed out, as "a fictive Now": "it is not a Then in the directly or indirectly experienced past of the reader or the author, for this past is not a part of the experience of fiction."[20] According to

Hamburger, the "here and now, i.e., presentified" (96) is created not by the insertion of the date itself but by the choice of narrative tense. The present tense, which Philippe Hamon has appropriately described as "le présent d'attestation"[21] ("the attesting present") is the intrinsic factor in evoking the now in which the narrator is telling the story and into which the reader is being asked to enter. The switch to the present tense for the beginning of the action reinforces the exact dating by not only placing the fiction temporally but also by fostering the illusion of its actuality.

The frequent, exact temporal markers both illustrate how the realist novel sets about the task of creating its internal time frame and support the argument that even at the point of its first publication it was not, strictly speaking, about contemporaneous happenings.[22] But the political and social conditions, which form the frame for the fictive action, were still sufficiently available in the minds of readers of that period to be readily retrievable. They were certainly within the boundaries of human memory and oral reminiscence in the same way as the Vietnam era or the Second World War still remain in collective memory today. So, normally, the narrator assumes that readers will have a certain familiarity with the situations alluded to, although varying amounts of explanatory commentary may also be included.

While such an assumption of familiarity was justified for the vast majority of nineteenth-century readers because of their relative closeness to the events in question, that is hardly the case nowadays. What is the position of readers of today, distanced by over a hundred years from the settings of the nineteenth-century novel? What then was barely gone by has, through the passage of time, become a far more remote past, retrievable no longer by memory or word-of-mouth report, but solely through the annals of history—or the words of the text. How does this fundamental shift of perspective affect our reading of these novels? What narrative strategies are instrumental in informing readers of the temporal parameters of the fiction? What are the differing means whereby the time frame of the novel is created? And how do readers of today manage to grasp and process the data contained in the text?

Two quite disparate lines of approach are possible. Curiously, although they are so divergent as to be virtually antithetical, they remain nonetheless mutually compatible. The first and more direct is to treat the texts as having acquired de facto the status of historical novels, period pieces that may be used as adjuncts to social history. The other, more complex perception is to regard the temporal markers as a kind of code, as one of the sustaining conventions of realist fiction, which readers recognize as such without having to master the particularities of the actual historical circumstances. I will briefly outline the first approach before elaborating further on the second, more provocative one.

To read nineteenth-century fiction as history has become fairly common. Attempts have been made, often very successfully, to reconstruct the Paris of Balzac or Zola, the Lübeck of Thomas Mann's *Buddenbrooks*, the Chicago of Dreiser's *Sister Carrie*.[23] With the increase of interest on the part of many historians in the lives of ordinary people, the nineteenth-century realist novel has come to be seen as a valuable repository of information about such matters as family relationships and women's experiences. Obviously, any discerning historian will evaluate this kind of evidence with due caution, mindful always of the underlying fact that fiction is fiction, and that its aims differ from those of biography or history. Nevertheless, despite this reservation, the nineteenth-century realist novel yields significant insight into social customs at various levels on the class spectrum. For instance, women's working conditions are vividly shown in many of these texts: the formation and role of the governess in *Jane Eyre, Villette,* and *Agnes Grey,* the vicissitudes of a servant's employment in George Moore's *Esther Waters,* the business of laundering in Zola's *L'Assommoir,* the occupation of dressmaker in Elizabeth Gaskell's *Mary Barton,* and the pursuit of prostitution in Zola's *Nana* and the Goncourt brothers' *Germinie Lacerteux.* To read through the lens of the historian is, literally, an act of retrieval in which the novel is cast into the role of a primary document, a nearly contemporaneous eye-witness account of places, customs, and predicaments, as they appeared to one particular observer. It is to confirm Balzac's grandiose vision of the novelist as "the secretary" to the nineteenth century, recording for posterity a present that has since become a past, yet that remains vivid forever through the images evoked by the text. The undesirable corollary to such a method is its tendency to reduce the fiction to mere material by disregarding its aesthetic configuration.

The aesthetic configuration, on the other hand, is central to the alternative mode of reading the past in nineteenth-century realist fiction. The act of retrieval here has an entirely different thrust: instead of envisaging the historical allusions as reflections of a once existent actuality, it seeks for recognition of their representative status as signals of contextuality. This is a predominantly literary mode of apprehension, because it focuses on the overall tactics of the discourse and their impact on readers rather than on the details of specific happenings, or even the truthfulness of the account. The fiction embraces historical materials, assimilating them into its fictive fabric. The narrative thus draws on temporal elements as a scaffold, a means not only of ordering its own time but also of placing itself on the timescale of historicity. Areas of overlap between historic and fictive time are partnered by points of disjuncture as the historiography within the text stands at the crossroads between functionality and performance.[24] Such a conception envisages the novelist not primarily as a historian, as Balzac would have it, but rather as a creative writer who chooses to graft the historical onto the arena of the fiction. This reordering of priorities does not impugn the veracity of the historical moment, as presented in the text. On the contrary, historical facts are brought into the fiction primarily to buttress its semblance of truth. Dates, like names, have been deemed "hostages to verifiability."[25] The introduction of the historical dimension into realist fiction is clearly intended as a warranty of authenticity, but it fulfills this purpose by more oblique means than is generally thought.

There are several ways of introducing historical allusions into a fictional text. At one end of the spectrum is Balzac, whose narrator functions openly as a chronicler, expounding the geographic location and the social and economic background to the plot before it gets under way. So *Eugénie Grandet* has a packed thirty-page overture, which tends to exasperate most readers eager to hear her story. The voice of the narrator, plainly addressing postulated readers in the second person ("vous"), first describes in highly evocative detail the street, the house, and the town where the Grandets live. From this present time of the narrative he moves thirty years into the past to 1789 to trace Old Grandet's rise to fortune and eminence during the tempestuous post-Revolutionary years. The various financial transactions and speculations by which he made his money over the years are explained with the utmost precision in a series of figures, which may not mean much in themselves to readers today, but which do convey a clear idea of Grandet's shrewd and inventive business acumen. What makes his career so fascinating is its direct connection to the economic and political vicissitudes of France during and just after the Napoleonic period. The narrator enumerates exactly where Grandet stood financially and socially in 1789, what steps he took in 1793, 1806, 1811, 1816, and 1817 in order to arrive at his present, that is, 1819 wealth and power in the little town of Saumur. He is a product of his time who has cleverly been able to turn the rapid shifts in government from Consulate to Empire to Restoration to his own advantage. The sale of clergy property put him on the path to prosperity, and he has used his position as mayor to build roads that further his business interests by providing better access to his vineyards.[26]

Readers who are not trained historians of the French Revolution, which is to say most of us, are bewildered by this plethora of economic data, and very likely tempted to skip a few pages, merely registering that Grandet is very rich, and that he has become so by rather devious manipulations. Such a hasty skimming of the text at this point is a pity because the account of Grandet's ascent is given for good reason. It is far more than a reflection of Balzac's own passionate involvement with money matters, or even than an expression of his chosen intent to reveal the hidden mainsprings of the nineteenth century. In the transformation of French society through the emergence of a more powerful bourgeoisie to replace the weakened aristocracy, the redistribution of capital is a central factor. Grandet, with his millions made in the wine trade, his authority as mayor of Saumur, and his prestige as a holder of the Legion of Honor, is an exemplar of this new breed. From this perspective already, Grandet's background is important to the novel; the knowledge readers are given of him serves to ground the text in a historical context.

Beyond that, however, the plausibility of the created story of Eugénie is enhanced through its roots in her father's career and its embedment in the historical situation. The credibility evinced by the outer historical setting, whose accuracy is open to substantiation, is extended to the fictitious areas of the text, which readers know to be invented, but whose capacity to convince is sustained by the high truth quotient of its frame. The possibles of realist fiction derive much of their force from the deliberate ways in which they are related to the actuals of history. The belief that readers are prepared to invest in Grandet's life history, because it coincides with facts ascertainable from other sources, such as documents of the period, is, as it were, transferred onto the fictitious life story of Eugénie. Without merely playing on words, story can here be seen as partaking of history and as growing out of it, seeking through that conjunction to accredit itself as truth and to command readers' trust. The specifics of Grandet's finances, tedious though they may be in themselves, produce something tantamount to the Barthian "reality effect," the impression through the accumulation of particulars that the text is indeed a representation of reality. So does Balzac's evident attachment to worn, old, shabby objects, which have had adventures and thus possess a historical past correlative to that of their owners.[27] His pronounced interest in old houses is one more manifestation of his tendency to view people and things with an archaeologist's eye, with a sense for qualities beneath their surface that point to a past still latent in the present. Similarly, his technique of recurrent characters ("retour des personnages"), some of whom make multiple appearances in *La Comédie humaine*, is a further device to create historical depth as the life and career of, for example, Rastignac, is traced over the years. The most curious aspect of Balzac's practice in *Eugénie Grandet* and elsewhere is that once the historical frame is in place, he more or less forgets it as soon as the plot is launched. The progress of fictional time is noted with care (ten years in *Eugénie Grandet*), but there are no further extraneous historical markers. The world of the fiction becomes sufficient unto itself.

Balzac's practice differs from that prevailing in most other nineteenth-century realist novels, where there is a continuing dialogic interchange between history and fiction as the characters not only comment on the events of the day but become involved in them, and find their lives directly affected by them. So the protagonists themselves, rather than the narrating voice, become the source of historical intelligence. The historicity retains the same function as in Balzac, providing a larger enframing dimension for the fiction and a link to a reality external and prior to the narrative. Yet at the same time it is subsumed into the fabric of the fiction. Such use of historical allusion can well be illustrated in George Eliot's *Middlemarch*, Zola's *L'Assommoir*, and Thomas Mann's *Buddenbrooks*. All of them draw on history to help to establish the validity of the fictional realm, though they do so in somewhat different ways and through diverse lenses.

Middlemarch, published in 1872, has its action take place between 30 September 1829 and the end of May 1832. A date, 1829, is specified only once in the novel in chapter 15;[28] nevertheless, the historical undercurrent is strong and extremely important. Eliot's notebooks, published as the *Quarry for "Middlemarch"*,[29] reveal the care with which she collected her data. The first part of the *Quarry* is devoted largely to medical matters, such as the then current views on delirium tremens (35–36), the spread of cholera (36), the distinction between typhus and typhoid fevers (29), microscopic discovery and cell theory (25), and the organization and remuneration of the profession as recorded in the *Lancet* of 1830 (21–25). The second part of the *Quarry* begins by mapping the dates of the major happenings of the fiction. Eliot's veritable passion for exactitude is shown in her listing of the dates of university examinations at Oxford and Cambridge (44) in order to fix when Fred Vincy could have taken his degree. In the outline (46–

51), a month is assigned to each of the novel's eight parts: part 1 begins in December, 2 in February, 3 in April, 4 in October, 5 for August, another October for 6, December again for 7, and finally February for 8, so that both the total time span of the action and the timing of each part is precisely mapped. The main dates of political events between 1830 and 1833 are listed (43–44 and 55–56); though fragmentary, the information is remarkably specific. These public dates are related to the "private dates," that is, the principal events in the lives of the protagonists such as births, marriages, and deaths (45–46). The fictive characters are established with the same insistence on precision; for instance, the ages of all the Garth children are set out, as well as those of Bulstrode, Raffles, Joshua Rigg, and even his mother, who never makes an appearance in the novel (52). Likewise, the names, occupations, and votes of the members of the hospital board of directors are listed (44–45). The Quarry therefore affords a unique and fascinating glimpse into the process whereby Eliot created her fictive world and simultaneously mounted it onto actual events.

The centrality of history to Middlemarch is revealed by another facet of its genesis. Originally Eliot was working on two separate narratives: one about Miss Brooke set in a town called Misterton, and the other about a physician in Middlemarch. Her decision to conflate the two tales was prompted by her realization of their contemporaneity: both take place in the period immediately preceding the passing of the First Reform Bill. In a letter of 5 April 1871 to her American publishers, Osgood, Ticknor, and Company, she underscores the spatial and temporal setting of the novel: "It a story of English provincial life—time 1830— and will be in three volumes."[30] The transitional state of provincial England at that particular time therefore forms one of the major organizing elements in Middlemarch. Politically, the death of George IV, to which indirect reference is made, and the campaign for the First Reform Bill, which was passed on 7 June 1832, that is, shortly after the end of the fictional time span, mark the passage from one era to the next. Socially, the transitions are adumbrated in the mention of the Catholic Question early on, in the evidence of some increasing mobility between the classes in the marriages that are, despite opposition, contracted, and above all in Lydgate's endeavors to modernize the system of medical care, which fail because of the entrenched conservatism and suspiciousness of the leading citizens of Middlemarch. Economically, a rural artisan mode of production is on the verge of industrialization: there is some talk about machine breaking as a problem of the day and lengthy discussion of the impact of the railroad line to be cut near the town. The progress of the Reform Bill acts both as a guiding thread in its physical incidents and as a structural metaphor to symbolize the efforts of individuals to evolve or reform themselves.

So the mythopoeic as well as the factual aspects of historicity are brought into play. In the opening words to the Prelude, readers are invited to ponder on the processes of history, and to view the happenings of the fiction through the lens of history as well as of myth:

> Who that cares much to know the history of man, and how the mysterious mixture behaves under the varying experiments of time, has not dwelt, at least briefly, on the life of Saint Theresa? (25)

This is one of the few direct invocations of history by the narrating voice. Eliot's predominant procedure is, as Jerome Beaty has aptly described it, "history by indirection,"[31] as significant events and trends are adduced piecemeal and almost casually. The interval of a quarter of a century between the time of writing and fictional time acts as a means of distancing. The narrative is deliberately conscious of its historicity and carries the implication that the past is a mode of the present. The world contained within the fiction is one where events have already happened, but because of the human inclination to repetition, are liable to be reiterated, mutatis mutandis. The comparison of Dorothea to Saint Theresa draws a large temporal arc that places Middlemarch in the context of a historicomythical schema that transcends the limits of the fiction's temporal parameters.

Eliot's method is in sharp contrast to that of the Balzacian narrator, who stands up at the beginning to recite a cohesive account of the characters' past in relation to their time. The tactics of indirection are more subtle; although they make greater demands on the reader, they implement a deeper fusion of history and story. History becomes central to the plot insofar as it represents the limitations encountered by the protagonists, and as they experience the thwarting of their desires, we as readers come to have a live sense of the time and place. Middlemarch itself, with all its gossip and web of personal and family connections, is the incarnation of a mentality, one that resists progress and opposes innovation. Mr. Brooke, who supports the Reform Bill, is not elected to Parliament. Dorothea is not able to carry out her benevolent schemes for cottages, her dream of social improvements for the poor, nor is she ever recognized as an intellectual equal of men. "Young ladies," she is told, "don't understand political economy" (39) and "women were expected to have weak opinions" (31). Lydgate's advanced plans for an isolation hospital for such contagious diseases as cholera, derived from his partly European training, arouse so much hostility and distrust of his judgment as a doctor that he has to leave Middlemarch for lack of patients and income. In all these instances, historical situations are immanent to the text, present in dim silhouette by allusion, yet decisively active in the unfolding of the plot as they determine the lives of the protagonists. Through this circumspect, yet calculated infusion of historical matter into the scenario of Middlemarch, the macrocosm of the world beyond the microcosm of this small provincial town is adumbrated. This lends the place both a wider universality and a heightened air of reality as the frontiers of fact and fiction become blurred within the novel. The response of fictive characters to actual happenings or dilemmas of their time is a fine practical instance of that technique of montage characteristic of realist fiction, whereby the fictive story is mounted into a knowable context, which serves by metonymic implication as a warrant for its authenticity.

There are similarities but also some cardinal differences between Middlemarch and L'Assommoir. Like George Eliot, Zola practices "history by indirection," weaving allusions to current concerns into the characters' conversation. However, he also resembles Balzac in conceiving the novelist as a social historian. The subtitle of the cycle of twenty novels, of which L'Assommoir is the seventh, is Histoire naturelle et sociale d'une famille sous le Second Empire (Natural and Social History of a Family under the Second Empire). This provides explicit temporal boundaries in the dates of the Second Empire (1852–70), as well as an avowal of the writer's intention to proceed as an analytical annalist of the period. The action of L'Assommoir, which was published in 1877, takes place between 1850 and 1869, and is punctuated by references to events of the day, as in Middlemarch. But while the main characters in Eliot's novel are educated middle to upper class, those in L'Assommoir are working class, struggling to survive in the slums of Paris. Their perspective is affected by their lowly position in society. Although they speak about voting in elections, about Bonaparte, the head of state, and about revolutions and republics, they have no immediate stake in these political developments. They are much rather the recipients, the victims of circumstances, watching passively on the margins as changes are enacted that will shape their lives too. Historicity enters into the fiction as a determinant of human lives, but on a less conscious and intellectual level than in Middlemarch. The fact that many of the political discussions are held while the characters are drunk both accounts for and denotes their lack of comprehension. The historical markers also become more scant in the latter part of the novel; as the family declines into abject poverty and alcoholism, they are increasingly preoccupied with mere day-to-day existence, intent on their own pressing problems with food and heating to the exclusion of larger issues.

As in *Middlemarch*, the women never voice any political views or have any say in discussions. In contrast to this absence, however, a more domestic aspect of history is registered largely through the eyes of the main female figure, Gervaise. The time span of *L'Assommoir* coincides with the architectural transformation of Paris by Baron Haussmann into a modern, designed city with avenues fanning out from the Arc de Triomphe. As Gervaise wanders through the streets of the area where she lives, she sees the reconstruction in progress with the demolition of the old hovels and their replacement with what seem to her like monuments: houses with six storys, their facades sculptured like churches, with bright windows hung with curtains, all exhaling an aura of prosperity. She feels disturbed and threatened by this splendor, dislodged from her familiar district, which is being gentrified beyond her means. Like the men with politics, she does not understand the causes or the significance of what she sees; hers is an instinctive reaction from her angle of vision. But for readers these allusions to the rebuilding of Paris are a clever way of referring to a known project of that time, and so again of locating the fictive characters and happenings in relation to an actual time and place.

The same strategies occur in Thomas Mann's *Buddenbrooks*. The social level is closer to that of *Middlemarch*, perhaps even somewhat higher, for the Buddenbrooks are patricians, deeply involved in the government of the north German Hanseatic city where they have lived for generations. The historical panorama emerges, as in *Middlemarch*, through the experiences and conversations of the characters, not through recital by a narrator. The opening chapter is devoted to the celebration of the Buddenbrooks' new house; the protracted festive dinner gives ample opportunity for the exposition of the political, social, and political problems of the day as they concern the protagonists.

This is one example of the great deftness with which the historical context is sketched to form a verifiable external frame of reference for the fictive action.[32] The time span of *Buddenbrooks* extends from 1835 to 1875; exact temporal indicators, such as dates, occur at or near the beginning of each section, and are generously interspersed elsewhere. Each of the first three generations is shown in response to the events of the day. Old Johann has doubts about the July

Monarchy of 1830, while his son, Jean, prefers Louis-Phillippe. The views of the young medical student, Morten Schwarzkopf, who is the object of Tony's first love, have also been decisively shaped by the upheavals of 1848 toward a championship of freedom, equality, and democracy. During the turbulence of that year, the peace of the Buddenbrook household is rudely disturbed by the maid's open insurrection. That little domestic scene is a vivid instance of Mann's ability to integrate the macrocosm of history into the microcosm of the fiction as the "neue Geist der Empörung"[33] ("the new spirit of rebellion") penetrates even into the sanctum of the dining room. The Austro-Prussian war of 1870, too, makes both physical and financial incursions on the Buddenbrooks: Prussian officers are billeted for a while in the Buddenbrook residences, and the following year the firm suffers big losses in the postwar reorganization.

As political and economic happenings impinge on the Buddenbrooks' lives, the boundaries between the actual and the fictive are thrown open. The historical is interwoven into the fictive in an extraordinarily adept and quite unobtrusive manner: for instance, the part played by street lighting in quelling the 1848 riots, and, later, Thomas's progressive advocacy of gas lighting. The coverage of problematical sociohistorical issues, such as the formation of the North German Customs Union and the development of railway communications amounts to much more than local color; the history of Lübeck is subsumed into the plot as the factors shaping its fortune simultaneously affect those of the Buddenbrooks. The eclipse of the old-style patricians and the concomitant empowerment of a vigorous new capitalist bourgeoisie is a fundamental aspect of the change traced in the novel. The commerce between public and private, which corresponds to that between historical and fictive, gives a live insight into the decline of the conservative ruling class, who are ousted, in an overtly symbolical ploy, from their house as well as from their position of preeminence by the risk-taking nouveaux riches. By the end of the novel, with the male Buddenbrook line extinct, the family is to all intents and purposes disenfranchised from political and historical activity.

Such interplay of fact and fiction as occurs in Middlemarch, L'Assommoir, and Buddenbrooks represents the dominant pattern in the nineteenth-century realist novel. These works stand toward the center of the spectrum of approaches to the task of evoking the "not so long ago." At one end of that spectrum is Balzac, whose narrator, as it were, stands up before the class of readers to give them instructive information. In the middle and in the majority are those writers such as George Eliot, Zola, and Thomas Mann, who cunningly fuse history and fiction, making readers cognizant of the historical situation vicariously through the protagonists' experience. An extreme variant on this is Henry James, who is at the opposite pole to Balzac in providing readers with virtually no data, letting everything transpire from the interaction of the characters.

This is the method in *The Bostonians*. The paramount historical fact underlying *The Bostonians* is the Civil War, over twenty years past at the time of its publication in 1886, and a good ten years anterior to the fictive action. Although the internal passage of time is carefully followed, the year is left open as 187–, and even that is not mentioned until page 129, contrary to the customary practices of realist fiction. On the other hand, there are multiple overt references to the war as a recent, traumatic event that has fundamentally affected every one of the main characters. The war and the toll it has taken in lives and economic ruination in the South are a constant presence throughout the novel.

It is reiterated too in the plot, in the confrontation between the Southerner, Basil Ransom, who has come north to start up as a lawyer, and the Northern establishment incarnated in his Bostonian cousin, Olive Chancellor. In the opening scenes, Basil has to spend much time waiting: so the Southerner, manipulated by wily Northerners, experiences alienation through reification and expropriation, just as does Lydgate in *Middlemarch*. The tensions between North and South are compounded by the parallel antagonism between men and women in the early phases of the feminist struggle for women's suffrage. In the rivalry between Basil and Olive for the affection of Verena Tarrant a segment of political history is enacted through the plot of the novel. The historical situation has a motivational and explanatory function. One of the novel's great climaxes comes in the episode when Verena shows Basil round Harvard and takes him into Memorial Hall, which commemorates "the sons of the University who fell in the long Civil War" and which makes the Southerner forget "the whole question of sides and parties" in a reverie of remembrance that "arched over friends as well as enemies, the victims of defeat as well as the sons of triumph" (198). In this scene it becomes very clear how historical fact, that is, the existence of Memorial Hall at Harvard and its public meaning, are incorporated into the fiction to serve its purposes, in this case to reveal the Southerner's changing understanding of the Civil War and the North. Since power is conceived in *The Bostonians* as the ability to establish one's own sense of time and one's own version of history, this episode marks, structurally, a pivotal turning point in the middle of the novel.

And more important, Basil's response to the tablets inscribed with the names of the dead also consummates the interface of fact and fiction.

The narrator in *The Bostonians* makes historical allusions on the patent assumption of readers' familiarity with the Civil War. At the time of publication that was undoubtedly justified, and probably even a hundred years later most readers command a sufficient outline of American history to construct the plot without difficulty, grasping the implications of the conflict between the North and the South. The Jamesian narrator always postulates readers as erudite and globe-trotting as he is himself, whereas Balzac conceives readers as in need of instruction.

ঈ৯

The contrast between Balzac's and James's methods of appropriating the historical raises a basic issue about the introduction of historical allusions into fiction: the kinds of assumption made concerning readers' knowledge. This question is of fundamental importance. Without examining their underlying presumptions, critics have been tempted to cast historical materials in fiction as an anchor mooring the fictional world to an ascertainable extraneous reality. Such a reading derives in part from the implicit belief that readers have an easy familiarity with eighteenth- and nineteenth-century history, which may well not be the case by the late twentieth century. The mere presence of a historical substratum to the plot has generally been interpreted as evidence of factuality. "We are more easily prey to referential illusion," Inge Crosman Wimmers observes, "when the work we are reading abounds in historical or geographic detail, evoking a whole era or milieu."[34] Drawing on Umberto Eco's theories of semiotics, she points to the cultural connotations of words and particularly of names such as "Napoleon." For informed readers such connotations can be vital clues emanating from the text to trigger a chain of associations, which can be brought to bear on the process of reading, turning it in part into a system of recognitions. But how do those many readers fare whose notions of history are rather vague?

The answer to this predicament is connected to the changes in the perception of history that have radically queried the traditional view that the reading of history (and of realist fiction) is essentially a matter of recognition. The fluidity and precariousness of what once were regarded as "facts" is nowadays widely acknowledged by historians who opt to explore a range of possible interpretations of events in the same way as literary critics do with a text. The current historiography of the French Revolution illustrates just how divergent the readings may be and how acute the differences of opinion. The former assured distinction between historicity and fiction has been replaced by an awareness of their reciprocal porosity and the similarity of the two modes. In the late 1920s E. M. Forster could still see the novel as "bounded by two chains of mountains, neither of which rises very abruptly—the opposing ranges of Poetry and of History."[35] This cozy dichotomization is refuted by Hayden White, who conceives the writing of history as an act of reconstructive narration akin to that of fiction. Such a vision has especially resonant repercussions for realist fiction:

> In my view, the whole discussion of the nature of "realism" in literature flounders in the failure to assess critically what a genuinely "historical" conception of "reality" consists of. The usual tactic is to set the "historical" over against the "mythical," as if the former were genuinely *empirical* and the latter were nothing but *conceptual*, and then to locate the realm of the "fictive" between the two poles. Literature is then viewed as being more or less *realistic*, depending upon the ratio of empirical to conceptual elements contained within it.[36]

In lambasting the old, polarized conceptualization of both historicity and realism, White insists on the coextensiveness of history and fiction. The boundary is open in both directions: the role of fictionalization is conceded in the writing of history, just as the input of historicity is prominent in the creation of the fictive universe. In realist fiction those boundaries are constantly crossed in the close interface between the strands of historicity and fictiveness. In most realist novels the two are so intimately intertwined as to be virtually inseparable. Lives, and plots, are dependent on circumstances.

This fundamental reassessment of the relationship between history and literature has far-reaching implications for readers of realist narrative. It is particularly consequential for those readers who do not (or not yet) command an extensive array of cultural connotations, yet who are nonetheless well able to construct the text. For it proves perfectly feasible to read *Middlemarch* without much knowledge of British constitutional law or the advance of industrialization or medical history, and the same holds true for *L'Assommoir* in regard to the politics of the Second Empire in France and the reconstruction of Paris by Baron Haussmann, and of *Buddenbrooks* in relation to the Austro-Prussian war of 1865, the North German Confederation of 1867, and the steps toward the unification of Germany under Bismarck in 1870. It is a rare reader who would be conversant with the Preston weavers' strike of 1853, which forms the core of Dickens's *Hard Times*, or the 1884 strike of miners at Anzin in Northern France in Zola's *Germinal*, or the British Chartist movement of the early 1840s in which John Barton in Elizabeth Gaskell's *Mary Barton* takes part as a delegate in the march from Manchester to London to present a petition to Parliament. In none of these instances are readers at all likely to be well informed of the factual basis of the narrative, but in every case the plot remains readily intelligible. In other words, it is not by virtue of our expertise as historians but rather through our competence as readers that we are enabled to grasp the historical strands of these novels. The intelligent exercise of the accepted strategies of reading supersedes the necessity for proficiency in history.

In this revised scenario for reading the "not so long ago," how do readers accomplish their quasi-automatic retrieval of the past? What is the inherent process? Unless they are consciously reading as social historians, the extent of their knowledge (or ignorance) of the historical data ultimately matters very little. Readers do not need to have the various dates and developments at their fingertips because they do not construct the text by direct reference to an external chronological format. Within the economy of the fictive realm the historical allusions function as a code that represents past happenings. Once the dimension of historicity is conceived in this way as essentially a code denoting a past time, it becomes apparent that rigorous knowledge of its intricacies is not a prerequisite for reading. Indeed, the annotations and footnotes, however illuminating they may be informationally, tend to interfere with our capacity to organize the narrative because they intrude materials extraneous to the realm of the fiction in which we are engrossed.

To acknowledge historicity as a code accounts for readers' capacity to retrieve the past directly from the promptings of the text without prior or additional instruction. As a recognizable code, the historical elements in realist fiction fulfill in many respects a function parallel to the "long ago and far away" of romance. Just as that formulaic phrase signals entry into a sphere of fantasy, dream, and desire, remote from the here and now, the historical allusions in realist fiction give access, through the gates of horn, to a fictive universe that purports to offer a true and faithful image of an actuality of not so long ago. The interweaving of historical allusions into the texture of the fiction invites readers to pretend to believe in the truthfulness of the narrative. It is, therefore, a manipulation of readers by verbal means, again like "long ago and far away" dependent on cultural programming: in this instance, our tendency to associate history with fact, and fact with truth. The process in realist fiction turns out in the last resort to be not so different from that in romance, although the tactics are more intricate, comprising a detour via history.

When reading becomes a matter of recognizing in the historical allusions a code associated with truth telling, and accepting it as a cipher for trustworthiness, it is in effect a form of inventiveness and invention. As Clayton T. Koelb has maintained, "The inventions of reading are no less inventions of history."[37] The temporal factor of the chronotope furnishes another of the crossovers in which realist fiction abounds, enabling readers to cross not so much from fact to fiction as from function to performance. The brilliance, resourcefulness, and cunning of realism's strategies can once again be uncovered beneath its patina of artlessness.

Historicity is thus a most potent prop of realist fiction. The word "prop" is used here in both its senses: as a support, and as stage decor. Historical allusion sustains the realist novel's claim that "*all is true*," while at the same time contributing to the evocation of a credible setting not so long ago. As an actuality of the recent past becomes the present of the narrative, an "air of reality" is lent to the fiction. When history merges into fiction, fiction legitimizes itself as history.

5

The Game of the Name

ॐ

What's in a name?—Shakespeare

Lookers-on see most of the game.—Proverb

ॐ "Might not the magic lie partly in the *name* of the place—?" Eudora Welty interjects this provocative question into her suggestive essay, "Place in Fiction."[1] She immediately answers in the affirmative by pointing to the far greater evocative force of "The Hanging Gardens of Babylon" than just "The Hanging Gardens." In this instance, clearly, the name, with its allusions to mythical and biblical narratives adds intertextual and associative dimensions to the phrase. What Welty illustrates does indeed amount to a kind of magic in readers' reaction to place-names. Since naming is one of the recurrent devices of realist fiction, it needs to be further sounded. What are the sources of this "magic"? How does it work? Specifically, in what ways and to what effects are place-names introduced into realist narrative? How do they contribute to drawing readers into the fiction's realm of pretense?

The hitherto dominant view has taken its cue from a comment by Henry James in the preface to *Roderick Hudson*: "To name a place in fiction, is to pretend in some degree to represent it."[2] The emphasis has, under the sway of mimetic readings of realism, almost invariably been on the representational aspects of names. Even in criticism published in the 1980s this traditional position has been reiterated, if not convincingly reinforced. H. Meili Steele, for instance, in his discussion of *The Golden Bowl* by Henry James maintains: "The text has many features of realistic discourse that ground the action in London society of approximately 1900. . . . The most obvious referential force is the use of historical place names: 'London,' 'Brighton,' 'Paris,' 'Rome.' "[3] Similarly, Henri Mittérand sees the name of the place functioning as an absolute guarantee of authenticity:

C'est le lieu qui fonde le récit, parce que l'événement a besoin d'un *ubi* autant que d'un *quid* ou d'un *quando*; c'est le lieu qui donne à la fiction l'apparence de le vérité. . . . Le nom du lieu proclame l'authenticité de l'aventure par une sorte de reflet métonymique qui court-circuite la suspicion du lecteur: puisque le lieu est vrai, tout ce qui lui est contigu, associé, est vrai.[4]

It is place that forms the foundation of narrative because the action needs an *ubi* [where] as much as a *quid* [what] or a *quando* [when]; it is place that gives fiction the appearance of truth. . . . The name of the place proclaims the authenticity of the adventure by a kind of metonymic reflection which short-circuits the reader's suspicion: since the place is true, all that is connected and associated with it is true too.

An even more sweeping generalization is made by Leonard Lutwack, who asserts: "Realistic writing is philosophically committed to the faithful rendering of actual places in order to qualify as realism."[5] This is a circular argument, based on an unexamined acceptance of the realists' own claims. Evidently, the self-image they propagated has persisted in some critics' minds with extraordinary tenacity.[6]

However, the poststructuralist perception of realist fictions as verbal compositions rather than as imitations of reality has initiated new approaches so that the time has come for a reassessment of the deployment and function of names. The current apprehension underscores "a most complex and unstable relationship between texts and worlds, with various levels of heterogeneity preventing texts from faithfully depicting worlds."[7] The implications of this tenet have been explored in interesting directions by Sandy Petrey in *Realism and Revolution*. He begins with this reminder: "As theorists of language from the Greeks to Derrida have pointed out, proper nouns are in important and persuasive ways the best evidence for the thesis that the function of words is to designate things that are not words."[8] Taking examples from Le Père Goriot, Petrey goes on to illustrate some of the slippages inherent in the use of names by fictive characters. The duchess of Langeais not only reduces Napoleon to Bonaparte, but also strips Goriot of his patriarchal dignity and distorts his name into Doriot, Moriot, Loriot. In part these displacements denote, of course, the aristocrat's contempt for both the upstart and the bourgeois. Yet they also suggest the precariousness of linguistic denomination. Petrey adds: "When the firmest of all linguistic units becomes loose and flighty, it is impossible to imagine how realist language could achieve its traditional task of conveying the reality of a world prior to language" (87).

Once the automatic referential conjunction of word and thing is opened up to such fundamental query, proper names, too, forfeit something of their old status as emblematic icons. The change of focus can best be summarized by reverting to James in order to put the spotlight now onto the idea of "pretend" instead of onto "represent." To discern the mechanisms of that pretense is to go a long way toward understanding the operative strategies of realist fiction. Names are an excellent instance because they play so crucial a role in the game of pretense that lies at the heart of realism. They are even more challenging than historicity because of the fundamental asymmetry of time and place in narrative. While a correspondence may be established in terms of time between the structuring of the text and that of the world, no parallel constant correlation can be evinced between the locale of the nineteenth-century realist text and that of readers' world.[9]

That so many nineteenth-century novels include a place-name or an element of localization in their titles is certainly no coincidence: Mansfield Park, Northanger Abbey, Wuthering Heights, La Chartreuse de Parme, Middlemarch, Barchester Towers, The Bostonians, The Europeans, The Spoils of Poynton, Le Curé de Tours, The Mayor of Casterbridge, The Master of Ballantrae, Tartarin de Tarascon, Die Leute von Seldwyla, Immensee, Cranford, North and South, Lourdes, Rome, and Paris, are a few random examples. In part this tendency reflects the reduction of interest in the journey, the picaresque adventures common in the fiction of the previous century. The greater proportion of female protagonists also fosters stasis, since women, with the exception of a few unconventional adventurers, had far less freedom and mobility than men. The typical woman's life was often indeed a tale of confinement amounting almost to imprisonment. So the nineteenth-century novel is more stationary, more rooted in a single central location as well as enmeshed in domestic trammels. The limitation to a single place is one of the characteristics of realist discourse as enumerated by Philippe Hamon: "Les références à un *ailleurs* (exotisme) seront donc réduites, et le héros réaliste voyagera sans doute fort peu loin de son milieu. L'Histoire viendra à lui, plutôt que lui n'ira au loin chercher l'Histoire (des histoires)"[10] ("References to an *other* [exoticism] will therefore be reduced, and the realist hero will doubtless not travel far from his environment. History will come to him, rather than his going far to look for History [stories]"). As a result of this restriction of the action to one major locale, that one place is evoked with far greater attention than was feasible or necessary for the multiple sites of previous narratives.

The necessity springs from the new role ascribed to milieu. Only in the late eighteenth and early nineteenth centuries does fiction begin to develop environment as a matrix in which character is formed, and with this, the close articulation of places and people. Earlier, place had mainly functioned allegorically in works as diverse as the *Odyssey*, Dante's *Divine Comedy*, and Bunyan's *Pilgrim's Progress*. In the seventeenth century, as M. H. Abrams comments:

the "composition of place" was not a specific locality, nor did it need to be present to the eyes of the speaker, but was a typical scene or object, usually called up before "the eyes of the imagination" in order to set off and guide the thought by means of correspondences whose interpretation was firmly controlled by an inherited typology.[11]

Defoe was the first writer who visualized the whole of a narrative as though it occurred in an actual physical place, but his gardens are still closer to stylized emblems, serving a redemptive, ethical purpose, rather than realistic natural settings. Similarly, according to Paul de Man, Rousseau in *La Nouvelle Héloïse* "does not even pretend to be observing. The language is purely figurative, not based on perception, less still on an experienced dialectic between nature and consciousness,"[12] so that Julie's garden is fashioned out of intertextual echoes of other texts. A significant turning point comes in the later eighteenth century with the rise of two new kinds of interest in physical surroundings: on the one hand, the romantics' enthusiasm for the picturesque, manifest in an aesthetics of landscape, and on the other, curiosity about the practical, industrial processes and social organization of human existence. The stark symbolism of allegory combines with the digressive prolixity of travel writing to produce the technique of detailed and cumulative notation of place normally associated with realism. At the same time, romantic local color, which was extrinsic to the plot and superimposed on it as an exotic frame for often sensationalist action, was superseded by the trend toward a psychologically and socially oriented form of local color such as is found in George Eliot, Zola, and Thomas Mann. With the growth of belief in determinism in the course of the nineteenth century, place in this sense comes to be an increasingly intrinsic factor in the plot. In short, it is transformed from mere decor to formative milieu.

The shift from the allegorical to the specific was also instrumental in bringing the provinces into prominence as a site of a narrative's action. What had been held against the provinces by the romantics, namely their ordinariness, was precisely what endeared them to the realists. *Madame Bovary* bears the subtitle *Moeurs de province* (*Provincial Manners*); Flaubert's analysis of limited mentalities could be set only in the provinces. *Middlemarch*, too, was consciously conceived as a study of provincial life, although to Eliot the provincial meant the average rather than necessarily the stupid, as it did to Flaubert. The foremost nineteenth-century chronicler of provincial life is, of course, Balzac, for whom the notion of the provinces carried ideological connotations of various kinds. To locate the action in the provinces denoted for Balzac both a protest against the exoticism of his immediate predecessors and a declaration of "une intention moderniste."[13] The provinces offered many advantages in Balzac's eyes: they were a new topic, they added a sociological dimension, and they were of a generic nature. Since he believed all provincial towns to be fundamentally alike in character, he could venture to write about them without first-hand intimacy. The pretense of knowledge on the narrator's part thus prefigures the pretense of belief on readers' part.

The rise of the provinces led to another device for creating particularity: the introduction of local dialect, such as the distinctive north German of the *Wasserkante* (literally, Water's Edge) in *Buddenbrooks* and the rural dialect in *Middlemarch*. Colloquialisms and slang, as in *L'Assommoir*, could serve rather the same purpose. However, as a designation of otherness, dialects and slang often carry more of a sociological class characterization than a geographic denotation.

Whether it be province, capital, or country, the citation of names is a basic and ubiquitous strategy in the evocation of place. Not only the titles, the texts too have an abundance—at times, an overabundance—of geographic appellations: Paris, London, Berlin, Venice, Rome, Florence, Manchester, Liverpool, Southampton, San Remo, Le Havre, Chinon, Azay, New York, Boston, Cape Cod, Topeka, Hamburg, Rostock, Travemünde, Munich, Smithfield, Cheapside, the Louvre, Notre-Dame, Versailles, Vesuvius, Charles Street, the Fischergrube, and so on. These place-names are handled in widely varying ways. At one end of the gamut Balzac insists on telling readers more about Saumur (in *Eugénie Grandet*) than most of them care to hear. At the other extreme, Henry James will introduce names without a word of explanation. In this respect, the exposition of names parallels that of historicity, stemming from the same divergent hidden assumptions about readers: in Balzac's case these assumptions lead to a didactic stance because readers are envisaged as in need of instruction, whereas the Jamesian narrator projects readers as cosmopolitan as he himself is.

But in the last resort, irrespective of the quantity or quality of the information tendered, a place-name is marked by only one unmistakable and unambiguous clue to its presence: the capital letter at its beginning at once lifts it out of its textual context. As a visible typographical symbol, the capital letter is an objective signal in the text wholly divorced from epistemological questions about the ontological standing of what it denotes. At the beginning of the nineteenth century, an initial letter followed by a dash was still customary usage. The M—— in Kleist's *Die Marquise von O——* shares with London, Paris, Middlemarch, and Yonville-l'Abbaye in *Madame Bovary* the capital letter as their lowest common denominator, without regard to the amount of description or the degree of their faithfulness to a putative reality. The ability to grasp the import of the capital letter, that is, that it denotes a proper name, is the sole absolute prerequisite that can properly be made of readers in their construction of a name.

The reason for the profusion of names is closely related to the realist novel's underlying aims. As Welty points out, "Fiction depends for its life on place."[14] She adds, "Being shown how to locate, to place any account is what does most toward *making* us believe it" (60). The intimate connection between localization and plausibility is one of the cornerstones of realism. For this reason particularity of place has been singled out ever since Ian Watt's *The Rise of the Novel* as one of the quintessential hallmarks of the emergent realist novel.[15] The posture of realism is predicated on its insistent endeavor to stabilize the illusion it seeks to foster. One immediate way for the novel to enhance the plausibility of its created universe is by endowing it with specificity of both time and place. Their cardinal importance devolves from their efficacy in validating the probability of the fiction by anchoring it in an order that exists outside the realm of the fiction. "Place," Welty concludes, "is the named, identified, concrete, exact and exacting, and therefore credible gathering-spot of all that has been felt, is about to be experienced, in the novel's progress."[16] The plausibility of the entire fiction is buttressed by, and to a considerable extent dependent upon, what Bakhtin has deemed its "chronotope" at the intersection of time and place. If these attendant circumstances are convincingly posited, readers will be likely to extend their belief in them onto the fictive world which they encompass. In this larger context the persuasive power invested in names becomes a vital instrument for the successful establishment of a trustworthy illusion.

Naming place and describing or evoking it is thus a central convention for the creation of the Barthian "effet de réel" ("reality effect"). Names in themselves, however, do not produce a fictive reality; the mere citation of names is a scant strategy of persuasion despite their perhaps punctilious correspondence to contemporary maps and almanacs. Names serve rather to adumbrate a landscape of possibility by exerting a "prompting function"[17] on readers' imaginings. They play the enormously important "role of props in generating fictional truths. . . . They give fictional worlds and their contents a kind of independence from cognizers."[18] To back this argument, Walton cites a fifteenth-century handbook for young girls, which advises them to imagine the Passion story by first fixing the places in their minds (27). The primacy of place-names in the creation of the fictive world derives from the category of data into which they fall. Their fictional truth value is enhanced by their special position astride the external and the internal fields of reference. Straddling the two, they are particularly effective stepping-stones for the transition into the game of make-believe.

The impact of naming is, therefore, similar to that ascribed by Philippe Hamon to description: "[D]ans le texte lisible-réaliste . . . la description est aussi chargée de neutraliser le faux, de provoquer un 'effet de vérité' "[19] ("In the readable realist text . . . description also has the task of neutralizing the false, of provoking an 'effect of truth' "). The ambivalence implied by Hamon is present too, though rarely noted, in Henry James's phrase: "the air of truth."[20] This suggests, rightly, that fiction cannot be true, only appear so. As Robert constantly reminds us, "[L]a réalité romanesque est fictive, ou plus exactement, c'est toujours une réalité de roman"[21] ("The novel's reality is fictive or, more precisely, it is always the reality of fiction"). She goes on:

Le Prague de Kafka n'est pas plus iréel que le Londres de Dickens ou le Saint-Pétersbourg de Dostoïevski, les trois villes n'ont que la réalité empirique des livres où elles sont crées, celle d'objets dont rien ne tient lieu et qui ne remplacent rien, . . . Le degré de réalité d'un roman n'est jamais chose mesurable, il ne représente que la part d'illusion dont le romancier se plaît à jouer.

Kafka's Prague is not less real than Dickens's London or Dostoevsky's St. Petersburg; the three cities only possess the empirical reality of the books that created them, the reality of objects that are substitutes for something else. . . . The degree of reality of a novel is not something quantifiable; it depends on the amount of illusion the writer chooses to activate.

In the creation and maintenance of that illusion through the complicity between narrator and readers, names are a powerful tool. The invocation of names is an important facet of that delineation of the here and now that is the sine qua non of realist fiction. Naming a place is, in the last resort, an act akin to conjuration.

ॐ

Through their capacity to conjure up "the air of truth," names exert a quasi-magic power. They perform in ways beyond what Welty claimed. For not only is location "the crossroads of circumstances,"[22] where the dynamics of the plot can begin to unfold. It also marks, quite literally, a crossroads for readers' construction of the text, one of the main points where readers imperceptibly cross the boundaries between the world of their reality, where they sit reading, and the realm of the fiction, inhabited by the protagonists. Because of their potential dual existence in both actuality and the fiction, names can act as a bridge of continuity, along which readers may move from one sphere to the other without becoming conscious of the transition.

In this respect the realist text differs from, and is far more elusive than its romantic antecedents. The romantic text characteristically exhibits "junctures of pronounced discontinuity where the act of validation or establishment is most explicit."[23] In Coleridge's "Kubla Khan," for instance, that discontinuity is at once exposed through the incongruence between the subtitle, "A Vision in a Dream," and the paratextual introduction. The words "vision" and "dream" remove the fictive location from readers' common domain into a private, subjective dimension. The scene of the vision is designated in the autobiographical preface in prose as "a lonely farm-house between Porlock and Linton, on the Exmoor confines of Somerset and Devonshire." While Porlock and Linton could equally well be invented or actual names, Somerset and Devonshire are existent British counties that Coleridge could expect his readers to know. So he is contextualizing the "vision in a dream" of his poem in a knowable location, and at the same time disengaging it from this homely environment.

"Xanadu," the second word of the poem, compels immediate attention by its acoustic strangeness. The contrast between the plainness of the "farm-house between Porlock and Linton, on the Exmoor confines of Somerset and Devonshire" and the exoticism of Xanadu with its "sacred river" Alph, its "caverns measureless to man" and its "sunless sea" is a measure of the distance between them. The physical description of Xanadu remains so general and schematic as to discourage any material concretization in readers' minds:

> And here were forests ancient as hills
> Enfolding sunny spots of greenery.

On the other hand, the atmospheric animation is forceful, not least because of the recourse to constative statements:

> A savage place! as holy and enchanted
> As e'er beneath a waning moon was haunted
> By woman wailing for her demon-lover!

or:

> It was a miracle of rare device,
> A sunny pleasure-dome with caves of ice!

The reiterated emphasis on the outlandishness of Xanadu underscores its remoteness from everyday reality. What is exacted of readers is a leap of faith: they have to believe in Xanadu as a place of the imagination experienced by the poet in a vision in a dream, and mediated through recollection. Through its very differentness from those in the preface, its name signals entry into a realm of fantasy. In "Kubla Khan" the distinction between the two spheres also becomes visually and aurally manifest in the switch from prose to verse.

The disjunction between real and fictive place is rarely as pronounced as in Coleridge's poem. More often, romantic fiction juxtaposes the two, sometimes letting them overlap, yet maintaining their separate identities. E. T. A. Hoffmann's *Der goldene Topf* (*The Golden Pot*), for example, is specifically located in Dresden, which is mentioned in the first sentence. Various geographic landmarks are cited as the action progresses with the student Anselmus moving about the city: the bridge over the Elbe, the bathing resort on the left bank about a mile above the bridge, the Kosel Garden with its open-air restaurants and concerts, the Prince Anton Gardens in the southeast suburb of Pirna, Konradi's pastryshop in the Schlossgasse which connects the old marketplace to the main square, the Neumarkt, the Moritzstrasse, and taverns such as the Golden Angel, the Helmet, and the City of Naumburg. Mention of the black gate in the northwest of the newer area of the city ("Neustadt") even allows limitation of the temporal frame, since it was erected in 1802 and demolished in 1812.

The absence of physical description does not diminish readers' belief that *Der goldene Topf* is grounded in a particular place at a particular time, but it leaves the scene more open to the transformations that are the crux of the plot. For the tale is presented as "ein Märchen aus der neuen Zeit" ("a latter-day romance"), and this subtitle fulfills a function parallel to that of the preface in "Kubla Khan" as a reading cue. Like the mysterious transformation of the face on the doorknocker under Anselmus's gaze, and like Veronika's metamorphosis into the snake, Serpentina, so the concrete Dresden of the physical world is transfigured into the mysterious Atlantis of imagination and myth. As Anselmus shuttles from the one to the other and back again, the names of locations map both his whereabouts and the stages of his quest. Each of the two spheres, as in "Kubla Khan," has its own aura and validity; but though conjoined, they are held in discrete suspension as the opposing poles in a tension, or the twin sides of a coin. Yet despite its incessant shifts, the disposition of the romantic text is relatively transparent compared to the more devious design of the realist text.

For realist fiction, in an attempt to enact its own claims to truthfulness, practices the art of disguise by taking pretense to its uttermost limits. In pretending to be a faithful representation of reality, it proceeds on the unvoiced hypothesis of a natural continuity between actuality and fiction. What is more, it actively encourages readers to make the same assumption. Place-names can serve as an ideal link between the two spheres since they have meanings in both adjacent worlds, the one extraneous and the other intrinsic to the fiction. The continuum, and the concomitant blurring of the boundaries, only enhances the importance of names in the game of pretense being played in realist fiction. The "magic" of names resides precisely in their aptitude for luring readers to join in that game by inducing them to believe in the reality of the fictional construct.

The naming of places inaugurates a system of slippages that enables the fluid interchange between reality and fiction to develop. This porosity is promoted by the relative independence of names as elements of discourse free of the embedment that defines, and limits, the scope of most other verbal units. Thus names represent an open space in which readers' imagination may engage simultaneously with prior experience and with the text. Hence it is in the forum of names that the process of fictionalization itself can best be observed.

Within the fundamental elasticity common to all names, some broad distinctions can be drawn among the different types for heuristic purposes. The first category of names cited in nineteenth-century fiction comprises places of world renown such as London, Paris, New York, or Berlin. It is reasonable to presume that all readers, then and now, would recognize these names as denotative of real locations. By "real" I here mean actual cities, whose situation can be ascertained at a certain latitude and on a certain longitude on a globe of the world. Often readers will have acquired vicarious knowledge of such places through other literary texts, or films, or television. In most instances the description of these celebrated cities tends to be more cursory than that of more recondite spots. Balzac, for example, always devotes far more attention to the specification of provincial settings than to those in Paris, where he is content to sketch the atmosphere and social level of a particular area.

By virtue of their very familiarity, the names of eminent places act as a cipher of an order of existence anterior to the fiction. Merely to invoke such names is, therefore, one expression of the "magic" that Welty attributes to them. The site of the fictive action in *Middlemarch* is instantly endowed with a degree of credibility through its relationship to a named place such as London, whose authenticity is widely accepted. So these famous names have a twofold function: their presence alone carries the suggestion of veracity, while the acknowledgment of their real existence provides a backcloth onto which the fictional realm can be mounted. Ultimately, these readily recognizable names may be compared to a kind of anchor, which grounds the created universe of the fiction in a knowable dimension of actuality. Like the historical allusions, they form a code to which readers are able to relate, and whose ulterior message is a corroboration of the realist novel's aspiration to truthfulness.

Other, lesser-known place-names have generally been taken as exerting the same legitimizing impulse. But on closer scrutiny, some of the fallacies inherent in such an interpretation become apparent; more interestingly, so too do the games that the text plays with readers through the widespread recourse to names. Those that fall into this second category would include Saumur (in Balzac's *Eugénie Grandet*), Rouen (in Flaubert's *Madame Bovary*), Leeds and Avignon (in *Middlemarch*), Travemünde (in Thomas Mann's *Buddenbrooks*), Albany, Calais, San Remo, Turin, and Ancona (in James's *The Portrait of a Lady*), and Topeka (in his *The Bostonians*). None of these is so prominent as to be immediately located by readers, most of whom would indeed experience some discomfort if asked to mark them on a map. And the exegesis contained within the text may be unilluminating or partial. To tell readers that Saumur is in Tourraine, as the Balzacian narrator does at the opening of *Eugénie Grandet*, is not helpful to readers unacquainted with either. Nor, curiously, is the venerable riding school mentioned, with which the name of Saumur is associated by French natives. This omission becomes comprehensible as soon as it is understood that the description of Saumur is by no means a guidebook account, geared to accuracy. The riding school is not introduced because it has no relevance to the plot. The description is an overture to the narrative, so the emphasis, in this tale of greed and domination, must be on the economic and political factors that determine life in this small provincial town. The chosen site is presented "à la fois comme une ville ordinaire, et comme la ville qui convenait à l'histoire racontée, celle dans laquelle cette histoire a pu ou aurait pu prendre sa forme la plus signifiante"[24] ("simultaneously as an ordinary town, and as the town that fitted the story told, that in which this story did or could find its most significant form").

Places such as Saumur, Leeds, or Topeka are no less real than London, Paris, or New York insofar as they, too, have a geographic existence. But the efficacy of these names as shorthand warrants of veracity is severely undercut by a combination of factors. Foremost among them is the limitation of readers' horizon: how much prior knowledge can readers be expected to bring to the construction of the text? Everything depends on the individual reader's educational level and the happenstance of where one was born and raised as well as how extensively one has traveled. These variables, though unpredictable, cannot be totally ignored. The problem of geographical remoteness is compounded nowadays by that of the intervening historical distance, discussed in the previous chapter. The hazardousness of recognition as a methodology in dealing with names becomes fully apparent when Saumur, Leeds, or Topeka is the scene of the action instead of London, Paris, or New York. So the contention, put forward in connection with the Vauquer boardinghouse in Balzac's *Le Père Goriot*: "Anyone who has lived in a boarding-house will recognize the atmosphere"[25] represents the worst possible approach in its surrender to subjectivity. Even the term "boardinghouse" may denote something other to an American than to a European, and certainly "atmosphere" is open to multiple interpretations. This pragmatic objection is finally overridden by the more fundamental theoretical one, namely: that to assess the impact of a text by reference to an anterior reality is to distort the process of reading as construction by inverting the priorities and subjecting the text to a controlling medium other than that of words.

The real but less well-known names are the supreme illustration of the slippages inherent to place-names. Readers unfamiliar with regional or provincial names will harbor genuine doubts as to whether they are actual or invented. In so doing they will become aware of the continual interchange between reality and fiction. At best the names may be taken as real through an act of supposition devolving from trust in the integrity of the narratorial voice.

This view contravenes that of Philippe Hamon, who envisages names as appropriating a function similar to that of "*citations*": "[I]ls assurent des points d'ancrage, rétablissant la performation (garants-*auctores*) de l'énoncé référentiel en embrayant le texte sur un extra-texte valorisé"[26] ("They assure points of anchorage, reestablish the performance [*authorially* warranted] of the referential statement by imbricating the text in a validated extraneous text"). Underlying this argument is Hamon's concept of the documentary as the "discours de l'autre" ("discourse of the other"), to be naturalized into the narrative by diverse procedures. Proper names are seen as "des entités sémantiques stables, qu'il ne s'agit d'ailleurs pas de comprendre que de reconnaître comme noms propres"[27] ("stable semantic entities which are not so much to be understood as to be recognized as proper names"). This is an alluring but dangerous path that rests on cultural hypotheses about the knowledge held by implied readers. Yet there are readers to whom Paris means a small town in Texas or Missouri as well as the capital of France. Admittedly, they are exceptions, who stand out, perhaps as a joke, against consensual opinion. Nonetheless, Hamon's assertions jump a step by not confronting the precariousness of positing recognition. As a critical approach, recognition can all too quickly lead into the quagmire of readers' subjectivity.

๛

Once the fluidity of the lines of demarcation between fact and fiction has been conceded, the difficulty of reading place-names and of appreciating the games being played with them (and with us as readers) increases incrementally. At some point, all readers, however knowledgeable and well traveled they may be, reach and cross the threshold of uncertainty. To take a simple example: Yonville-l'Abbaye in *Madame Bovary* is, according to the narrator's account, eight miles from Rouen between the Abbeville and Rouen roads on the borders of Normandy, Picardy, and the Ile-de-France, just off the new Abbeville-Amiens highway.[28] So far, so good, particularly to anyone who has driven through northern France.

Not only is the location very specific; the narrator's tone is that of factual reportage, as in travel writing. But these fairly well-known names (Normandy, Amiens, Rouen) soon give way to ones that very few readers are likely to have heard outside the confines of the novel: Bray, Boissière, Leux, Argueil, Saint-Jean (73), Doudeville (266), Longueville, Saint-Victoire (13), Quincampoix (261), Vissonville (32), Goderville, Normanville, Cany (28), Thibouville (58), Barneville near Aumale, Bas-Diauville (119), Buchy (139), and so on. This sample suffices to make the point. What are readers to do with such names? Ought they to get a very large-scale map of the area? Are they victims of their ignorance? The only thing beyond dispute is the palpable decline in readers' sense of assurance in regard to the factuality of the text, and hence a heightened awareness of their dependence on the narrator and the discourse. Parallel instances occur with Gottfried Keller's Seldwyla (in the cycle *Die Leute von Seldwyla* [*The People of Seldwyla*]), Elizabeth Gaskell's Cranford in the novel of that name, and Thomas Hardy's Casterbridge, all of which sound quite possible place-names. So do Donchéry, Briancourt, Marancourt, Vrignes-aux-Bois, Doudy, Sarignan, Rubécourt, Pouru-aux-Bois, Francheval, Villers-Cernay, and Saint-Monges in Zola's *La Débâcle*. But, as Michael Riffaterre has shown,[29] our reading is not significantly affected by his impish substitution of names from the local telephone book: Geaume, Hagetmau, Montfort, Ondes-aux-Bois, Momuy, Cambrans, Coudures, Pontes-les-Forges, Mugron, Oeyreluy, La Chapelle, and Saint-Criqu!

Riffaterre's amusing little controlled experiment lends strong support to the postulate that readers' apprehension of place-names derives not from their geographic expertise but from their competence as readers. As Riffaterre insists, the explanation of the literary phenomenon lies in the relation between text and reader, not between either text and author, or text and reality. "If," he maintains, "there is any difference between texts like Rabelais's and the Surrealists and those by Balzac and Zola, it is that the former openly proclaim that they are verbal calisthenics, while the latter conceal the fact" (24). Taking this view to its logical conclusion, he asserts that "*the referent has no pertinence to the analysis.* No advantage can be gained by comparing literary expression to reality or by evaluating a work of literature in terms of such a comparison" (25). Therefore, he adds, "[a] description can be false without striking us as wrong or improbable, for the representation does not refer to reality but, instead, replaces it" (22). To bear out Riffaterre's argument, we may take readers of *Eugénie Grandet* who happen to know Saumur and are dismayed by the lack of any mention of the riding school; they are in fact handicapped in the formation of the mental image evoked by the text by the intrusion of material extraneous and alien to the text.

Extreme though Riffaterre's position may seem at first glance, it is far more productive than its opposite, which relies on appeals to readers' perhaps idiosyncratic knowledge of boardinghouses, and so on. Steering somewhere between the two is Benjamin Harshav's theory of the dual fields of reference in fiction (discussed in chapter 2). The attractiveness of Harshav's model lies precisely in the possibility it offers of admitting the input of both external and textual information. For Harshav, with greater subtlety than Riffaterre, concedes the "double-layered nature of literary reference."[30] Thus a fiction may have a referential grounding (and a realist fiction certainly will), within and upon which it builds its own internal universe. This is well illustrated by Fontane's *Effi Briest*, which takes place in north Germany. The mention of Berlin, a universally known place, provides a clue to the locale of the action on a large scale. In the scenes in Berlin, Fontane forgoes description in favor of naming streets, districts, parks, public buildings, shops, and restaurants on the assumption that the city is sufficiently familiar to readers to enable them to complete the picture conjured up by the various landmarks. He is, therefore, in this case drawing primarily on an external field of reference that is absorbed into the fictional realm as the urban center that forms an axis of the plot. Hohen-Cremmen, on the other hand, the country estate of Effi's parents, is a fictitious place created internally by means of a brief narratorial account of its physical features, to which a coloration of feeling is added through Effi's deep emotional ties. The same procedure is followed in regard to Kessin, where she lives for a while after her marriage. It falls into the uncertain category midway between actual and fictitious, since it is reputed to be modeled on the small town of Swinemünde. Readers are unlikely to know this, much less to have specific associations with the name. In any case, it is not even introduced, the more euphonious Kessin being substituted. Like Hohen-Cremmen, Kessin comes to life for readers through a minimum of narratorial exposition, which is filled out piecemeal by Effi's experiences of the house, the town, its inhabitants, and surroundings. Fontane's practice of fusing external and internal fields of reference is parallel to Flaubert's in *Madame Bovary*. Such easy passage between the worlds of actuality and of pretense is so common in realist fiction as to be one of its distinguishing traits. But contrary to Pavel's contention that "there is no detectable difference between nonfictional and fictional proper names,"[31] the well-known names (Berlin, Paris, London, New

York) are generally described more scantily on the presumption of greater knowledge on the part of readers, although ontological distinctions are eschewed so as not to disrupt the fluidity between the external and internal fields of reference.

In the interlacement of these two fields, names have a very special role as the favored vehicles of transition. Because of their frequently indeterminate status, they may be part of either or both fields of reference. Even when a place-name has an acknowledged existence in the external field, it may assume a variety of meanings internally. A good example of such a spectrum is the transformation of Paris as it appears in Le Père Goriot, L'Assommoir, and Rilke's Die Aufzeichnungen des Malte Laurids Brigge. All three narratives are set in the same city, the capital of France. Yet it has widely differing connotations to the central protagonists. To Rastignac, the ambitious young man from the provinces, Paris is a forum of opportunity, a challenge to his resourcefulness, a social circuit whose particular laws have to be mastered. To Gervaise, the young woman from the country, it spells both hope and fear, and proves a script largely undecipherable to her. To Malte, the hypersensitive scion of an aristocratic family, it seems an objectification of his anxiety and dread in the face of life and the future.[32] In these instances the translation from external to internal field of reference occurs without any spatial displacement, merely by the move into the consciousness of the protagonist. In other cases, the transfer involves also a psychic shift, which coincides with the crossing from reality into fiction.

This does not imply any discontinuity. On the contrary, realist fiction actively encourages a pretended continuity in the coexistence of the internal realm as an extension of the external. With a canny concealment of any cracks, fictional referents are presented as prolongations of referents known outside the fictions. Although the two frames of reference overlap and share, they do not meet. The internal is adjacent and parallel to the external. So the text projects a new referent, constructing its own reality while simultaneously describing it. This internal reality draws on a selection of attributes from the actual world, physically and socially, that function as "reality keys."[33] The antecedents are related to the text by a process of fictionalization, whereby both historical and geographical data are annexed into the fictive realm as warranties of realism's pretended authenticity.

This motivation emerges clearly from one of Flaubert's letters about Madame Bovary: "Mon livre sera incomplet sans lesdits turbans alimentaires, puisque j'ai l'intention de peindre Rouen"[34] ("My book will be incomplete without the aforesaid special loaves because I make the pretense of *painting* Rouen"). The emphasis here might rather be put on "make the pretense." Such pretense making is evident in the production of Yonville-l'Abbaye as it is introduced in a quasi-guidebook discourse that informs readers of its location, the quality of its soil, its agricultural products, and its climate. To bolster the "reality effect," Flaubert sketched a map of the main street on which the locations of the pharmacy, of Guillemin's house, and the Bovarys' residence are marked. But its pretentiously high-flown hyphenated name, which suggests the romantic spot of Emma's desires, is promptly subverted by the parenthetical aside that it is called after an old abbey, of which not even ruins remain. The conflict of codes between the expository and the ironic opens up an aperture of doubt that throws the existential status of Yonville into question. Such a deliberately ambivalent image, similar to the *sfumato* technique in painting,[35] leaves the reader undecided as to the ontological standing of the locale, suspended between the potentially real and the fictive. The description of the one-street town is

far from innocent: it is neither a neutral background description to help situate the couple in their new milieu nor a description of their point of view as they arrive in the new place—either one of which would have been in keeping with narrative logic and economy. Instead, we are presented with a highly selective, evaluative description of the town and its surrounding countryside—not an impartial, panoramic view from lofty heights, but a biased view from an ironic distance. This ironic mode is communicated through the almost exclusive focus on the negative aspects of the place, backed up by a series of derogatory and disparaging analogies. This excess of information through the steady focus on negative details puts us on our guard.[36]

Not only are readers put on their guard by the narrator's obvious bias toward the negative in the description of Yonville; they are also alerted to its essentially literary texture, in which all the details are calculated to create a certain impression. It is as much the mood of Yonville that is evoked as its physical appearance. The symbolism is quite transparent in the positioning of the somewhat dilapidated church on one side of the street, and opposite it, near the market square and the town hall, the striking and colorful storefront of the Homais pharmacy. While tradition is declining, modern science (or pseudoscience) is in the ascendant here. The short main street leads nowhere but to the cemetery. Even before Emma has set foot in Yonville, this description forecloses her life there, and hints that her only exit will be into death.

The Game of the Name

In the production of Yonville, the internal field of reference, created by the narrator's survey of the town, is predominant. The place takes on an autonomous existence as an active agent in the story of Emma's life. It does so by virtue of the internal textual signals, not by reference to any extraneous reality. That Yonville-l'Abbaye may have been modeled on the small Norman town of Rye is wholly irrelevant. The linguistic elaborations in themselves (i.e., "-ville-l'Abbaye") are strong indicators of the imaginative transfiguration that has intervened between the real place and its fictive appearance. In mounting Yonville-l'Abbaye into the landscape of Normandy, Flaubert has related the scene of the action to an external field of reference, which in turn yields to the internal field established through the ironic and symbolic description of the town.

A parallel process can be observed in *Middlemarch*, into whose genesis George Eliot's notebooks, the *Quarry*, give illuminating insight. Middlemarch is situated in the northeast corner of Loamshire, which is an invented British county, and which therefore betokens the fictitiousness of the location. The names, too, Middle-march and Loam-shire, carry clear symbolic overtones. To flesh out this internal field of reference, Eliot, in the second part of the *Quarry*,[37] drew a schematic map on which the exact distances between Middlemarch and the protagonists' abodes, Tipton, Lowick, and Freshitt are specified in miles. At the same time, like Yonville-l'Abbaye, Middlemarch is related to the larger world of London, Paris, Rome, Lausanne, Lyons, Avignon, Leeds, and Manchester, which represent the external field of reference, onto which the fictive scene is grafted. Again like Yonville, Middlemarch has a putative prototype in Eliot's native Coventry, but this piece of information is immaterial to an understanding of the novel. Unlike Flaubert, Eliot offers virtually no physical picture of Middlemarch, preferring such indirect means as the widespread recourse to gossip to elicit the mentality of the place, which will be discussed in the next chapter. Its vitality, as well as its plausibility for readers, rests not on topographical data, but on its ethical and social import as a complex system of values. Though coexistent and continuous temporally and geographically with the contemporary circumstances in which it is embedded, Middlemarch, like Yonville-l'Abbaye and the unnamed place in *Buddenbrooks*, is essentially a verbal product of the text.

These examples illustrate the primacy of textual and reading strategies over recognition in the construction of names. The physical existence of a named place is in the last resort of very little import. For place is "not a datum but the product of the work of the writer."[38] What the fiction therefore demands of its readers is not extensive geographic erudition, but acts of belief and pretense stimulated by an alertness to the signals emitted by the text itself. Even that most far-fetched name, Xanadu, proves the point. By dint of ingenious research, John Livingstone Lowes discovered its origins in Coleridge's reading of *Purchas His Pilgrimage* by Samuel Purchas and *Purchas His Pilgrimes*, in which the travels of Marco Polo were included.[39] In the first edition of *Purchas His Pilgrimage* of 1613, the name takes the form of "Xaindu," while in the second of 1617, which is more likely what Coleridge saw because Wordsworth owned a copy, it appears as "Xamdu." These cacophonous versions were transformed by Coleridge into the euphonious and rhythmically pleasing "Xanadu." Readers do not need to know anything about the Purchas volumes, nor about Marco Polo, much less about the exploration of the summer capital of Kubla Khan. They must instead allow themselves to respond imaginatively to the spell cast by the magic of the outré and exciting name that beckons into a visionary realm of the wondrous.

"Xanadu" also reveals the difficulties encountered in reading fiction in dissociating "real references" from "pretended acts of referring." That distinction has been put forward by John R. Searle, who argues that not necessarily all references in a work of fiction are "pretended acts of referring."[40] Geographic place-names might be presumed to fall into the latter category; London, Paris, or New York would fit this paradigm. But whenever readers experience doubts as to the existential status of the places named in a fiction, they are unable to decide on the proportion of reality to pretense contained in the reference. The situation is particularly vexed in realist fiction because it purports to be wholly true to reality, and therefore deliberately sets out to subvert the kind of differentiation attempted by Searle. A much more workable hypothesis is put forward by Barbara Herrnstein Smith, who contends that a " 'saying' " that has "no original sayer . . . appears uncontaminated by ordinary human error or bias, and thus 'oracular.' "[41] Herrnstein Smith's " 'oracular,' " though clothed in the language of scholarliness, is another way of expressing Welty's insight into the "magic" of names.

That magic may stem from an acoustic, onomatopoeic appeal, as in Xanadu or Yonville-l'Abbaye, or it may be provoked by a metaphorical, symbolizing suggestivity, as in Middlemarch, Lowick, and Freshitt. Its power derives essentially from its readability, from the connotative force it is able to convey to readers. Readability is a function of the total context, of the ways in which the external and internal fields of reference coalesce. The centrality of the entire context to the potential for assertability has been underscored by Hilary Putnam in his article "Is There a Fact of the Matter about Fiction?" (77). Petrey, too, emphasizes the need for "establishing a context in which their [the fictional statements'] constative validity is secure."[42] While the speech act cannot create reality, it can indeed produce a reality internal to the fiction. Insofar as realism plays with possibles, it conjures up a world bordering on the one known to readers. In the crossing of the unmarked boundaries between these contiguous realms, names have a vital role because of their dual existence. The credibility of the St. Petersburg in Tolstoy's *Death of Ivan Ilyich* is not lessened by the work's status as a fabricated biography that pretends to be an actual life (or death) story. To cite Walton once more:

Correspondences between work worlds and the real one can affect the richness and vivacity of appreciators' games, no doubt. But the character of the games depends substantially on the manner in which fictional truths are generated, not just which ones are generated.[43]

To envisage realist fiction in this light, not necessarily as a mimetic replica but rather as a possible continuance of reality, obviates several of the problems that have beset the question of realism. With the displacement of mimesis in favor of textual strategies as the mainspring of realist writing, reading, as a corollary, is converted from an exercise in recognition and memory into one of competence at linguistic analysis. Names are constructed by a process of cognitive mapping in readers' minds according to a schema projected by the text. And accuracy as a criterion for assessing the effectiveness of descriptions of place must yield to the power of rhetoric within and beyond the limits of the fiction.

The capacity of the referent to project a new referent is most concretely illustrated by the after-history of *Buddenbrooks*. The Buddenbrook house, which now decorates the cover of the popular German paperback edition,[44] with its typically north German gables, is modeled on the house where Thomas Mann's aunt used to live. Within the novel it assumes symbolic significance, marking first the family's ascendancy to dignity as they move into the imposing edifice, then their gradual, hidden decline as the rear areas are allowed to slip into disrepair, and finally their fall when the house has to be sold to the Hagenströms, the upstarts who have displaced the Buddenbrooks financially and socially. Invested in this way with meanings within the text, it has subsequently taken on a life of its own as a tourist attraction touted in Lübeck's publicity material. The fiction, through its symbolizing transfiguration of an actual antecedent, has spawned a mythology that fuses the referential with the textual and comes to acquire a quasi-autonomous existence. A similar instance is the celebration of Leopold Bloom's Dublin on Bloomsday; actual sites undergo fictionalization through appropriation into *Ulysses*, and then materialize with the status of a new reality.

These curious developments suggest that the invocation of place-names is a more complex tactic with a more equivocal impact on readers than has hitherto been assumed. On the one hand, names, especially those of world renown, can impart an "air of truth" by appearing to anchor the fiction in reality. On the other hand, however, they represent a major bridge for the readers' crossing of the boundaries between reality and fiction that eventually leads to a whole-hearted belief in the fiction. Thus names also facilitate that casting of the anchor to reality in the surrender to the fiction as a substitute reality. The landscape of actuality hovering on the margins of the fiction is superseded by an overriding landscape of consciousness within its parameters as the internal field of reference comes to supplant the external one.

The essential lesson of the game of the name is the fluidity and porosity of all categories. The real and the fictive are reciprocally permeable. For this reason, the antithetical polarities traditional in criticism of realism, such as Marianne Moore's "real" and "imaginary,"[45] George Levine's "truth" and "lying,"[46] even Hayden White's "empirical" and "conceptual,"[47] are misleading dichotomizations. Only through a willing and conscious participation in realism's performative pretense can readers begin to understand its games.

6

Landscapes of Consciousness

☞

Das Plastische entsteht nicht durch Schauen, sondern durch Identifikation.

The plastic comes into being not through looking, but through identification.

—Hugo von Hofmannsthal

☞ "Le fait n'est donc plus rien en lui-même, il est tout entier dans l'idée que les autres s'en forment"[1] ("The fact no longer has any validity in itself; everything depends on the perception that others form of it"), Vautrin explains to Lucien de Rubempré in Balzac's *Illusions perdues*. With his cynical but accurate insight into social mechanisms, Vautrin is here fulfilling the same pedagogic function toward the still naive newcomer to Paris as he does for Rastignac in *Le Père Goriot*. His lesson here is that fact commands little regard, whereas image reigns supreme; in other words, that the figure lodged in the mind of perceivers exerts greater power than the original data.

Vautrin's axiom has a direct relevance to the landscapes in realist fiction, where "l'idée que les autres s'en forment" proves to be more consequential than "le fait" itself. The "others" in this instance are the protagonists within the text, including the narrator as a more or less defined persona. The characters are, as it were, readers of the places they inhabit through the mental images they form of their worlds. Theirs, as much as the narrator's, become the dominant organizing centers of consciousness. Sometimes the shift of focalization is clearly visible, as at the beginning of *L'Assommoir*, where the Parisian slum is first presented in the third person through the mediation of an anonymous narrating voice, but by the end of the opening chapter is described as experienced by the fictive persona. This represents another kind of porosity, in this case, the transmutation of an external view ("le fait") into the internal one held by the character(s) ("l'idée que les autres s'en forment"). This narrative technique is more common later in the century than earlier. With the increasing refinement of narrative strategies from Flaubert onward, the narrator's optic, so dominant in Balzac, tends to recede and to yield to the protagonists' vision. As a result, the realist novel's much vaunted objectivity is permeated with subjective apprehensions, which throw into question this traditional dichotomization into opposing pairs.

The long customary dismissal of the subjective from realist fiction was already disputed by Richard Brinkmann in *Wirklichkeit und Illusion* (*Reality and Illusion*), which appeared in 1957 and put forward a concept of realism quite revolutionary for its time. Taking three German texts hardly known internationally, Grillparzer's *Der arme Spielmann* (1848), Otto Ludwig's *Zwischen Himmel und Erde* (1856), and Eduard von Keyserling's *Beate und Mariele* (1903), Brinkmann argued that objectivity is "keine angemessene Kategorie"[2] ("not an appropriate category"). He went on to elaborate:

Je genauer sie das besondere individuelle Tatsächliche in der Sprache zu erfassen und darzustellen versucht, um so mehr treten an die Stelle reiner intentionaler "Gegenständlichkeit", an die Stelle der "Gegenstände" die subjektiven Bestimmungen, mit denen sie in ihrer Besonderheit dargestellt werden sollen. (311)

The more precisely it [realist narrative] attempts to grasp and represent the specific individual fact in language, the more purely intentional "objectivity" and "objects" are displaced by the subjective conditions with which they are to be evoked in their specificity.

Those "subjective conditions" are the mental processes of the characters, whereby "objects" are registered. In a later essay, "On the Concept of Realism for Nineteenth-Century Narrative," Brinkmann restates his hypothesis with a somewhat different emphasis: "Was die sogenannte realistische Erzählkunst auf vielfältige Weise beschwört und vorstellt, das ist die zunehmende Subjektivierung der Wirklichkeit gerade in der Erfahrung einer neuen Fülle und neuer Formen des Tatsächlichen"[3] ("What the so-called realist art of narration conjures and evokes in manifold guise is the increasingly subjective nature of reality precisely in the experience of a new plenitude and new forms of the objective"). As a corollary to this insight, Brinkmann, in an apparently paradoxical reversal, locates reality in the subjective consciousness. The logical outcome of this extreme position would be to declare James Joyce, Virginia Woolf, and Faulkner as the consummate realists in their exploration of stream of consciousness. Yet despite his tendency to overstatement, Brinkmann provided a salutory corrective to the ingrained and mistaken insistence on the objectivity of realist narrative.

Brinkmann was also one of the first to direct attention to the role of consciousness in narration. This has gained far greater importance over the past twenty or so years as a result of the systematic analysis of narrative, particularly in reader-oriented criticism. In "Reading as Construction," Todorov identifies the three factors through which readers filter the information they receive from a text as "mode," "time," and "vision." "Vision" offers answers to the question, "To what extent is the story distorted by the various 'centers of consciousness' through whom it is told?"[4] While "distorted" is an infelicitous term insofar as it may imply the existence of some undistorted, pure truth,[5] the concept of "centers of consciousness" is an eminently useful heuristic tool for an understanding of the processes of narration.

Those "centers" denote primarily, though not exclusively, the protagonists as they experience—and frequently become affected by—the places where they are, so to speak, placed. Thus in realist fiction, place has a dual function: as the outer physical location of the action and as the inner force it attains through its absorption into the protagonists' consciousness. The phrase "landscapes of consciousness" derives from Jerome Bruner's *Actual Minds, Possible Worlds*, which examines the procedures by which the mind comes to create imaginary worlds. To Bruner, the "landscape of consciousness" is "what those involved in the action know, think, or feel, or do not know, think, or feel."[6] The presence of such landscapes of consciousness in realist fiction presupposes, or prompts, the admission of the subjective element and the concomitant acceptance of an interface, not a separation, between objective and subjective.

Objective and subjective can be seen as equivalent to Balzac's pair, fact and perception, twin aspects of place that coexist, at times in a relationship of correspondence, at others of divergence. It has generally been assumed that the scene of the action, emanating from the author/narrator, is an "objective," factual description, while the protagonists' perception, stemming from their cognizance of and their feelings about their environment and its impact on their lives, is predominantly subjective. Their personal gaze lends an individual connotation to the surrounding place just as their interpreting minds endow it with particular meanings. They are the internal readers of their place, literal and figurative, in the realm of the fiction. But the distinction between their internal scenarios and the narrator's supposedly objective one is not clear-cut. That the narrator in realist fiction may himself hold a personal, to some degree subjective, view of a place has not been adequately acknowledged because of realism's own emphasis on factuality, which has gained widespread acceptance.

To envisage the realist text as a self-producing artifact, in which the narrator functions as both a voice and a persona, is to contravene what has recently been described as "the postulate of realism: the popular belief that objects invariably precede words independently of any viewpoint, and that words, secondary with regard to these objects, only designate them."[7] This would be tantamount to equating the word with the fact at the expense of the "viewpoint" or perception. My argument, on the contrary, is in favor of the viewpoint insofar as the landscape of consciousness is filtered through the mind and words of its perceivers, and is, therefore, a product of the text. As such, it comprises a spectrum of possible readings of a place rather than any limited (mimetic) reflection; it is a "Liber mundi personnel" ("a personal "Book of the World"),[8] a vision of the experiencing subject that turns the outer arena into a psychic reality.

Such a conceptualization modifies the theory put forward by Barthes in his influential article, "L'Effet de réel" ("The Reality Effect"). To Barthes "l'illusion réferentielle" stems from belief in the direct collusion between the real and the signifier, with the signified expelled from the sign.[9] He goes on to comment that the aim of realism is "faire de la notation la pure rencontre d'un objet et de son expression" (88; "to make notation a pure encounter between an object and its expression" [17]). This proposition, curiously, overlooks the mediating, enframing presence of the narrating voice that intervenes between object and expression, rendering a "pure encounter" impossible. In an attempt to minimize such intervention, the narratorial role may be attenuated into an allegedly anonymous voice. Or it can function as a covert immanence, often by means of indirect discourse, via the consciousness of a protagonist, who becomes the narrating medium. The protagonists' account is, in a strange omission, totally disregarded by Tzvetan Todorov in his outline of the reading process: according to his schema, the author's account stimulates the imaginary universe evoked by the author, which in turn leads to the imaginary universe constructed by readers and hence to readers' account.[10] Yet, as I shall argue, it is precisely the protagonists' account, that is an important source for readers' imaginative construction. Much closer to the mark is the observation that in realistic novels narrators become increasingly involved with and affected by the characters and actions of their stories. "This involvement results in a loss of authority and reveals itself in a mingling of voices—narrator's and characters'—and ultimately a representation of multiple perspectives."[11] It is, in part, this "representation of multiple perspectives" that creates what James calls "the air of reality."

The multiplicity of perspectives is achieved by manipulation of viewpoint and frequent changes in focalization, conventions of realist fiction. Such a technique differs from that of romantic narrative, which tends to be more univocal, often recording in diaries, letters, or monologue the musings of a single figure in the first person. When the persona's perspective is supplanted by another, as in the editorial framework to Goethe's *Werther*, there is a palpable sense of intrusion, even of violation, as the subjective account is amended by another's view. By contrast, realist fiction permits easy transitions from mind to mind, creating a distinctive heteroglossia, not least through slides into indirect discourse. In such a narrative disposition, the narrator is often credited with omniscience because of his insight into the protagonists' psyche.[12] But many narrators, as was shown in chapter 3, freely confess to limitations on their knowledge, infusing into the narratorial voice a certain tentativeness that reduces its authority as the omniscient source of all information.

In light of the fluctuations and shifts of focalization in realist fiction, it is fallacious to categorize the information within a text as "subjective" or "objective," as even recent critics have done:

Subjective information reveals the character (temperament, personality, beliefs, responses) of a perceiver; it is discourse about persons as subjects. Objective information consists of descriptions about objects or persons-as-objects.[13]

The so-called objective information comes from an audible voice, readily identifiable as that of the narrator, drawing on his own experience and knowledge. In most of Balzac's novels, for instance, it is this narratorial voice that presents and describes the locale of the action, normally at the outset, though further descriptive passages may also be interspersed later, as in *La Cousine Bette* or *Illusions perdues*, where each new interior is catalogued in precise detail. This third-person narratorial voice pretends to objectivity, in contradistinction to the pronounced subjectivity of the protagonists' perceptions. However, it is legitimate to see the narrator, too, as a kind of filter, through whose consciousness the scene is mediated. The ideal of narratorial impersonality, launched by the realists themselves as an integral part of their claim to truthfulness, is exposed for what it is: a mere myth. If, as Terence Doody puts it, "realism achieves its objectivity by recognizing the inviolable subjectivity of all its human characters, the potentially equal value and authority of every individual, the possibility of another point of view," then the narrator must be included among "its human characters."[14] But in that case the word "objectivity" loses its force as it coalesces into "another point of view," that is, another facet of subjectivity.

The narrator's partiality is apparent in the opening of *Eugénie Grandet*. The novel begins with a general statement:

Il se trouve dans certaines villes de province des maisons dont la vue inspire une mélancolie égale à celle que provoquent les cloîtres les plus sombres, les landes les plus ternes ou les ruines les plus tristes.[15]

There are, in certain provincial towns, houses, the sight of which inspires a melancholy equal to that provoked by the gloomiest cloisters, the bleakest heaths, or the saddest ruins.

Despite the composure of this assertion, it is permeated with an atmosphere of dejection that must strike every reader. The naming of "melancholy" as the dominant mood is immediately backed by the comparison of those lugubrious houses to emblems of isolation or desolation: cloisters, heaths, and ruins. The rhetoric of the thrice reiterated "les plus" serves to underscore by insistent repetition the extremity of the proposition. The elements chosen for comparison all suggest silence, stasis, decay, and death. Moving in for a close-up, the description passes from the house onto the street before coming to rest on an uncannily motionless figure, silhouetted in the window, transfixed to the spot as if no longer alive. The Gothic undercurrents to this provincial domestic drama are implicit in the opening words. The narrator purports to present what he sees, offering his own intimacy with the scene as validation for the accuracy of his testimony. But the impression made by this passage springs above all from its rhetoricity, its pattern of images and personifications, its intertextual resonances, in short, its imaginative, evocative qualities, not its truthfulness as an account of

Saumur. The interjection of the narrator's subjectivity animates the entire tableau. This is as much a landscape of consciousness—the narrator's consciousness—as any projected by protagonists.

The porosity between subjective and objective renders the distinctions tenuous at best, and at worst, misleading. The objective becomes suffused with the subjective to the point where the two are wholly interdependent and hardly distinguishable. To cite Doody once more:

[T]he novelist who wants to create a thing and remain impersonal will necessarily be willing to undermine, distribute, or share his own authority in order to define his meaning by the proposal of a consensus rather than by an appeal to some superior or antecedent norm.[16]

That consensus must, obviously, embrace the protagonists' readings of their place. But while the narrator pretends to superior authority through more extensive anterior knowledge, he is no more in a position to present the "facts" about a place than are the internal readers. He has his own agenda and perception, just as they do. Each operates from a specific point of view, and that of the narrator is as much determined by the demands of the narrative as the protagonists' is by their situation. Balzac's inclusion in the introduction to *Eugénie Grandet* of a great deal of information about the economics of viniculture, but no reference to the riding school for which Saumur has been famous since the eighteenth century has already been discussed in chapter 5. The selection of what to incorporate and, conversely, what to omit is purposefully guided by the plot to be unfolded. Balzac, as many critics have noted, is most deliberate in his use of settings, which are often, as in *Eugénie Grandet*, strictly utilitarian in regard to human activity. Grandet's house "is a presence and an influence that counts throughout . . . particularly in . . . the sense of the moral and social foundation of the story."[17] Or, as Lukács put it:

Balzac's descriptions never create a setting in the sense in which the word was later used in positivist sociology and it is for the same reason that for instance Balzac's very detailed descriptions of people's houses never appear as mere stage settings.[18]

When facts are thus seen as subordinate to images, the concept of unbiased objectivity can no longer be upheld as a viable frame of reference.

The coexistence of two possibly quite disparate perceptions of the same place emerges from the description of the view from Olive Chancellor's windows in *The Bostonians*:

The western windows of Olive's drawing-room, looking over the water, took in the red sunsets of winter; the long low bridge that crawled, on its staggering posts, across the Charles; the casual patches of ice and snow; the desolate suburban horizons, peeled and made bald by the rigour of the season; the general hard, cold void of the prospect; the extrusion at Charlestown, at Cambridge, of a few chimneys and steeples, straight, sordid tubes of factories and engine-shops, or spare, heavenward finger of the New England meeting-house. There was something inexorable in the poverty of the scene, shameful in the meanness of its details, which gave a collective impression of boards and tin and frozen earth, sheds and rotting piles, railway-lines striding flat across a thoroughfare of puddles and tracks of the humbler, the universal horse-car, traversing obliquely this path of danger; loose fences, vacant lots, mounds of refuse, yards bestrewn with iron pipes, telegraph poles, and bare wooden backs of places. Verena thought such a view lovely, and she was by no means without excuse when, as the afternoons closed, the ugly picture was tinted with a clear, cold rosiness.[19]

To the narrator, whose voice dominates this passage, the view is replete with negative connotations implied in the words chosen: "the long *low* bridge that *crawled*"; *staggering* posts"; "the *desolate* suburban horizons, *peeled* and made *bald* by the *rigour* of the season"; "the general *hard cold void* of the prospect"; "*sordid* tubes of factories," and so on (italics are mine). These oblique but highly evocative suggestions of a dismal industrial scenario are followed by direct narratorial comment in the sentence beginning "There was something inexorable in the poverty of the scene, shameful in the meanness of its details," a statement that introduces a list of the displeasing, derelict aspects of the vista, culminating in the telling metaphor: "bare wooden backs of places." Then comes the abrupt shift of focalization with: "Verena thought the view lovely." The contrast between the rebarbative features that have been underscored at some length and "lovely" is startling. It may serve it part to point to Verena's innocence, an ambivalent quality since it can comprise lack of judgment as well as a fresh capacity for wonder. The ambiguity is left unresolved, the innocence perhaps exposed to gently comical satire on the part of the experienced narrator. To him "the picture" continues to be "ugly" even as Verena's opinion of it is supported when it is "tinted with a clear, cold rosiness." The glow of the sunsets, which Olive and Verena come to admire, transforms the crassness of the objects: they now become "no longer vulgar, but almost silvery." The entire tone of the vocabulary changes with the use of terms with a more attractive aura: "pink flushes," " 'tender' reflections,"[20] "dusky undulations against the fading glow," "deep and delicate," "tinkle like crystal." Ultimately, both landscapes are upheld: the narrator's as that of a sober, somewhat sour critical gaze in the harshness of daylight, and Verena's as that of an entranced, youthful vision at sundown. Their equal validity illustrates the cardinal role of the filtering center of consciousness.

More commonly, the discrepancy between adjacent, perhaps conflicting perceptions is the outcome of a slippage, as is evident in the description of Yonville-l'Abbaye, with which the second part of *Madame Bovary* begins. Here the narratorial voice assumes the stance of a dispassionate reporter, adopting at first the tone and mode of a guidebook in his directives: "On quitte la grande route à la Boissière et l'on continue à plat jusqu'au haut de la côte des Leux, d'où l'on découvre la vallée"[21] ("One leaves the main road at Boissière and continues straight on to the top of the Leux hillside, from which the valley can be seen"). The panorama of the valley is then sketched, with the river bisecting the area into two distinctive regions: to the left, pasture, and to the right, crops. The contours of the valley are delineated in concrete, measured terms, although the paragraph ends on a poetic flourish as the countryside is likened to "un grand manteau déplié qui a un collet de velours brodé d'un galon d'argent" (73; "a great cloak, unfolded, which has a velvet collar embroidered with a silver edge"). The simile appears like a flash in the pan, for the description continues for another few lines in the former sober manner, naming geographic locations and tracing topographical features.

Then suddenly the tone changes with the surfacing of evaluative adjectives which carry, without exception, negative connotations:

On est ici sur les confins de la Normandie, de la Picardie et de l'Ile de France, contrée *bâtarde* où le langage est *sans accentuation*, comme le paysage *sans caractère*. C'est là que l'on fait les *pires* fromages de Neufchâtel de tout l'arrondissement, et, d'autre part, la culture y est *coûteuse*, parce qu'il faut beaucoup de fumier pour engraisser ces terres *friables pleines de sable et de cailloux*. (74; italics are mine)

Here one is on the borders of Normandy, Picardy, and the Ile-de-France, a *bastard* area where the language is *flatly unaccented*, just as the landscape is *devoid of character*. It is there that the *worst* Neufchâtel cheeses in the whole area are made, and, on the other hand, agriculture is *expensive* because a lot of manure is required to enrich this *brittle soil full of sand and stones*.

In this infertile terrain, the advent of a new road linking Yonville to the main Abbeville-Amiens highway has wrought little change. The village's intractable backwardness is conveyed in such phrases as "stationnaire" (74; "stationary"), "le bourg paresseux" ("the lazy township"), the cowherd "couché" ("lying") by the river to take a siesta, as well as the observation: "Au lieu d'améliorer les cultures, on s'y obstine encore aux herbages, quelque dépréciés qu'ils soient" ("Instead of improving the crops, they still obstinately cling to grasses, however depreciated they may be"). In the aspect of the village, too, the same willful stagnation is suggested by the houses "encloses de haies" (74; "enclosed by hedges"), the thatched roofs "comme des bonnets de fourrure rabattus sur des yeux" ("like fur hoods pulled down over the eyes"), by the narrow courtyards, and the paltriness of the occasional pear tree. The main landmarks are the church on one side of the road, and on the other, the pharmacy with its garish advertisements for patent medicines. Both are drawn with an abundance of detail reminiscent of Balzac, but also with a pronounced ironic edge in the excesses of overstatement (75–76).

This picture of Yonville masquerades as a description of a place, especially at the outset. However, even in the initial phrase, an undercurrent of irony is discernible: "Yonville-l'Abbaye (ainsi nommé à cause d'une ancienne abbaye de Capucins dont les ruines mêmes n'existent plus) est un bourg à huit lieus de Rouen" (73; "Yonville-l'Abbaye [so called after an old Capucin abbey, of which not even the ruins remain] is a village eight miles from Rouen"). The affectedness of its high-flown name, which no doubt appeals to Emma, is swiftly and deftly deflated by the parenthetical aside, which strips the spot of its past and its romance, leaving a dreary, becalmed country village, devoid of any allure. Flaubert has devised a setting in complete consonance with his announced plan to write a book about nothing. Under the guise of an objective exposition, he has sketched a metaphoric landscape of consciousness.

A remarkably parallel procedure is followed in the narration of Emma's experience of La Vaubyessard (part 1, chapter 8). The section opens with an apprehension of the place as it might be seen by arriving visitors. The first paragraph consists of a largely visual enumeration of the style and components of the castle and its gardens: it is modern, Italianate, with two wings and three terraces, an immense lawn surrounded by rhododendron, syringa, and viburnum bushes, between which a curved path wends its way. There is a stream with a bridge, and in the background, through the mist, a cluster of buildings with thatched roofs can be glimpsed amid the wooded slopes: stables, carriage houses, and the preserved remains of the old demolished castle (49–50). While the few adjectives are thoroughly positive ("immense"; "grands arbres espacés"

[49; "large well-spaced trees]), the gaze records fairly neutrally the visitors' first impressions without manifest emotional coloring, although this is clearly a charming pastoral idyll.

The arrival of Charles's carriage at the main entrance introduces a brief transitional paragraph of one sentence, divided into several sequences: the carriage stops, servants appear, the count comes forward, offering his arm to the doctor's wife to lead her into the hall (50). So Emma, named only generically as the doctor's wife, is brought into the castle, and at the same time into the center of the picture.

As in the description of Yonville, here too the impersonal tone is still maintained for a while as the interior of the castle is surveyed. The emphasis is on its sumptuousness: its marble floor, on which steps resound as in a church, its large staircase, its gallery with a vista of the garden and a billiard room from which comes the clack of the ivory balls. The information at this point is both auditory and visual, and the perceiving mind unspecified, though presumably that of Emma as she moves forward into the castle. This supposition is confirmed in the phrase: "Emma vit" (50; "Emma saw"), which marks the transition to the predominance of her viewpoint. If she (and Charles) have till then been the hypothetical beholders, from now on hers is the perceiving filter. A series of sentences follows her notation of the portraits in the hall of the venerable former lords of the castle with their biographical inscriptions, which she reads (50–51).

Only a couple of paragraphs later, with the entry into the dining room for dinner, is the shift into Emma's consciousness fully accomplished: "Emma se sentit, en entrant, enveloppée par un air chaud, mélange du parfum des fleurs et du beau linge, du fumet des viandes et de l'odeur des truffes" (51; "Emma felt herself, on entering, enveloped in warm air, a blend of the perfume from the flowers and the beautiful linen, from the aroma of the meats and the odor of the truffles"). The crucial enframing phrase is the initial "Emma felt herself." The rest not only of this paragraph but of the entire chapter, although it alternates between narration and indirect discourse, presents the ball at La Vaubyessard through Emma's eyes and reactions. This technique results in sharp irony, quite different from the benign tolerance of the Jamesian narrator toward Verena in The Bostonians. Emma systematically idealizes everything, transforming even the slobbering old man into a source of admiration: "Il avait vécu à la Cour et couché dans le lit des reines!" (52; "He had lived at court and slept in the bed of queens!"). In this scenario, Emma sees herself as "une actrice à son début" (52; "an actress making her debut"), and she falls into her chosen role with grace and joy. The action is interspersed with her thoughts and memories, particularly of the relative crudeness of her father's home as against the refinement of the castle, represented by the maraschino ice-cream, which she eats out of a vermilion shell, holding her eyes half-closed as she puts the spoon into her mouth (55). She is yielding to reverie, elevating La Vaubyessard into a symbol of the elegant life for which she yearns. It becomes a landmark in her mind, a repository of nostalgia, longing, and regret (60). The subjective nature of her reactions is brought out by the contrast with Charles's: he feels constrained by the tightness of his trousers because of the weight he had gained, altogether gauche and ill at ease, and relieved to return home to his onion soup. The differing response of the two characters to the same place shows the extent to which Emma's view of La Vaubyessard is an outcome of her tendency to sentimentality. There is here again a paucity of objective fact and an abundance of subjective landscape.

Zola uses the same manipulations of viewpoint as Flaubert to create internal landscapes, but he lets readers witness the shifts into and out of the protagonists' minds rather more readily. Changes in the grammatical structure of the sentences mark the transfer from the narrator's point of view to Gervaise's in the first chapter of L'Assommoir. It begins with a third-person narratorial account of her sitting at the window: "Elle regardait à droite," "Elle regardait à gauche," "elle levait les yeux," "elle apercevait"[22] ("She looked to the right," "She looked to the left," "she raised her eyes," "she noticed"). Shortly, it glides into a less determinate focalization, which fuses her angle of vision with the narrator's in an intermediary state, characterized by the equivocal "il lui semblait" (2: 380), which could mean either "it seemed to her" or "it seemed to him," although the former is more likely. The chapter ends, however, within her consciousness in the transposition of the key reiterated sight of the slaughterhouse and the hospital into indirect discourse:

C'était sur ce pavé, dans cet air de fournaise, qu'on la jetait toute seule avec les petits; et elle enfila d'un regard les boulevards extérieurs, à droite, à gauche, s'arrêtant aux deux bouts, prise d'une épouvante sourde, comme si sa vie, désormais, allait tenir là, entre un abattoir et un hôpital. (2: 403)

It was onto this sidewalk, into this furnace-like atmosphere, that she was being cast all alone with the little ones; and she threw a glance up the exterior boulevards, to the right, to the left, gripped by a silent terror, as if her life from now on was to be lived out there, between a slaughterhouse and a hospital.

The repetition of her act of looking to the right and to the left up and down the boulevards underscores the parallelism of this situation with the one at the beginning of the book, although by the close of the chapter the perception is an internal one, animated by Gervaise's fear.

A similar duality of viewpoint occurs in the episode when the wedding party looks back on to their little district of Paris from the top of the Vendôme column. This is registered successively in the third person through the eyes of various participants, then in indirect discourse in their own words ("Non, décidemment, ça vous faisait froid aux boyaux" [2: 419; "No, for sure, that gave you the creeps"]), back to third-person narration, and finally shifts to a poetic description by a narrator far more cultured and sensitive than the wedding group:

Paris, autour d'eux, étendait son immensité grise, aux lointains bleuâtres, ses vallées profondes, où roulait une houle de toitures; toute la rive droite était dans l'ombre, sous un grand haillon de nuage cuivré; et, du bord de ce nuage, frangé d'or, un large rayon coulait, qui allumait les milliers de vitres de la rive gauche d'un pétillement d'étincelles, détachant en lumière ce coin de la ville sur un ciel très pur, lavé par l'orage. (2: 450)

Paris, around them, spread its gray immensity to the bluish distances of its deep valleys, where a bevy of roofs huddled together; the whole right bank was in the shade, under a big rag of coppery cloud, fringed with gold; and from the edge of this cloud flowed a large ray of sun that lit up the thousands of windows on the left bank with a burst of sparkle, silhouetting this corner of the city against the very pure sky, cleansed by the storm.

The narrator's patently literary, totalizing vision of Paris is in startling counterpoint to the wedding guests' myopically disjunctive apprehension of isolated details. Like Gervaise, they all lack the capacity to grasp the whole of the city's extent and beauty, remaining confined to the ghetto of their slum. Neither their view nor the narrator's is factual; both are imaginative landscapes of consciousness, produced verbally by the text, not mimetically by reference.

The way in which a text can create a place for readers is nowhere more apparent than in *Buddenbrooks* in the presentation of Travemünde. Travemünde is part of a factually existent reality: it is an actual town that can be found at a certain latitude and on a certain longitude on a map of Germany. But its referential charge is rather weak since it is not a well-known place such as London, Paris, or Boston, immediately recognizable as actual. The name may strike a non-German and certainly a non-European as possibly fictitious. However, for the reading of Buddenbrooks this proves immaterial, because Travemünde comes less to denote a physical spot than to connote a state of relaxed happiness. It is a resort town with a park, a beach, a small harbor, and a lighthouse, but above and beyond that, it is a place of the mind, an alternative mode of life to the enclosed austerity of the Buddenbrooks' native city. The open vistas of the beach and the unrestricted space of the sea suggest a freedom for the individual to expand at will in a way not granted by the narrow streets of the hometown.

Travemünde is endowed with this signification within the fiction as the action develops with repeated visits there. When Tom and Tony arrive for the first time: "Sie übersahen eine Weile Bucht und Bollwerk, die roten Dächer des Städtchens, und den kleinen Hafen mit dem Segel- und Tauwek der Böte"[23] ("They looked for a while over the bay and the rampart, the red roofs of the little town, and the small harbor with the boats' sails and masts"). The description is so nonspecific as to be applicable to almost any seaside town with the result that Travemünde is virtually as generic as Middlemarch. What is important is not the features of Travemünde that Tom and Tony register, but that theirs is the registering gaze. The transfer of the viewpoint from the narrator to the protagonists is crucial here as the gateway into a landscape of consciousness. For Tony, Travemünde is the unforgettable scene of her early and only love for Morten Schwarzkopf, while for Hanno it is a blessed release from the tyranny of school, a haven of dreamy dolce far niente. So Travemünde becomes a symbolical cipher for a paradise of ease denied to the Buddenbrooks except for brief, tantalizing intervals. It continues to play the same role later in the novel when Thomas, suffering from increasing nervous exhaustion, is packed off there by his doctor for a break from the stresses and strains of his everyday existence.

On this metaphoric plane, readability is wholly independent of geographic referentiality. It is through the fictive context and its associations, that is, textually, that Travemünde assumes its meaning. The text has fashioned its own internal field of reference, which does not exclude the outer frame of reference but complements and transcends it. Place is not portrayed from the outside or through the narrator's eyes, but as the characters see it and experience it in their minds. The reading of Travemünde in Buddenbrooks throws into question one of the claims made for realism, namely: "Als literarische Richtung appelliert der

Realismus in erster Linie nicht an die ästhetische Kompetenz des Rezipienten, sondern an seine Alltagserfahrung"[24] ("As a literary tendency realism appeals not the receiver's aesthetic competence, but to his/her everyday experience"). To read realist fiction requires the same degree of aesthetic competence as any other genre and not necessarily more extraneous knowledge.

⚜

Both *Buddenbrooks* and *Middlemarch* are remarkable for the spectacular absence of concrete descriptive information, in contrast to the lengthy, copious expositions of provincial milieux or the social dissection of certain districts of Paris through the lens of the narrator in Balzac's oeuvre. Such physical description has generally been considered one of the hallmarks of realist fiction that distinguishes it from the seventeenth- and eighteenth-century novel in which objects do not figure prominently. As both Butor[25] and Lukács[26] have pointed out, in the stable, hierarchical pre-Revolutionary society, furnishings at every social level were a matter of convention, and therefore not an issue for eighteenth-century novelists. By the nineteenth century, however, the relationship of the individual to society had become more open as well as more complex. Possessions were indicators of class, making detailed description a necessity in order to define social position. Hence the protagonist's exact place and surroundings acquire a specificity, a significance, and an autonomy previously unknown in fiction.

Allied to this is the rise in the belief in the formative and restrictive impact of social milieu in the wake of determinism. The association between people's character and the appearance of their dwellings had been made earlier too. The clearest example is Darcy and his estate, Pemberley, in *Pride and Prejudice*. But this shows how the eighteenth century subscribed to the individual's power to modify and improve environment, whereas the nineteenth was struck by the opposite: the power of environment to shape and modify character. "As a man's surroundings, so will his life be" is J. Hillis Miller's succinct summary of this theory.[27] With the increased emphasis on external things as both a cause and an effect of character, descriptions tend to expand to unprecedented length, occasionally even threatening to break free of their moorings in the text continuum to form set pieces, such as the verbal pictures of Charles's cap and of Emma's wedding cake in *Madame Bovary*. Against this tendency to exuberance must be set Zola's dictum that "dans un roman, dans une étude humaine, je blâme absolument toute description qui n'est pas . . . un état de milieu qui détermine et complète l'homme"[28] ("in a novel, in a study of human beings, I totally disapprove of any description that is not . . . an environmental state that determines and completes the figure"). Though apparently exclusionary, this demand actually justifies such passages as those about the cap and wedding cake insofar as they are revelations and completions of character. Thus, action only seems to stop for description; in effect, settings are involved in the action from the outset, instilled with implications, and rich in connotations.

In the context of this tradition, the sparsity of physical description in *Middlemarch* and *Buddenbrooks* is at first sight surprising as an apparent transgression of one of realism's central conventions. Closer analysis suggests, however, that it is the accepted view of those conventions that is in need of amendment. The absence of the kind of tactile, visual description found in Balzac and Flaubert is certainly not due to any lack of familiarity with the locations on the authors' part. It is well known that *Buddenbrooks* takes place in Lübeck, Mann's hometown, while the model for Middlemarch is Eliot's native Coventry. Like Flaubert with Yonville, Eliot drew a diagrammatic sketch of the various locations in *The Quarry* for "Middlemarch," noting the distances between them. Yet Middlemarch is a town without a physiognomy, without a grid of streets, shops, and landmarks such as Yonville has. As for *Buddenbrooks*, Lübeck is not once actually named as its locale, although many of its streets and precincts including the Fischergrube, the Beckergrube, the Königsstrasse, the Burgtor, the Jerusalemsfeld, the Marienkirche are freely invoked, as well as the neighboring towns of Hamburg, Travemünde, Rostock, and the railroad junction at Wismar. However, the narratorial account of street- and landscapes is perfunctory and schematic. Travemünde, for instance, is given short shrift with a few nondescript adjectives: the sea is "blau" (1: 119; "blue") and "friedlich" ("calm"), and the lighthouse "rund" ("round") and "gelb" ("yellow"). The impressions made by smells and sounds are noted with greater precision: for example, in the city's harbor, the smells of tar, seawater, oil, and fish, and the dialect spoken by and to the workers.

In both novels, moreover, interiors are carefully delineated. This is very much in keeping with the conventions of the novel of manners, which has a marked preference for closed/enclosed spaces over open ones. Because homes are created by their inhabitants, people have more control over them than over their outer surroundings. With the growth of mass production in the course of the nineteenth century and the mania for the possession of things as status symbols, houses assume greater semiotic significance in defining and revealing personality. As a cultural artifact, "la maison est une des plus grandes puissances d'inté-gration pour les pensées, les souvenirs, les rêves de l'homme"[29] ("the house is one of the most powerful forces for the integration of the human being's thoughts, memories, dreams"). The house is, especially in northern climates, the forum for conversations and dialogues, the locus for the enactment of ten-sions and conflicts, the scene for the abundant talkers and listeners in realist fiction. Another reason for the precedence of interiors is the increasing centrality of middle-class female protagonists. The woman's sphere invariably turned on the household and domestic obligations: it was her task to make the home, and it in turn made her. Isabel Archer's entire career in *The Portrait of a Lady* is presented in terms of a succession of houses.

Houses are symbolic milestones in Dorothea Brooke's life too. Her first visit to Lowick, Mr. Casaubon's home, might have deterred her from marrying him, if she had been more experienced. As it is,

Dorothea, on the contrary, found the house and grounds all that she could wish: the dark book-shelves in the long library, the carpets and curtains with colours subdued by time, the curious old maps and bird's-eye views on the walls of the corridor, with here and there an old vase below, had no oppression for her.[30]

Almost as ominous is the room that is to be her sitting room:

The bow window looked down the avenue of limes; the furniture was all of a faded blue, and there were miniatures of ladies and gentlemen with powdered hair hanging in a group. A piece of tapestry over the door also showed a blue-green world with a pale stag in it. The chairs and tables were thin-legged and easy to upset. It was a room where one might fancy the ghost of a tight-laced lady revisiting the scene of her embroidery. A light book-case contained duodecimo volumes of polite literature in calf, completing the furniture. (100)

Dorothea even rebukes her uncle for calling the room "a little bare now" and proposing new hangings and sofas. Her determination not to see her future husband's shortcomings is skillfully conveyed by her response to his house. Not surprisingly, the most cherished room is Casaubon's sanctum, the library. The gloom, mustiness, and sterility of Lowick, whose name itself alludes to a dim light about to extinguish, contrasts with the bright domesticity of Freshitt, where Dorothea's sister lives after her marriage to Sir James, and the easygoing casualness of her uncle's home, the Grange. In every case, *nomen est omen* in both appearance and atmosphere.[31]

Similarly in Buddenbrooks the family's living room, the so-called "Landschafts-zimmer" ("landscape room"), the recurrent setting of many of the novel's major events, is portrayed with minute attention in the opening pages. It signals the Buddenbrooks' class, prosperity, and taste. In its orderliness, its light but muted colors, its idyllic, rather artificially pretty iconography, as in its self-conscious harmoniousness, its somewhat old-fashioned elegance, and its controlled spaces, it is a summation of the neat, settled world that the Buddenbrooks would like to inhabit. The whole room bespeaks a sense of restraint guided by security, an ease within a known and mastered universe. Nature is here filtered, tempered, and tamed in the same way as each of the Buddenbrooks will be expected to check his or her passions for the sake of maintaining the order sacrosanct in the family. Later, as decline begins to set in, the rear of the house is not maintained; the cats running wild in the former billiard room are an invasion of primal animal indifference into what was the civilized, well-tended play area of serious men of affairs. The delapidation of the interior behind its still impressive facade echoes Thomas's nervous exhaustion, masked by his exaggerated personal grooming and meticulous clothing. His new house carries patrician distinction to extrava-gant lengths; fully a quarter of its living space is occupied by the music room, while the bedroom is connected to an ample bath and dressing room. On the other hand, it is entirely lacking in office premises. It represents in Tony's eyes, "die Macht, den Glanz, und Triumph der Buddenbrooks" (1: 362; "the might, the splendor, and the triumph of the Buddenbrooks"), but it also embodies in its design the turn away from commerce to aesthetics.

This insistence on interiors and the relative dearth of exteriors in Buddenbrooks and Middlemarch is clearly no coincidence. The attenuation of the outer landscape is a precondition for the primacy of the inner landscape of consciousness. The subtitle of Middlemarch, A Study of Provincial Life, intimates that an entire way of life, rather than just a single place, is under scrutiny. The anonymity thus serves the purpose of generalization. Parallel to this is the title of Mann's speech, "Lübeck als geistige Lebensform"[32] ("Lubeck as a Spiritual Way of Life"), delivered in 1926 on the occasion of his return to his native city as an honored Nobel Prize laureate. As a commentary on Buddenbrooks, it discloses the deliberateness with which the physical is relegated in preference for the spiritual.

To assign to place a decidedly spiritual dimension in the action clearly amounts to an internalization. This tendency becomes increasingly manifest in the course of the nineteenth century. In the earliest major practitioner of realism, Balzac, the presentation of place functions mainly as a preface and frame to the plot. Indeed, the locations of Balzac's novels are so loosely connected to their plots that they could easily be switched. For the tales of human passion have such universality that the scenarios of, say, *Eugénie Grandet* and *A la Recherche de l'absolu* could be transposed without substantial alteration of the novels. Place is not as intrinsic to Balzac's fictions as it was to become in the latter part of the century. With the growing importance of determinism, which envisages the individual life as essentially shaped by milieu as well as by heredity, environmental forces come to play a far more prominent and direct part in the plot development than previously. Not only the social, political and economic constellation, such as had furthered Grandet's advancement, but also more ineffable factors, such as the prevalent mentality of a certain place at a certain time come to be of vital consequence in the motivation of the action.

As a result, the static description of place, the norm in Balzac, gives way to the dynamic experience of place found in *Middlemarch*, *Buddenbrooks*, and Henry James's novels. The outer scene becomes in effect and in technique an inner scene, filtered through the consciousness of the protagonists. As Eudora Welty has pointed out, "*feelings* are bound up in place,"[33] because place has the function of "furnishing a plausible abode for the novel's world of feeling" (61). So, Welty argues, place is central to "making the characters real" (61), exerting "the most delicate control over character too: by confining character, it defines it" (62). Place is no longer just the setting for the action, but through the interaction between milieu and persona, through the process of conditioning personality, it comes to have a cardinal role in determining the course of the characters' lives.

Another manifestation of this change is found in the representation of the city, which similarly modulates from stasis to flux. Burton Pike has traced this evolution in the perception of the city less and less as elements fixed in relation to each other, and more and more as a succession of fluid and unpredictable juxtapositions. "During the nineteenth century," he asserts, "the word-city was increasingly represented in literature as an unstable refraction of an individual consciousness rather than as an object fixed in space."[34] In short, reality falls into the orbit of consciousness, acquiring credibility not so much through the description of exteriors as through the inner moral power it attains in the characters' mental landscape and hence in the narrative as a whole.

Such internalization of place is, literally, enacted in the first chapter of *L'Assommoir*, where the Batignolles slums are converted into a landscape of consciousness through the grammatical shift into indirect discourse, and with it into the nightmare of fear in Gervaise's mind. The same kind of internalization occurs on a larger scale in *Middlemarch* and *Buddenbrooks*, where the places of the mind carry a strong figurative charge.

In *Middlemarch*, it is one of smallness, and by implication, of commonness, in the dual sense of the word as frequency and as paltriness. The microcosm of the fictional forum, the transparently allegorical Middle-march in "the northeast corner of Loamshire" (33), is contrasted with the macrocosm of the expansive world on the horizon in the allusions to London, Paris, Rome, Lausanne, Lyons, Avignon, and so forth. The village of Tipton strikes Dorothea as a "little pool" compared to the "lake" (47) beyond; the adjectives applied to it are "narrow," "petty," and "small," and the images those of confinement ("hemmed-in," "a labyrinth," "a walled-in maze") as against "the grandest path" and "the greatest things" (51) ascribed to what transcends the boundaries of provincial life. The echoing reiteration of Dorothea's experiences in Lydgate's career confirms that her reading of Middlemarch is more than an innocent young woman's mirage. Middlemarch's self-enclosure becomes evident in the multiple interconnections between the families, in the close interlacing of public and private affairs, in the constant exchange of gossip, and not least in the image of the web. The web denotes the tissue research that Lydgate has brought back from his studies in Paris, but at the same time it signifies the enmeshing mentality of Middlemarch, which stifles his lofty ideals just as it thwarts Dorothea's aspirations.

The landscape of *Middlemarch* thus turns out to be not only the arena where the protagonists' lives are enacted, but itself a participatory determining agent. Through its central and commanding role in the novel, it is transformed from a passive frame of the plot into an active motivational force. Its mechanisms are most cogently illustrated in the intrigues governing the administration of the hospital which make Lydgate aware of "the hampering threadlike pressure of small conditions" (210), and lead him to understand how most of Middlemarch's citizens "regard every institution of this town as a machinery for carrying out their own views" (214). As the same foreclosure of desire and relegation to second best *mutatis mutandis* cumulatively befalls Lydgate, Dorothea, Fred Vincy, Mary Garth, and Bulstrode, each in his or her own way having to submit to the limitations imposed on the individual by this environment, Middlemarch assumes a reality in the fiction as a determinant of action and lives. The characters are created and, to some extent, explained by the milieu in which they live. It comes across as a place of the mind, a texture of entrenched opinions, a mentality resistant to change or innovation. Neither Dorothea nor Lydgate, neither Mr. Brooke nor Casaubon manages to accomplish her or his aims. The repeated incidence of such disappointing, restricting outcomes, in concert with the exiguity of tangible designation, makes Middlemarch not only a generic but also a quasi-mythical place.

Place thus appears in realist fiction as an ideology, as the incarnation of the spiritual order reigning in the fictional world: "every milieu becomes a moral and physical atmosphere,"[35] indeed "a system of symbolic space."[36] "Reality" therefore comes to be understood as the product of collective agreements and interpretations, that is, as a consensus gathered from a variety of perspectives. This aggregate of the assumptions, values, and concepts that inform the affective and ethical life of individual members of a particular society is often implicit in the apparently casual conversations of subsidiary characters, who act as the representative carriers of the ethos governing that group. This is certainly the case in Middlemarch, Buddenbrooks, and Balzac's Illusions perdues, all of which are long narratives whose seemingly digressive episodes are in fact vital to the creation of the place's atmosphere and ideology. The discussions about the building of a railway line in Middlemarch, the exchanges between the barber and his clients on his morning rounds in Buddenbrooks, and the unfolding of the literary scene in Paris by the people to whom Lucien listens in Illusions perdues are good examples of such an oblique method of evoking places. So place is at once functional as the setting for the plot and indicative of the ideology that is the sum of the practices and beliefs of that locale at that point in time. It transcends its basic purpose as the physical site of the action to become part of the narrative's meaning, too, as the metaphor for the forces that determine the protagonists' lives. This ethical charge of place comes to the forefront in nineteenth-century realist fiction because it is so concerned with the problem of the individual's position in society and with the adjustments necessary for a successful compatibility between the ideals of the individual and those of the community. As a morally loaded entity, place is a grid and a standard against which the direction of the self can be assessed in relation to the social environment. Whether characters stay in one place or move on is also closely connected to the degree of their consonance with the normative ways of life where they are. Discontent or a sense of disjointedness is a primary cause for moving in a search for a more congenial arena.

However, this ethical quality of place is not to be confused with the "controlled use of the physical setting to reflect mood," which has been hailed as one of the practices of realism.[37] The phrase is more appropriate to the romantic *paysage-état-d'âme*, an antecedent to the nineteenth-century landscape of consciousness. The *paysage-état-d'âme* consists of a tableau into which are invested the emotions of the pivotal persona, often a first-person narrator. One of the outstanding and earliest examples of this technique occurs in the musings prompted by the advent of autumn in the second "walk" in Rousseau's *Les Rêveries du promeneur solitaire* (*Reveries of the Solitary Walker*):

Depuis quelques jours on avait achevé la vendange; les promeneurs de la ville s'étaient déjà retirés; les paysans aussi quittaient les champs jusqu'au travaux d'hiver. La campagne encore verte et riante, mais défeuillée en partie et déjà presque déserte, offrait partout l'image de la solitude et des approches de l'hiver. Il résultait de son aspect un mélange d'impression douce et triste trop analogue à mon âge et à mon sort pour que je ne m'en fisse pas l'application. Je me voyais au déclin d'une vie innocente et infortunée, l'âme encore pleine de sentiments vivaces et l'esprit encore orné de quelques fleurs, mais déjà flétries par la tristesse et desséchées par les ennuis. (47)

The wine harvest had been completed a few days earlier, the visitors from the city had already gone, and the peasants too were leaving the field until it was time for their winter work. The countryside, still green and pleasant, but partly stripped of leaves and already nearly deserted, bore everywhere an image of solitude and of the approach of winter. Its appearance gave rise to a mixed impression of sweetness and sadness too closely analogous to my age and to my fate for me not to apply it to myself. I saw myself at the close of an innocent and unhappy life, with a soul still full of intense feelings and a mind still adorned with a few flowers, even if they were already withered by sadness and dried up by cares.

The thrust of this passage springs above all from the feelings released by the autumnal scene, which crystallizes the spectator's inner state of mind and becomes the occasion for an associative outpouring of affective resonances. The state of mind, however, precedes the glimpse of the phenomenon that triggers its expression. So the outer scene becomes the carrier of an already existent mood. In a manner typical of the pathetic fallacy, the countryside, tinged with the persona's subjective perception of self, is transformed into an objective correlative of the inner state.

The autumnal season, with its undertones of decline and impending death, is a particularly apt vehicle for romantic melancholy. Echoes of Rousseau run through the extensive romantic (and postromantic) poetry of autumn.[38] In prose, there is a parallel to Rousseau in the lapidary words of Goethe's Werther:

Wie die Natur sich zum Herbste neigt, wird es Herbst in mir und um mich her. Meine Blätter werden gelb, und schon sind die Blätter der benachbarten Bäume abgefallen.[39]

As nature inclines toward autumn, so it is becoming autumn within and around me. My leaves are turning yellow, and those of the neighboring trees have already fallen.

Like Rousseau's solitary walker, Werther is isolated on the margins of a society he has rejected. The pictorial incarnation of this romantic stance is captured in Caspar David Friedrich's "Der Wanderer über dem Nebelmeer" ("The Wanderer above the Sea of Clouds") in which the human figure, again alone, is precariously perched on a mountain top, looking out to the surrounding peaks through the mists. The homelier countryside of the valley below is not discernible. In all these instances, the social cadre is noticeably absent, while the persona is frozen into an introverted stasis.

The landscape of consciousness in realist fiction differs from this earlier model in several cardinal respects. Foremost among them is the potent, indeed often pressing presence of those social and political circumstances so markedly missing in the eighteenth-century scenario. In contrast to the romantic loner's dissociation from the commonplace, everyday world, the protagonists of nineteenth-century realist fiction are invariably embedded and enmeshed in a complex skein of material concerns, frequently in problems of a financial, marital, or societal nature. Though life is not necessarily lived on the bare subsistence level of *L'Assommoir*, the Buddenbrooks, the Bovarys, like Lydgate, Bulstrode, the Vincys, and the Garths in *Middlemarch* are all subject to anxieties about money, marriage, and status. Their struggles stem from their dynamic interaction with vicissitudes arising from factors outside their psyche or their control: the rains that ruin the grain harvest and bring to a disastrous end Thomas Buddenbrooks's sole speculative venture; the accident of Coupeau's fall from the roof that breaks his leg and his will to work, and so eats up Gervaise's savings in *L'Assommoir*; the return of Raffles, which precipitates Bulstrode's disgrace in *Middlemarch*: these external factors have an immediate urgency for the characters in realist fiction in a way that they do not for their eighteenth-century predecessors. Whereas the latter are under the sway of their moods, the former are under the pressure of social and political circumstances. They therefore respond to the landscape in which they are placed, often caught, rather than creating it, as the solitary walker and Werther do. The primacy of emotions is replaced by the preponderance of sociopolitical exigencies, which the protagonists negotiate in their own way, but can neither determine nor transform.

This reciprocal interdependence of individual and society in nineteenth-century fiction has been well summarized by Steven Marcus:

> In George Eliot's novels society and individual persons are conceived as being related in determinate ways. Society, in these novels, is represented as a living whole, composed or articulated of differentiated members, each of which fulfills or possesses a special function. As a consequence, the individual person is not separable from the human whole; and in turn the social whole is equally dependent on each individual person, since each contributes to the common life.[40]

This holds as true for *Buddenbrooks* and *L'Assommoir* as for George Eliot's novels. In all these instances, moreover, the ubiquity and prominence of gossip illustrates the intricate involvement of the various individuals with each other as well as with social issues at large. The importance of the social texture confirms Sandy Petrey's thesis that realism finds "its expression as social truth."[41] However, this "social truth" must in itself be recognized as a fabrication of the text, empowered with meanings within the parameters of the fiction, not a self-sustaining autonomous entity.

Yet some vestige of the *paysage-état-d'âme* lingers into nineteenth-century realist fiction in a certain complicity of landscape, time of year, and weather with mood. In *L'Assommoir*, Gervaise's conversation with Goujet, in which he proposes that they leave to start a new and better life together in Belgium, takes place on a narrow strip of greenery with a few tufts of yellowing grass, a tethered goat, and a dead tree in the bright sunlight between a button factory and a mechanical saw workshop. The pathetic incongruity of Gervaise's perception of this bleak, barren spot as almost "the country" ("la campagne" 2: 614) serves further to underscore the misery of her customary surroundings. In *Middlemarch* it is the turn of the seasons that is, at several points, in consonance with the action. Thus Dorothea's first visit to Lowick is in late autumn (98), while snow is falling on her return from her honeymoon in January (306); the beginning of Lydgate's married life coincides with the emergence of light green buds against the dark evergreen (459). In *Buddenbrooks* climatic phenomena are invoked as metaphoric figurations of the current situation. So, during Thomas's and Christian's youth:

"In jenen Tagen herrschte Sonnenschein im Hause Buddenbrook, wo in den Comptoirs die Geschäfte so ausgezeichnet gingen" (1: 66; "In those days sunshine reigned in the Buddenbrook house, where business was going so well in the offices"). Grünlich's arrival, on a June afternoon, is fittingly into a somewhat contrived bucolic courtyard:

> Der Himmel, an dem unbeweglich ein paar weisse Wolken standen, begann langsam blasser zu werden. Das Stadtgärtchen lag mit symmetrisch angelegten Wegen und Beeten bunt und reinlich in der Nachmittagssonne. Der Duft der Reseden, die die Beete um-säumten, kam dann und wann durch die Luft daher. (1: 92)

> The sky, on which a few white clouds hung quite still, began slowly to pale. The little city garden, with its symmetrical paths and flowerbeds, lay bright and neat in the afternoon sun. The scent of the resedas, which edged the beds, drifted on the air now and then.

Grünlich's deceitful pretentiousness, with its specious affectations, is the precise human counterpart to this overwrought garden. And a tremendous thunder-storm, which finally breaks the mounting tension of the oppressive humidity, is graphically limned at the very moment when Johann Buddenbrook is felled by a stroke (1: 251–53).

These narrational strategies already indicate the metaphorization of place in the semiotic interdependence of person and place. Again it is houses that lend themselves most readily to such treatment: the Vauquer boardinghouse in Le Père Goriot, Lowick in Middlemarch, Thomas's luxurious new home in Buddenbrooks, the daunting tenement in L'Assommoir,[42] and a whole spate of Jamesian homes: Mrs. Montgomery's in Washington Square, the Wentworths' and Robert Acton's in The Europeans, not to mention such Dickensian abodes as Peggotty's house in David Copperfield, Tom-All-Alone's in Bleak House, and that of Arthur Clenman's mother in Little Dorritt. The city, too, in the later nineteenth century becomes the organizing metaphor for mental anguish as buildings translate into places of desire or dread. If, as Bruner asserts, "the artist creates possible worlds through the metaphoric transformation of the ordinary and conventionally 'given,' "[43] then place must be acknowledged as a major locus for such metaphorization in realist fiction. Place frequently becomes the "kind of emblematic object"[44] that lends unity to a complex work by embodying its pervasive themes. The most striking example is Middlemarch as it shows, repeatedly, the inescapable necessity of remaining in the middle marches of human existence.

Metaphoricity is innate to the landscape of consciousness insofar as it presents a view of a place in its relation to the persona and/or the action. To maintain that the "problem of realism" is "an endemic bifocalism that interrupts the account of an individual's inner life or his progress in the world with the narrative of the artifacts of a civilization"[45] is to misunderstand the narrational tactics of realism. The "narrative of the artifacts of a civilization" is not only a salient way of creating a sense of time and place, but also to present a metaphoric "account of an individual's inner life or progress in the world." No need to look further than the artifacts in Madame Vauquer's boardinghouse or in Casaubon's Lowick, or in the Buddenbrooks' "landscape room." As an essential expression of personality, the objects accumulated over the years[46] simultaneously tell a story and reveal a character. Thus the metonymic facets of realism are alloyed with its metaphoric aspects.[47]

For this reason it is not uncommon "que la description double, ou anticipe le récit fondamental"[48] ("that description reduplicates or anticipates the underlying narrative"). The evocation of the Pont-Neuf passage in Paris, with which Zola's Thérèse Raquin opens, is a model of the figurative implications inherent in what seems to be a physical description. From the first paragraph onward, the negative aspects of the Pont-Neuf passage emerge: it lies at the end ("au bout")[49] of the rue Guénégaud, forming "une sorte de corridor étroit et sombre" (15; "a sort of narrow, dark corridor"), thirty steps in length and at most two in width, paved with "dalles jaunâtres, usées, descellées, suant toujours une humidité âcre" (15; "yellowish, worn, loose stones, always moist with an acrid humidity"), and covered with glass panes "noir de crasse" (15; "black with grime"). On fine sunny summer days, a whitish light comes through the dirty panes, "et traîne misérablement dans le passage" (15; "and drags wretchedly through the passage"). On bad, foggy winter days, night reigns over the sticky paving stones, "de la nuit salie et ignoble" (15; "a filthy, sullied night"). The repetition of "nuit" ("night"), together with the long narrow shape of the passage, its decrepitude, dampness, and somberness strongly suggest the image of a grave. The place where Thérèse is forced to exist is, indeed, a living death to her. The shops, "pleines de ténèbres" (16; "full of darkness"), are "autant de trous lugubres dans lesquels s'agitent des formes bizarres" (16; "so many lugubrious holes where strange shapes flit about"). Their windows cast greenish reflections on merchandise lingering there for twenty years, displayed along the shelves painted "d'une horrible couleur brune" (16; "a horrid brown color"). The intrusion of the evaluative, emotive adjective "horrible" betrays the perceiving narrator's reactions, as does the later adverb, "lamentablement" (17; "lamen-tably"). The exposition ends on a crescendo with: "Au-dessus du vitrage, la muraille monte, noire, grossièrement crépie, comme couverte d'une lèpre et toute couturée de cicatrices" (16; "Above the panes, the wall rises, dark, vilely pitted, as if covered by leprosy, or all puckered by scars").

The themes introduced in this overture are reiterated, with variations, in the ensuing three pages. The murkiness and the dampness, as of a grave, are constantly underlined in the catalog of the faded, dusty, spoiled, greenish, sweating, rotting objects in the shops. The association with death is voiced in the statement that at night, under the dim, flickering lights of the gas lamps, "[l]e passage prend l'aspect sinistre d'un véritable coupe-gorge" (17; "the passage takes on the sinister appearance of a place where throats are cut"). The cataleptic fixity, the decaying stagnation, the hints at entombment are then extended to the human figures of Thérèse, her husband, and her mother-in-law, enclosed in the icy bareness of their room. As if to depersonalize and deaden them further, none of the protagonists is even named in the initial chapter; they are simply "she," "her husband," and "the old lady," imprisoned in a gruesome hole, and locked into a mysterious bond.

This brief chapter, laden with ghoulish undertones, inaugurates a tale of love, murder, and retribution, told, according to Zola's claims in the preface to the second edition, with scientific detachment as a neurological study, but actually vibrant with passion. The opening description is a fine instance of this duality insofar as the account of the Pont-Neuf passage is oriented in two directions at once: to the external field of reference in the Parisian locations ("rue Guéné-gaud," "rue Mazarine à la rue de Seine" 15), and to the internal field of reference in the plot that it "reduplicates and anticipates." Through the montage of the fictive action onto a Parisian location, a bridge is created between the extraneous world and the realm of the fiction. The place, while purporting and pretending to be real, only becomes so for readers by virtue of the symbolical, metaphorical force it assumes within the frame of the narration.

৯৭

How then is the landscape formed in readers' consciousness? The question is crucial to the topic of this inquiry. The answer lies in an intricate transaction between readers and texts, not in readers' prior knowledge of the location of the action and their recognition of it, as used to be thought. The intimacy that

Americans feel with Travemünde after reading Buddenbrooks, like that of European readers with Lycurgus in Dreiser's An American Tragedy, has nothing at all to do with recognition, and everything with narrational and reading strategies.

One of the major strategies of realist fiction, as has already been pointed out, is the manipulation of viewpoint. From this Elizabeth Deeds Ermarth has constructed a theory of realism under the title Realism and Consensus:

> Realistic novels demonstrate the power of narrative consciousness to occupy one mind after another; and in so doing, they confirm the potential continuity of consciousness between minds and even implicitly extend that continuity beyond the arbitrary limits of the text to include the reader. The narrator transgresses the boundaries of individuality not only between persons but also between persons and texts.[50]

Such continuity of consciousness allows readers to experience place coextensively alongside the protagonists. They, as internal readers, prefigure the exegetic model for us, the actual readers. The process is both specular and transferential. As the characters within the fiction engage in readings of their place and situation, they become "interpretants"[51] of their fictional world. If this term is adopted for the part they play, then the more customary "interpreter" can be reserved for the reader/critic. The distinction is helpful so long as it is taken purely as a heuristic device, not as the predication of an absolute dichotomy.

For, increasingly, it is the opposite that happens as we read our way through the often substantial volumes that realism produces in its desire to create an entire world fictionally: "[W]e maintain our sense of separateness, but the very act of reading forces us not to sympathize but to become the audience of the tale."[52] An audience is and is not a part of a performance; at one level it is engrossed in the action, while at another at least some of its members may muse on the characters, their choices, and their place. This suggests the possibility of a certain overlap between interpretants and interpreters, an identification that does not, however, rule out moments of detachment. Such a stance is facilitated by the smooth transitions in focalization, which enable readers to move in and out of various minds, seeing from multiple points of view serially and sometimes even simultaneously. So, in Madame Bovary, we are privy to both Emma's and Charles's daydreams as they lie in bed side by side: she fantasizes about exotic lands, camels, and dashing cavaliers, whereas he visualizes their daughter's future as she grows into a schoolgirl, a young woman, and a bride. More extensively in Middlemarch and Buddenbrooks, the same set of problematic circumstances is habitually examined through the lens of diverse percipients. The "dissolution of the boundaries between reported speech and reporting context" not only makes the text more "polyphonic" but also renders readers' task of interpretation "more active and problematic."[53]

The problematics are particularly evident in the role of indirect discourse and interior monologue, which give readers immediate access to the protagonists' consciousness, thereby encouraging empathy, yet that empathy can be inverted into recoil through the intervention of irony. That is what happens in *Madame Bovary*, certainly in regard to Emma, but the practice is none too common in realist fiction because it seeks as an *écriture* to efface the marks of its literariness, and thereby to come closer to passing for a true and faithful copy of an extraneous reality. The relationship between characters and readers is, therefore, not as perplexed as in self-conscious narratives, which make wider use of irony. Consequently, "feeling in the book has a close correlative in the quality of feeling aroused by the book."[54] This holds equally for feelings about place: readers feel the nostalgic affection for Travemünde that Tony, Hanno, and Tom do, the horror and anguish in the Batignolles slums through the eyes of Gervaise, and the frustration caused by the intransigence of Middlemarch with Dorothea and Lydgate. Place comes alive for the interpreters through the intermediacy of the interpretants.

This mechanism of identification corroborates Walton's hypothesis: "Appreciation of representational works of art is primarily a matter of participation."[55] This participation is predominantly "psychological,"[56] involving "imagining, from the inside, doing and *experiencing* things" (212). To which should be added: places. This is implied as Walton elaborates on his thesis:

> We don't just observe fictional worlds from without. We live in them (in the worlds of our games, not work worlds), together with Anna Karenina and Emma Bovary and Robinson Crusoe and others. . . . True, these worlds are merely fictional, and we are well aware that they are. But from *inside* they seem actual—what fictionally is the case is, fictionally, *really* the case—and our presence in them . . . gives a sense of intimacy with characters and their other contents. (273)

Foremost among "their other contents" are the places where they live out their fictional lives.

Walton concedes that "some representations positively discourage participation," so that "appreciation . . . is something of a spectator sport" (273–74). But this is definitely not the case with realist fiction, which encourages reader participation in the form of pretense. As a result, readers can hold a dual standpoint: they exist both fictionally and literally, that is, they are absorbed in the realm of the fiction as if it were real, yet they also remain aware of their actual position as readers of fiction. But this continuing cognizance of their rootedness in their own world does not detract from their capacity to pretend belief in response to the text's invitations to do so. As Walton comments, "From inside the fictional worlds which we share with Tom Sawyer and Willy Loman look very much as though they are real."[57] And we get "inside" through realism's use of such techniques as the manipulation of viewpoint and indirect discourse.

The effect of readers' ability to maintain a dual standpoint has not been sufficiently explored, and has led to simplifications and misrepresentations. Particularly nefarious is the assumption that the "reality" quotient of place in fiction must be assessed against the yardstick of an external, existent location, and, as a corollary, that its plausibility stems from the degree to which it conforms to contours known to the author and recognizable by readers. Such a model clearly devolves from the mimetic imperative. But place, like all else in fiction, is ultimately a verbal artifact, an illusion created by a particular selection and combination of words. Partly through the associative and suggestive force of language, the evocation of place acquires the power of a reality within the fiction. It is further validated by the role it comes to play within the frame of the fiction in shaping the lives of the protagonists, who experience directly the moral pressures it exerts on their aspirations and desires. Only through its function integral to the fiction can place become "real" to readers. The process is one of osmotic transposition as the interpreters assimilate the interpretants' readings in the landscapes of their consciousness.

The relative positions of fact and image prove to be more circuitous and porous than Vautrin supposes. For the plastic, as Hugo von Hofmannsthal understood, comes into being not through looking, but through identification. Or, as Saussure asserted: "c'est le point de vue qui FAIT la chose"[58] ("it is the point of view that MAKES the thing"). This other use of "fait" as a creative agent runs counter to Balzac's static postulate of "le fait" as the objective, independently existent fact. Instead, it empowers readers, in collaboration with the text and through the protagonists' vision, to make place, as an internal perception, into a potent, credible presence at the very core of our reading of the fiction.

7

Figuring the Pretense

❧

You may use any language you choose to indulge in,
without impropriety.—W. S. Gilbert

❧ The structuralists' insistence that "to read is, in fact, a labor of language,"
to revert to Barthes's dictum, has fostered renewed attention to the figuration of
texts, the patterning of the words themselves. Despite an indifference to the
"readerly" mode that amounted to a barely veiled contempt, the structuralists
introduced an intensive concentration on language that has been continued by
their successors and that brought to an end the tendency to neglect the linguistic
texture of realism. No longer is its language regarded as merely aimed at the
communication of meaning; its figuration is now given close scrutiny. The
alleged simplicity and naïveté of realist writing can indeed be seen as yet another
component of its pretense. The covert "writerliness"—and literariness—of the
readerly text is brilliantly uncovered in S/Z.

Barthes's underscoring of the labor of language as the essence of reading (and
even more so of rereading) has given impetus to close reexamination of realist
fiction for its specific use of words. So Kanes, in discussing the language of
Balzac, who used to be dismissed as a hasty, almost careless writer, now envisages "les opérations du langage comme découverte du monde"[1] ("the workings of language as the discovery of the world"). Readers, too, discover the
world of the fiction, making its order and its places with the narrator by means

of the language. This extends into apparently minor details of grammatical usage. For instance, one of Balzac's favorite constructions, a demonstrative followed by a relative clause (or clauses), establishes categories that form, as it were, bridges that enable readers to cross from their actual world to the fictive realm: "Ces salles basses, qui n'ont ni devanture, ni montre, ni vitrage, sont profondes, obscures et sans ornements extérieurs ou intérieurs"[2] ("These low rooms, which have no frontage or show cases or windows, are deep and dark, devoid of exterior or interior decoration"); "Le lendemain matin régnait à Paris un de ces épais brouillards qui l'enveloppent et l'embrument si bien que les gens les plus exacts sont trompés sur le temps" (2: 877; "The next day Paris had one of those fogs that blanket and darken to such an extent that even the most careful people mistake the time"); "Cet appartement, de mille écus de loyer, qui regorgeait de toutes les belles choses vulgaires que procure l'argent, prenait le premier étage d'un ancien hôtel, entre cour et jardin" (6: 236; "This apartment, that was rented for a thousand *écus*, and overflowing with all the pretty, vulgar things that money can buy, took up the first floor of an old mansion between the courtyard and the garden"). Admittedly, it takes readers willing to reread and to focus on the linguistic texture to grasp such strategies—in short, readers open to conceiving realist fiction not as mimesis but as a literary artifact.

Such an approach contravenes established habits of long standing. Because one of the ways of praising a work of literature was to say that it was very true to life, the role of language had of necessity to be minimized in order not to attract attention to the verbal fabric. This once dominant stance has been summarized by Fowler:

Generally, prose fiction of the eighteenth to twentieth centuries, unlike verse, avoids 'foregrounding' the physical substance of the text. Claiming to be rational, referential discourse pointing to a 'reality' beyond language, the novel pretends that its medium is transparent, playing down the visual and phonetic shape of the text.[3]

Fowler realizes that realist fiction is merely "*claiming* to be rational, referential discourse," and that it "*pretends* that its medium is transparent" (my emphasis). "Transparent," a frequent and prominent term to describe realist discourse, projects an image of both simplicity and nonstyle. Despite the findings of recent critics, who have taken issue with the word, disputing its appropriateness to realism,[4] this perception of the characteristic style of realism as a nonstyle has nevertheless been hard to dislodge. Even a critic as astute as Philippe Hamon has asserted: "Le discours réaliste, comme le discours pédagogique, réfusera en général la référence au procès de l'énonciation pour tendre à une écriture 'transparente' monopolisée par la seule transmission d'une information"[5] ("Realist discourse, like pedagogic discourse, will generally shun reference to the process of statement making in order to cultivate a 'transparent' mode of writing, monopolized solely by the transmission of information"). Hamon therefore sees realism as aiming "vers le *monosémie*" (437; "toward *monosemis*"), by which he means singularity of denotation.

Hamon's conception of realist discourse is reminiscent of Mukarovsky's definition of "standard language in its purest form, as the language of science with formulation as its objective" and hence "automatized," in contrast to the function of poetic language that "consists in the maximum of foregrounding of the utterance . . . to the extent of pushing communication into the background."[6] Yet despite the sharpness of this dichotomy, Mukarovsky is able to posit an intermediary status of language corresponding to the practices of the novel. For, he argues,

[it] holds, even for works and genres of poetry in which the subject matter is the dominant, that the latter is not the 'equivalent' of a reality to be expressed by the work as effectively (for instance, as truthfully) as possible, but that it is a part of the structure, is governed by its laws, and is evaluated in terms of its relationship to it. . . . It cannot be said of the novel that here the linguistic elements are the esthetically indifferent expression of content, not even if they appear to be completely devoid of foregrounding: the structure is the total of all the components, and its dynamics arises precisely from the tension between the foregrounded and the unforegrounded. (23)

This is a fundamental insight for the analysis of realist fiction, insofar as it opposes facile distinctions between a transparent nonstyle, such as has been attributed to Champfleury, and the so-called *style artiste* of Flaubert and the Goncourts.[7] The simplifying schema of a bifurcation is here replaced by an acknowledgment that slippages and amalgams between the modes are both normative and likely.

Slippages are inherent in the words themselves because of their connotative properties. It has been customary to differentiate, as does Mukarovsky, between denotative and connotative language, which coincides largely with what he calls "standard" and "poetic" language. "Denote" means "to note down," "to mark or mark out," "to be the visible sign of," "to indicate," and, in the field of logic, "to be a name of." The *Oxford English Dictionary*'s example of "denotative" is "Proper names are preeminently denotative," that is, Lilian Renée Furst denotes me, and no one else. "Connote," on the other hand, derived from *con notare* (to note with), means "to signify secondarily or in addition," "to include or imply along with the primary meaning," "to suggest." Whereas "denotation" specifies "a designation" or "the signification of a term," "connotation" characterizes "the signifying in addition," "inclusion of something in the meaning of a word besides what it primarily denotes," "implication." So a likely connotation of "home" is a place of warmth, security, and comfort. Denotation seeks to be univalent in its quest for precision, while connotation is polyvalent in its suggestivity. If scientific discourse aspires to denotation, literary discourse thrives on connotation, on the associations latent in words. In Genette's formulation,

ce que nous appelons le style—même le plus sobre—reste lié à ces effets de sens seconds que la linguistique nomme des connotations. Ce que dit l'énoncé est toujours en quelque sorte doublé, accompagné par ce que dit la manière, et la manière la plus transparente est encore une manière.[8]

what we call style—even the most sober style—remains linked to those secondary sense effects that linguistics calls connotations. What the statement says is always in some way doubled, accompanied by the manner in which it is said, and the most transparent manner is still a manner.

The connotative force of language therefore militates against transparency.

This connotative force has already been illustrated in chapter 6 in the discussion of the opening paragraphs of *Thérèse Raquin*, where language that purports to scientific detachment proves highly evocative. It is important to realize, however, that virtually all words, even those that seem most innocent, have a connotative potential. Ordinary adjectives such as "black" and "white" serve well to reveal the slide from the denotative to the connotative in their several meanings listed in the *Oxford English Dictionary*. "Black" is defined in these nine senses: "as a colour pertaining to objects dark even in full light; absorbing all light;" "with the names of various objects prefixed, e.g. jet, coal, pitch, raven;" "characterized in some way by this colour, e.g. hair, complexion, clothing, armour;" "characterized by the absence of light, enveloped in darkness; dark, dusky, swart;" "deeply stained with dirt, soiled, dirty, foul;" "having dark or deadly purpose; malignant, deadly, baneful, disastrous, sinister;" "foul, iniquitous, atrocious, horribly wicked;" "clouded with sorrow or melancholy; dismal, gloomy, sad, e.g. countenance, look) in contrast to bright and hopeful;" "indicating disgrace, censure, liability to punishment, e.g. book, list." The rapid movement from the physical color black to its secondary metaphoric meanings is very readily apparent here. A parallel instance is "white:" "of the colour of snow or milk; fully luminous and devoid of any distinctive hue;" "in a looser or wider sense: of a light, pale colour;" "in combination, e.g. white-hot, white-blue;" in special collocations, e.g. animals: fox, shark, heron;" "of or in reference to skin or complexion; applied to those races characterized by light complexion;" "in early use applied to illness marked by pallor; pallid, especially from fear or other emotion;" "clothed or arrayed in white, especially belonging to an ecclesiastical order, e.g. white friar; from seventeenth century associated with royalist or legitimist causes, e.g. white flag of the Bourbons;" "figuratively: morally or spiritually pure or stainless; spotless, unstained, innocent;" "chiefly of times and seasons, now rare: propitious, favourable, fortunate, happy;" "highly prized, precious, dear, beloved, favorite;" "(obsolete) fair-seeming, specious, plausible." Particularly interesting is the openness of "white" to both negative ("pallid," etc., as in the "white scourge" of tuberculosis) and positive connotations, with the latter predominating. "Black," too, can have contradictory undercurrents; although it is the color of mourning, it is also used in a complimentary sense in the trademark "Blackglama" for the most luxurious mink pelts.

The range of denotations and connotations attached to "black" and "white" offers a forceful argument against the conception of language as plain, neutral, or "transparent." The sentence "The walls of the room were black" prompts quite different responses from "The walls of the room were white." The first demands completion with "which made the ceiling seem low," while in the second, the ceiling would seem "high." These are, on the surface, purely descriptive statements, constative of a fact concerning color, free of judgment or comment. The two rooms may well be of the same size so that the relative height of the ceiling may be an optical illusion devolving directly from the color of the walls. Yet even in this straightforward case, strong associative overtones immediately come into play: white walls and the appearance of a high ceiling induce a feeling of spaciousness, airiness, pleasantness; conversely, black walls and the impression of a low ceiling elicit darkness, pokiness, enclosure, perhaps imprisonment. This example confirms Fowler's reminder "that rhetoric and attitudinal colouring are inevitable conditions of all language use. . . . Language is a powerfully committing medium to work in. It does not allow us to 'say something' without conveying an attitude to that something."[9] This connotative thrust of language precludes exclusively literal writing (except in a highly controlled, circumscribed scientific context, for instance in giving statistical results of an experiment, where the context itself instructs readers *not* to attend to connotations). Despite its desire to be read literally and as truth, realist fiction cannot shed the connotative, which frequently moves in the direction of the figurative.

ॐ

All the realists use language both denotatively and connotatively. However, some privilege its denotative aspects, while others favor its connotative potential. These preferences result in two different approaches to description: the emphasis on denotation is conducive to density, in contrast to the suggestiveness that is the outcome of connotation. In neither case is language foregrounded to the point of attracting primary attention to itself, as in poetry. The language of realism favors functionality, even if connotation by its very nature embraces a greater degree of figuration. Nor must the two tendencies be seen as alternatives despite certain writers' predilection for one over the other. Again it is Balzac and James who stand at opposite poles, the former espousing density, while the latter practices suggestiveness.

Density is characterized by a feast of information, whereas suggestiveness has a relative attenuation of concrete detail. These two approaches correspond well to the twin fundamental thrusts of description outlined by Philippe Hamon in his *Introduction à l'analyse du descriptif*. The one is "une tendance 'horizontale' d'exhaustivité" (61; "a 'horizontal' tendency to exhaustiveness") in which the thing to be described "est considéré comme une surface, un espace, rationalisé-rationalisable, articulé, découpé, segmenté, grillé d'un côté par les 'champs' lexicaux du vocabulaire, de l'autre par les divers savoirs officiels" (61; "is considered as a surface, a space, rationalized and rationalizable, dissected, sectionalized, segmented, regimented on the one side by the lexical 'fields' of vocabulary, and on the other by the various organized realms of knowledge"). In this type of description, technical language is borrowed, for instance, from horticulture to describe vegetation, from architecture for a building or monument, from technical specialities for a machine. The describing voice is that of a traveler, a surveyor of both spaces and libraries, who gives a "fragment," a "piece," a "slice of life," a "picture," a "case," a "cutting," a "class," a "detail," etc." (62). It is perhaps not inappropriate to interject that Hamon himself exhibits all the traits of exhaustiveness. The other tendency is "'verticale', *décryptive plûtot que descriptif*" (63; "'vertical,' *décryptive* rather than descriptive") as the thing to be described is not articulated into a mosaic of territories, fields, and discourses to be traversed, but rather is "*considéré comme constitué de deux (ou plusieurs) 'niveaux' superposés qu'il faut traverser en allant du plus explicite au moins explicite*" (63; "considered as constituted of two [or several] superposed 'levels' which must be traversed, moving from the more to the less explicit"). This sort of description is qualitative not quantitative, more intent on comprehension than on extension, motivated by a desire to penetrate beneath the surface in order to ferret out the intrinsic features.

These two kinds of description result from divergent methods. Density is the outcome of agglomeration, a metonymic enumeration of one detail after another that produces an overdetermined image in an apotheosis of totalization. "*La description, de toute façon, excède*"[10] ("The description is, in every way, excessive"), Raymonde Debray-Genette comments; yet she adds: "*c'est de cet excès qu'elle se nourrit en travaillant à se justifier*" ("it is on this excess that it feeds in striving to justify itself"). The superabundance that stems from fullness of specification, in rhetorical terms, from *amplificatio*, is generally regarded as one of the salient features of realism. However, overdetermination can impede or suspend the process of reading if readers feel overwhelmed by such an onslaught of information that they lose grasp of the whole as a result of the inflation of a particular segment. Density can thus prove self-defeating when it thwarts ease of readability, that ready understanding that is one of the ideals of realism. The part then becomes self-sufficient as a set piece, almost as an excrescence, an outgrowth of the narration that threatens to overshadow the global effect. It is as if immersion in the particular in all its minuteness blocks the larger system of which it is merely a subsidiary element. The proportions are endangered through what Zola recognized in himself as "*l'hypertrophie du détail vrai*"[11] ("the hypertrophy of accurate detail"). Such superabundance, according to Hamon, performs a function in the narrative by mobilizing readers' hermeneutic powers. Yet mostly, dense texts are self-interpretative through their inclusion of denomination and explanation. So superabundance runs the risk of alienating readers by its long-windedness and seeming redundancies, or of tempting them to impose arcane designs that militate against realism's pretense to simplicity.

Density is more prevalent in Balzac than in any later realist. His novels show, particularly in the preliminaries preceding the start of the action, "a desperate linguistic exuberance,"[12] an overdescription whose impact can be dizzying. In

Eugénie Grandet a full nineteen pages elapse before the titular heroine makes her first appearance.[13] Meanwhile, the exterior of the house, the street, the town of Saumur, its commerce, its leading citizens and factions, and the economic and social prehistory of Eugénie's parents is unfolded with an expansiveness that amounts to "the sublimation of details."[14] Before the narrative gets going, the narrator draws a word picture in the tradition of the rhetorical device known as ecphrasis. This was the concept most available to novelists at the beginning of the nineteenth century, and it clearly affected their practice. It was also, as Burton Pike points out, "not really until Balzac that the word-city itself was individualized."[15] For Balzac this involves the effort to translate the visual image into linguistic terms. So the exposition is ordered by a series of spatial directives: "ici" (3: 480; "here"), "là" (3: 481; "there"), "plus loin" (3: 481; "further on"), and "à côté de" (3: 480; "beside") as well as by that profusion of demonstratives that project specificity ("cette rue" [3: 480; "this street"], "ces salles basses" [3: 481; "these low-ceilinged rooms"], "ce mur" [481; "this wall"], "cette espèce d'antre" [3: 481; "this kind of cave"]) mentioned earlier. The language aspires to the denotative through its concentration on the financial data that have shaped both the town and Grandet, but its briskness is colored by the motif of melancholy introduced in the opening sentence and reiterated at the end of the first paragraph. The incongruence between Grandet's meteoric success in the world of commerce and the mysterious gloom in his house is certainly a factor likely to arouse readers' curiosity. Yet, readers' role here is complicated: mainly they are treated as outsiders in need of initiation into this scenario, although the addresses to them quickly solicit their active participation as if they had already become insiders. Similarly, they are swept along by the forward rush of the inordinately long paragraphs (which number only five in nineteen pages), while at the same time recoiling from the pace because of the difficulty of assimilating such quantities of information. It is a relief to hear (3: 497) that the description of the rest of the house will be postponed until the relevant point in the action, and to reach at long last its dramatic start on the day of Eugénie's birthday. No other writer after Balzac imputed to readers the patient willingness to handle at the outset so massive a descriptive preamble. Increasingly, as realism evolves, description is integrated into the action, tending to diminish in quantity and change in quality as density yields to suggestiveness.

The impulse to density may surface in localized areas of intense description. One such example is the famous—or perhaps, infamous—account of Charles's cap on the second page of *Madame Bovary*:

C'était une de ces coiffures d'ordre composite, où l'on retrouve les éléments du bonnet à poil, du chapska, du chapeau rond, de la casquette de loutre et du bonnet de coton, une de ces pauvres choses, enfin, dont la laideur muette a des profondeurs d'expression comme le visage d'un imbécile. Ovoïde et renflée de baleines, elle commençait par trois boudins circulaires; puis s'alternaient, séparés par une bande rouge, des losanges de velours et de poil de lapin; venait ensuite une façon de sac qui se terminait par un polygone cartonné, couvert d'une broderie en soutache compliquée, et d'où pendait, au bout d'un long cordon trop mince, un petit croisillon de fils d'or, en manière de gland. Elle était neuve; la visière brillait. (4)

It was one of those hybrid pieces of headgear, in which can be found traces of the busby, the chapska, the beret, the otterskin, and the nightcap, in short, one of those pathetic objects, whose mute ugliness has depths of expression like the face of an idiot. Ovoid, dilated with whalebone, it began with a circular headband composed of three sausage-like rolls; then lozenges of velvet alternated with others of rabbit fur, edged in red; next came a kind of bag, topped by a polygon reinforced with cardboard and embroidered in an elaborate braided pattern, from which, at the end of too thin a cord hung a small tuft of gold thread, intended as a tassel. The cap was new; its visor gleamed.

This ludicrous cap is the most striking thing about Charles on his entry into school. It is portrayed metonymically through conglomeration of its features except for the half sentence of narratorial comment in the middle that switches to metaphor and simile. It defies attempts at an allegorical interpretation of each of its components. But its overall signification is made quite plain. Its incongruity is contained in the weird concatenation of various kinds of headdress. And the narrator mediates its meaning by calling it "in short, one of those pathetic objects, whose mute ugliness has depths of expression like the face of an idiot." Only a boy so devoid of self-esteem as to allow his mother to dominate and manipulate him as Charles does would submit to being saddled with such a preposterous cap. Here the brief passage of overdescription has the larger function of characterization; it is the simultaneously concrete and figurative embodiment of the "*ridiculus sum*" (5) that Charles is made to write out twenty times in all its conjugations.

Density is also used for a specific purpose toward the end of *Buddenbrooks* in the third chapter of the closing section (*Gesammelte Werke*, 1: 775–79) about Hanno's death. It does and does not deal with his dying, for he is never actually named; it is not until the following chapter that reference is made to his burial six months back (1: 780). The narrator circumvents a painful episode by taking refuge in a strictly medical report of the course of typhoid fever without any mention whatsoever of the patient. The tone is set by the opening statement: "Mit dem Typhus ist es folgendermassen bestellt" (1: 775; "Typhus runs its course as follows").[16] The absolute impersonality of the construction is emphasized by the use of the stilted officialese, "folgendermassen" ("as follows"), redolent of a legal document. The ensuing two and a half pages offer a meticulous clinical account of the stages in the disease's symptomatology and their customary treatment in discourse that mimics a medical textbook. The bewildering over-description with its serried list of the frightening signs of disintegration is a cogent way to impress the inexorable decay caused by the fever. Not until the final paragraph, after the verbatim repetition of the initial sentence, does the mode shift into the figurative as the anonymous patient's reaction to the thera-peutic regime is internalized: will he respond positively to the beckoning voice of life, or will he shake his head at its summons, shrink back in trepidation and revulsion, and die? (1: 778–79). Density of specification inverts abruptly into suggestiveness.

Suggestiveness as a mode of description is essentially tentative and open-ended. It implies readers different from those projected by density; for density is prompted by the postulate of unknowing readers in need of initiation and instruction, while suggestiveness supposes knowing readers capable of making associations with certain places and even of identifying the social import of addresses without explanation. In Washington Square, for instance, James devotes the entire opening paragraph to elaborating on the "consideration which, in the United States, has always been bestowed on the medical profession," but on the next page the names "the Bay," "the Battery," and "Canal Street" are dropped on the assumption of readers' familiarity with that section of Manhattan. On his marriage Dr. Sloper had gone to live "in an edifice of red brick, with granite copings, and an enormous fan-light over the door, standing in a street within five minutes' walk of the City Hall" (11). How terse and sketchy that is com-pared to Balzac's eager exploration of every nook and cranny. The difference becomes even more apparent in the presentation of the house in Washington Square, the scene of most of the action, which is introduced in merely two sentences:

The ideal of quiet and of genteel retirement, in 1835, was found in Washington Square, where the Doctor built himself a handsome, modern, wide-fronted house, with a big balcony before the drawing-room windows, and a flight of white marble ascending to a

portal which was also faced with white marble. This structure, and many of its neighbors, which it exactly resembled, were supposed forty years ago to embody the last
results of architectural science, and they remain to this day very solid and honorable
dwellings. (11)

Here, as in *Eugénie Grandet*, the mood of the dwelling precedes its physical aspect: it
is to form "the ideal of quiet and of genteel retirement," yet ironically, both its
quiet and its gentility will be disturbed by the intrusion of Morris Townsend as a
suitor to Catherine Sloper. The house is seen at this point only from the outside.
The adjectives ("handsome, modern, wide-fronted," and "solid and honorable") all carry connotations of pleasantness, as do the "big balcony" and the
"white marble steps ascending to a portal which was also faced with marble."
Elegance reigns, although the house is not at all individual, exactly resembling its
many neighbors, which seems to reduce its worth as one of a series. Unlike
Balzac, James does not interpret the items in the description, leaving readers to
surmise the atmosphere of ease and comfort at a certain level on the social and
financial scale.

   This emphasis on the social predominates throughout *Washington Square*. The
characters' status and position on the social hierarchy is conveyed by the places
where they live. Mrs. Almond, Catherine's aunt,

lived much further up town, in an embryonic street, with a high number—a region
where the extension of the city began to assume a theoretic air, where poplars grew
beside the pavement (when there was one), and mingled their shade with the steep roofs
of desultory Dutch houses, and where pigs and chickens disported themselves in the
gutter. (12)

The unfinished state of this street is caught in the vivid metaphor, "embryonic."
Its remoteness and partial pavement immediately hint at an uncouth primitive-
ness that is confirmed at the end of the sentence by the presence of pigs and
chickens. James clearly suggests the literal and figurative distance between Dr.
Sloper's residence and his sister's without explicitly spelling it out. In this sense
he is indeed "decryptive," to invoke Hamon's neologism, cryptic and allusive
rather than ample and categoric. The interior of Dr. Sloper's house comes into
view only in fragmentary glimpses. Townsend on a visit sits "in the front parlor,
in the biggest armchair" (25). Just how big is it? what is the color, quality, and
condition of its upholstery? what does the cushion that he slaps with his stick
look like? Balzac would surely have told us. Similarly, when Catherine goes into

her father's study to announce her engagement, "she found him sitting in his chair beside the fire" (47). There is no description of the study, nothing beyond this minimal "chair beside the fire." What lies behind the facade of Dr. Sloper's house is virtually as inscrutable as what lies behind his facade. Once, a view of the drawing room is given when Catherine receives Morris "amidst the chaste upholstery of a New York drawing-room furnished in the fashion of fifty years ago" (43). It is the visitor who throws

a glance at the long, narrow mirror which adorned a space between two windows, and which had at its base a little gilded bracket covered by a thin slab of white marble, supporting in its turn a backgammon-board folded together in the shape of two volumes—two shining folios inscribed, in greenish-gilt letters, *History of England*. (44)

This decor suggests an aura of leisure and affluence, together with a certain pretentiousness, but Morris is too preoccupied with his own precarious situation to reflect consciously on what he glimpses.

Not so Dr. Sloper, when he calls on Mrs. Montgomery, Morris's sister, on the Second Avenue. He deliberates calculatingly on her home, deducing both her rank and her personality from its location and furnishings:

She lived in a neat little house of red brick, which had been freshly painted, with the edges of the bricks very sharply marked out in white. It has now disappeared, with its companions, to make room for a row of structures more majestic. There were green shutters upon the windows without slats, but pierced with little holes, arranged in groups; and before the house was a diminutive "yard," ornamented with a bush of mysterious character, and surrounded by a low wooden paling, painted in the same green as the shutters. The place looked like a magnified babyhouse, and might have been taken down from a shelf in a toy-shop. . . . She received him in a little parlor, which was precisely the parlor he had expected: a small, unspeckled bower, ornamented with desultory foliage of tissue-paper, amidst which—to carry out the analogy—the temperature of the leafy season was maintained by means of a cast-iron stove, emitting a dry blue flame, and smelling strongly of varnish. The walls were embellished with engravings swathed in pink gauze, and the tables ornamented with volumes of extracts from the poets, usually bound in black cloth stamped with florid designs in jaundiced gilt. (58–59)

It seems strange at first that by far the lengthiest and most particularized description of external and interior milieu in *Washington Square* should be attached to a minor character. The answer lies not in the perceived object but in the perceiving subject, Dr. Sloper. His is the controlling intelligence in the fiction; he is endowed with the insight to read place interpretatively in a manner out of the reach of the other protagonists. His posture is condescending: he is supercilious about the house's diminutive size and the dubious taste of its furnishings ("engravings swathed in pink gauze," "florid designs in jaundiced gilt"). In order to bring out caste, James here resorts to notation unusually dense for him, but, significantly, makes it emanate from the consciousness of a protagonist, not from the narratorial voice.

The Europeans follows the same pattern: here, too, the descriptions are mostly quite brief, no more than an overview, a rapidly summarizing survey, economical in expression and sparse in documentation, often pushing synecdoche to its furthest potential. This is the case in the opening tableau of Boston seen from a hotel window by a lady newly arrived there:

A narrow grave-yard in the heart of a bustling, indifferent city, seen from the windows of a gloomy-looking inn, is at no time an object of enlivening suggestion; and the spectacle is not at its best when the mouldy tombstones and funereal umbrage have received the ineffectual refreshment of a dull, moist snow-fall. (5)

All the adjectives ("narrow," "indifferent," "gloomy-looking") and the topoi ("grave-yard," "mouldy tombstones and funereal umbrage") have a decidedly negative charge, as if the city were a gateway to death. Its coldness is expressed in the meteorological metaphor of an unseasonable mid-May snowfall. It intimates a disheartening start for Eugenia, who has come from Europe with her brother, Felix, to seek a renewal of her life. The scene and the action are focalized from the point of view of these two outsiders as they become acquainted with the houses of their cousins, the Wentworths, and of their New England neighbors. "The large, clean-faced house wore, to his eyes, as the barouche drove up to it, a friendly aspect" (34): the intercalated phrase "to his eyes" underlines that this is Felix's perception and interpretation. "I see you have arranged your house—your beautiful house—in the—the Dutch taste!" (38), Eugenia comments on entering it. Just as Dr. Sloper's house is built exactly like those next to it, so the majority of the houses in The Europeans are, as it were, generic homes, representative of conformity to a sober, almost spartan lifestyle. The persistence of plurals indicates the repetitive typicality of the interiors: "large, clear-coloured rooms, with white wainscots, ornamented with thin-legged mahogany furniture, and, on the walls, with old-fashioned engravings, chiefly of Scriptural subjects, hung very high" (23). The very absence of individuality and colors, and with it of particularity of idiosyncratic detail, assimilates these homes to the dutiful traditions of their time and place. Their conventionality serves as a foil to the otherness of the European visitors. These cursory descriptions are supplemented by recurrent addresses to readers such as "You may imagine" (7), "as you see" (18), "you would have perceived" (21), "if you had been present, it would probably not have seemed to you" (44). The process of interiorization is thereby extended from the consciousness of Eugenia and Felix to that of readers. The technique of suggestiveness is carried to its extreme in the exhortation to readers to become knowing accomplices, sharing the Europeans' perceptions of New England, and filling out the picture in their own minds.

As in *Washington Square*, there is one notable exception to this method, one description that stands out from the rest for its extravagant density. It is of Robert Acton's home, appraised by Eugenia:

His house the Baroness mentally pronounced a very good one; more articulately, she declared that it was enchanting. It was large and square and painted brown; it stood in a well-kept shrubbery, and was approached, from the gate, by a short drive. It was, moreover, a much more modern dwelling than Mr. Wentworth's, and was more redundantly upholstered and expensively ornamented. The Baroness perceived that her entertainer had analysed material comfort to a sufficiently fine point. And then he possessed the most delightful chinoiseries—trophies of his sojourn in the Celestial Empire: pagodas of ebony and cabinets of ivory; sculptured monsters, grinning and leering on chimney-pieces, in front of beautifully figured hand-screens; porcelain dinner-sets, gleaming behind the glass doors of mahogany buffets; large screens, in corners, covered with tense silk and embroidered with mandarins and dragons. These things were scattered all over the house, and they gave Eugenia a pretext for a complete domiciliary visit. She liked it, she enjoyed it; she thought it a very nice place. It had a mixture of the homely and the liberal, and though it was almost a museum, the large, little-used rooms were as fresh and clean as a well kept dairy. (82–83)

Eugenia's assessment of Acton's home is motivated by her interest in marrying him. His house testifies to his sophistication, his wide horizon, his openness to the exotic, and more generous appreciation of comfort than is customary in New England. She reads his house as an externalized image of his personality as she weighs the desirability of such a match. This single passage of denser description plays an important role in the plot, parallel to Dr. Sloper's conclusions about Townsend's social standing from his estimation of his sister's abode. Yet even here plurals predominate, for Eugenia's racing gaze jumps metonymically from object to object without resting on anything long enough for a deeper scrutiny. A swift impression suffices for her. She realizes the contradictions in this house in her closing twin metaphors: "almost a museum" and "a well kept dairy." The drama of her hesitations in regard to Acton is perhaps already contained in this dualistic apperception of his house.

While Balzac and James offer the most conspicuous examples of density and suggestiveness, the denotative and the connotative as methods of description, their writings reveal at the same time the inextricable imbrication of the two modes. Density, even when pushed to the extremes found in Balzac, is never merely a record of a surface appearance. The details enumerated in the decor of the Vauquer boardinghouse in Le Père Goriot are simultaneously denotative and connotative insofar as they both delineate a scene and evoke an atmosphere. The same blend of dense description and evocative suggestion occurs at the opening of Eugénie Grandet. In their fusion of connotation with denotation these passages are remarkably parallel both to Dr. Sloper's reading of Mrs. Montgomery's abode in Washington Square and to Eugenia's view of Acton's home in The Europeans. The essential difference between the two resides in the viewpoint. As the focalization becomes increasingly internalized in the course of the century, places are perceived more from the perspective of the protagonists than of the narrator. It is through the eyes of Dorothea that Lowick is first recorded in Middlemarch, just as it is through Tom's and Tony's experience that Travemünde appears in Buddenbrooks. The protagonists can, solely according to their temperament, be made to draw on density or suggestiveness, the denotative or the connotative, the plain or the poetic in the language of the notations attributed to them. The shift into the consciousness of the persona is thus decisive in enabling realism to mobilize a wider range of narrative language and so to transcend the limitations it imposed on itself in its theoretical program. And once the truth is that of the fictive character, and the representation a pretense of truthfulness, the question of mimesis falls into abeyance.

༄

The same shift in focalization is also centrally implicated in the tensions between metonymy and metaphor. These categories sprang into the forefront of literary criticism in the wake of the distinction first instituted by Roman Jakobson in his essay "Two Aspects of Language and Two Types of Aphasic Disturbances," published in 1956 in *Fundamentals of Language*. The final section of that paper, entitled "The Metaphoric and Metonymic Poles," explores the applicability of the differentiation to discourse. Before Jakobson, rhetoricians from Aristotle onwards had generally regarded metonymy (and synecdoche) as forms or subspecies of metaphor, all being figurative transformations of literal statements. Jakobson went against this tradition by maintaining that metaphor and metonymy are opposed, because they are generated by contrary principles: metonymy is formed along the "axis of combination," whereas metaphor is created by the "principle of equivalence."[17] So metonymy becomes operative through substitutions dependent on contiguity, as when the name of an attribute stands in for the whole (e.g., "Ph.D." for "scholarliness"). The metonymic figure projects features on a preexistent chain from one end of the link to the other, so that the part is invested with all the features of the whole. Metaphor, on the other hand, is governed by the perception of similarity where no extrinsic link exists between the two parts of the relation; the tenor of meaning is transferred onto a vehicle from a different sphere (e.g., "my trusted steed" for "my car"). While it is possible clearly to distinguish between contiguity and similarity in the aphasic speech disorders that formed Jakobson's starting point, this is by no means the case in literary discourse, where contiguity can gradate into similarity ("Ph.D." could stand not only for "scholarliness" but also for "lack of street wisdom"). A certain ambiguity thus lurks at the heart of this attempted systematization, at least as far as literary discourse is concerned.

When Jakobson extended his dichotomy into the literary sphere, he aligned the romantic and symbolist modes with the metaphoric, the realist with the metonymic. The basis for this polarization is laid in *The Fundamentals of Language*:

Following the path of contiguous relationships, the realistic author metonymically digresses from the plot to the atmosphere and from the characters to the setting in space and time. He is fond of synecdochic details. (78)

This association of realism with metonymy is later reiterated when "realistic literature" is designated as "intimately tied with the metonymic principle."[18] In Jakobson's schema, then, the poetic (i.e., the literary) is homologous with the metaphoric, which in turn is opposed to the metonymic. Consequently, realist discourse, at least by implication, is relegated to a lesser status as not possessing the poetic quality of metaphor. It is regarded as a plainer style, whose actual language is of lower interest since its aim, like that of scientific writing, is set primarily on the transmission of a message. This view rests on the realist novel's disposition, since its beginnings in the seventeenth century, to model its tone on historical writing. The Goncourts revived Aristotle in coining the epigram that history is a novel that happened, and the novel is history as it might have happened. Although the understanding of history itself has changed significantly over the past thirty years with the recognition of the interpretative nature of its apparently factual reportage and hence the relativity of its formerly assumed veracity, the alliance of realism with history has nevertheless lent support to its location on the metonymic side. And the realists' own insistence on truthfulness as their cardinal purpose tended further to confirm its classification as nonpoetic.

For a while Jakobson's theory found widespread acceptance among literary critics partly because of his preeminent authority as an expert in linguistics and partly too because its polarities exactly suited the type of binary analyses favored by the structuralists. The opposition appears in Northrop Frye's enormously influential *Anatomy of Criticism* in another guise and in somewhat different terminology:

Realism, or the art of verisimilitude, evokes the response "How like that is to what we know!" When what is written is like what is known, we have an art of extended or implied simile. And as realism is an art of implicit simile, myth is an art of implicit metaphorical identity. . . . In myth we see the structural principles of literature isolated; in realism we see the *same* structural principles (not similar ones) fitting into a context of plausibility. (136)

Frye here grounds his reasoning for the metonymic nature of realism in the postulate of mimesis: the realist text is "an art of extended or implied simile" (which is a facet of metonymy) because, as "an art of verisimilitude," it is based on the perception of likeness. Frye is investing "likeness" with a meaning divergent from Jakobson's "similarity"; for Frye "likeness" occurs between things of the same kind, whereas for Jakobson "similarity" is between essentially disparate elements and therefore requires a leap of the imagination into the metaphoric. The discrepancy between Frye's notion of "likeness" and Jakobson's of "similarity" points to the potential confusion inherent in the entire formulation. The synonyms "likeness" and "similarity" have antithetical denotations for the two theoreticians: for Frye "likeness" is linked to metonymy, not to the metaphoric associated with "similarity" by Jakobson. Frye introduces a further complication and, incidentally, exposes the circularity of his argumentation, by equating "likeness" with mimesis. That he feels a certain unease about this conjunction is evident in his admission that "[t]he presence of a mythical structure in realist fiction, however, poses certain technical problems for making it plausible" (136). The attempt to segregate the realistic as metonymic from the mythical as metaphoric does not function well in practice because the division is by no means clear-cut. Moreover, as soon as plausibility is recognized as merely one of the pretenses of realism, the realist text can be emancipated from mimesis and granted independence as an aesthetic, linguistic construct in its own right, albeit determined by conventions different from those of the romantic/symbolical/ mythic construct.

The issue of metonymy/metaphor is openly confronted by David Lodge in a search for clarification.[19] While assenting to the usefulness of Jakobson's systematization, Lodge suggests a number of modifications that have the overall effect of moderating the intensity of the opposition. In answer to the question "How can the metonymic be assimilated into the POETIC?" he contends, for instance,

that, at the highest level of generality at which we can apply the metaphor/metonymy distinction, literature itself is metaphoric and nonliterature metonymic. The literary text is always metaphoric in the sense that when we interpret it . . . we make it into a total metaphor: the text is the vehicle, the world is the tenor. (109)

An even more decisive modulation of the antithesis is initiated by his observation that the metonymic text, too, "contains a good deal of local metaphor in the form both of overt tropes and of submerged symbolism" (111). This "submerged symbolism" coincides with what Frye calls "a mythical structure." But unlike Frye, Lodge accepts it as a normative aspect of the metonymic text rather than as a "problem." The situation of simile, metonymic for Frye, is dualistic for Lodge: while he envisages it as belonging to the metaphorical side in Jakobson's schema because it derives from the perception of similarity, he maintains that it can more easily be absorbed into the metonymic mode of writing since it does not involve as radical a substitution as metaphor (97, footnote, and 112–13). Ultimately, Lodge reaches this workable equipoise:

it must always be remembered that we are not discussing a distinction between two mutually exclusive types of discourse, but a distinction based on dominance. The metaphoric work cannot totally neglect metonymic continuity if it is to be intelligible at all. Correspondingly, the metonymic text cannot eliminate all signs that it is available for metaphoric interpretation. (111)

This adumbrates the possibility of a sliding spectrum instead of a divisive contraposition. In "revisiting" the texts he has discussed, Lodge arranges them in a horizontal order: the encyclopedia entry at one end and T. S. Eliot's *The Waste Land* at the other, with the newspaper article, E. M. Forster's *Passage to India*, and Dickens's *Bleak House* in between (103–8). Interestingly, the descriptive passages that Lodge has chosen to illustrate the slippage from predominantly metonymic to predominantly metaphoric all happen, surely not by accident, to be presentations of place.

It is also the evocation of place, London in Dickens's *Sketches by Boz*, that forms the fulcrum of J. Hillis Miller's deconstruction of Jakobson's categories in an important but relatively little-known essay, "The Fiction of Realism: *Sketches by Boz, Oliver Twist*, and Cruikshank's Illustrations." Miller is impelled less by a desire to qualify Jakobson, in the manner of Lodge, than to rewrite him quite fundamentally. He uses the example of *Sketches by Boz*, together with *Oliver Twist*, to query the validity of a diametric opposition between metonymy and metaphor for realist discourse. His enterprise is daring, not least on account of his choice precisely of *Sketches by Boz*, "an unpromising text for such a study" (86) since the "Sketches" still seem very rooted in the journalistic mode of Dickens's first way of writing as a parliamentary reporter. The "Scenes" give vivid vignettes of London life at the period of Queen Victoria's accession, such as Scotland Yard, Newgate Prison, Vauxhall Gardens, Greenwich Fair, pawnbrokers' and gin shops, theaters, coaches, cabs, buses, and so forth, which have normally been read as " 'social history' " and as "straightforward mimetic realism" (87). But, Miller asserts, "we have been inveigled into taking as *mimesis* solidly based on an extra-literary world a work which is in fact fiction and which contains the linguistic clues allowing the reader to recognize that it is fiction" (104). This contention is backed by a close and convincing analysis of "the linguistic clues" that point to the character of the *Sketches* as a devised literary creation: the pervasiveness of the themes of deception, playacting, and illusion, the notions of performance, copying, and repetition, and especially the theatrical images and metaphors, which come to supplant the metonymic sequences. In his discussion of specific passages Miller shows how "the metonymic reciprocity between a person and his surroundings, his clothes, furniture, house, and so on, is the basis for the metaphorical substitutions so frequent in Dickens's fiction" (97).[20] The strength of Miller's contentions lies in the corrective he offers to Jakobson's excessively stringent dichotomization. He allows that "poetry proper depends on metaphor, but realistic fiction defines people in terms of their contiguous environment. It favors metonymy over metaphor and the referential function of language over the set of language toward itself" (92). However, he amends this by pleading that "realistic fiction is a special case of the poetic function of language. Its peculiarity may be defined as the reciprocal relation within it between the story narrated and the question of what it means to narrate a story" (86). Hence, the literal and the figurative, the metonymic and the metaphoric, are engaged in an incessant mutual displacement, with the result that "this chain of substitutions and transformations creates illusion out of illusion, and the appearance of reality out of illusion" (123).

It is daunting, but necessary, to ask after such extensive and controversial debates, what is the validity of Jakobson's categories for our current rereading of realist texts? The first comment that needs to be made is a reservation about the word "categories," which implies a settled classification and has been interpreted by Jakobson and many of his successors as a polarity. But as J. Hillis Miller (and Genette) have argued, metonymy may generate metaphor. For contiguity is not separable from similarity; on the contrary, the two may be continuous and complementary. It is, therefore, a matter of an interface rather than of dichotomization. The balance of the interfacing elements allows for considerable variations: metonymy or metaphor can predominate but never to the total exclusion of the other. In pairing metonymy and metaphor in this way, it is vital to acknowledge them as means conducive to the attainment of certain ends. Thus metonymy is most pronounced where the pretense to objectivity is greatest and the narrator's voice most audible; contrariwise, metaphor gains prominence when the focalization shifts into the protagonists' consciousness so that the viewpoint is that of an assumed subjectivity. The pattern that emerges is an association of metonymy with denotation and density, and of metaphor with connotation and suggestiveness.

So Balzac's dense, denotative writing is that most given to metonymy. The description of the house at the opening of *Eugénie Grandet* (*La Comédie humaine* 3: 480–81) approximates most closely to the metonymic mode. The tone is of a reportorial sobriety as the narrator surveys and presents the panorama before his eyes in visual terms that foreshadow the cinematic. The enumerative technique is governed by contiguity as each detail follows on the one adjacent to it. This spatial progression corresponds to the movement of the gaze registering the scene. The passage is remarkable for the absence of figuration except for the extended simile in the first sentence introduced by the adjective "égale à" ("like"). The demureness of the ensuing pages sets these opening comparisons into relief. Through the collocation of the melancholy evoked by certain houses in the provinces to that provoked by "les cloîtres les plus sombres, les landes les plus ternes ou les ruines les plus tristes" (3: 480; "the gloomiest cloisters, the bleakest moors or the saddest ruins"), the mood not only of this description but of the entire fiction is named and evoked. The rhetoric of repetition, together with the powerful connotative implications of the places named in the simile, serves effectively to highlight this single (but triple) determining figure of speech.

The presentation of the Vauquer boardinghouse in Le Père Goriot (La Comédie humaine 3: 848ff.) is in many ways parallel in manner to Eugénie Grandet, though rather more complex. Again the narrator is palpably present as the source of information and as the registering eye. Again, too, the discourse is primarily metonymic and denotative, with a number of similes, but it also embraces some connotative metaphors. The putative traveler's descent into the Catacombs (2: 848), for instance, has both literal and figurative force. The neighboring dwelling is personified through the ascription to it of "un manteau de lierre" (3: 849; "a mantle of ivy"), which is a metaphoric turn, as is "une chaleur capable à faire éclore des oeufs" (2: 850; "a heat capable of making eggs hatch"). What is interesting about this set piece is the way in which it repeatedly draws attention both to its language and to the question of representation. Madame Vauquer's mispronunciation of the word for a lime tree, "tilleul," which she distorts into "tieuilles" (2: 849), mainly characterizes her deviation from the norm but also raises consciousness of the words themselves. Similarly, the smell in the house is designated as "sans nom dans la langue" (2: 851; "without name in language") as if to underscore the denotative inadequacy of language to convey the sensuous impression made by this house. The narrator adds: "Peut-être pourrait-elle se décrire si l'on inventait un procédé pour évaluer les quantités élémentaires et nauséabondes" (2: 851; "Perhaps it could describe itself if a procedure were invented to evaluate the elemental, sickening quantities"). The recourse to the strange reflexive form, "se décrire" ("describe itself") carries metaphoric suggestions: it adumbrates once more a personification of the place as if it were somehow able to speak for itself. In addition to these references to language, this narrator directly names tropes: "comparaison" (2: 848), "symboles" and "mythe" (2: 849), as well as introducing a statue (2: 849) and pictures (2: 850) that fulfill the function of representing representation internally in the text. This practice is not metaphoric in Jakobson's sense, yet it discloses realistic discourse as operating beyond the set toward the message for its own sake, and with that consciousness of its linguistic means and of the process of narration that Miller reads as a sign of its special status within the poetic sphere, despite its proclivity to metonymy.

The account of Lowick in *Middlemarch* is to some extent reminiscent of Balzac in mode. The house and its gardens are depicted largely by means of metonymic contiguity. The manor is personified and related to its owner in that both "had an air of autumnal decline" (99). Simile, regarded as a metonymic device, is used on several occasions to herald a movement toward metaphor laden with connotation: "seemed to melt into a lake under the setting sun" (98), "a room where one might fancy the ghost of a tight-laced lady" (100), and most notably, "Sir James, smiling above them like a prince issuing from his enchantment in a rose-bush, with a handkerchief swiftly metamorphosed from the most delicately-odorous petals" (99). Here the transformative substitution of "handkerchief" for "delicately-odorous petals" is actually voiced. The motif of representation makes two appearances: in the piece of tapestry hung over the door of the boudoir showing "a blue-green world with a pale stag in it" (100), and in the long library in "severe classical nudities and smirking Renaissance-Correggiosities" (99). The linguistically glaring "Correggiosities" is the most inventive sally in an otherwise quite restrained passage. Rhyming with both "curiosities" and "monstrosities," the bizarre, quasi-metaphorical formation "Correggiosities," gives an inkling of the undercurrent of strangeness and eccentricity in this dull dwelling by running so counter to the moderate tone dominant in the rest of the discourse.

The description of Yonville-l'Abbaye at the opening of the second part of *Madame Bovary* (73–76) also has some affinity to *Eugénie Grandet* except that the narrator is less apparent: a voice rather than a presence. The tone, especially at the outset, is that of reportage, with metonymic succession as its guiding principle. Some similes crop up: the landscape "ainsi ressemble à un grand manteau déplié" (73; "thus resembles a great mantle spread out"); the thatched roofs are "comme des bonnets de fourrure rabattus sur les yeux" (74; "like fur head-dresses turned down over the eyes"); the figure of Homais is silhouetted in his pharmacy "comme dans des feux de Bengale" (76; "as if illumined by Bengal lights"). Language is forefronted in the use of italics for the indirect discourse to mark the inhabitants' boast of their town hall: "construite *sur les dessins d'un architecte de Paris*" (76; "constructed *according to a Parisian architect's design*"). But elsewhere in *Madame Bovary* the discourse is more complicated, especially when Emma's musings drift from reflection into daydream:

Il lui semblait que certains lieux sur la terre devaient produire du bonheur, comme une plante particulière au sol et qui pousse mal tout autre part. Que ne pouvait-elle s'accouder sur le balcon des chalets suisses ou enfermer sa tristesse dans un cottage écossais, avec un mari vêtu d'un habit de velours noir à longues basques, et qui porte des bottes molles, un chapeau pointu et des manchettes! (43)

It seemed to her that happiness must flourish more fully in certain parts of the world, like a plant native to a particular kind of soil. If only she could lean on the balcony of a Swiss chalet, or enclose her sadness in a Scottish cottage, with a husband dressed in a dashing coat of black velvet, soft leather boots, a peaked hat and ruffles on his sleeves!

The start of this reverie is metonymic and denotative, enriched by a simile ("comme une plante") to make the point. With the move into indirect discourse ("Que ne pouvait-elle . . ." "If only she could . . .") is there a switch to metaphor? Are the Swiss chalet and the Scottish cottage generated by the principle of equivalence (i.e., equivalents to "some places on earth") or by a perception of similarity (i.e., substitutes for "some places")? The words and images certainly resonate with connotations, memories of Emma's adolescent self-education in romance. The disposition of the language in *Madame Bovary* is such as precisely to elide delineative contours, and thereby to uncover the ambivalences concealed beneath the innocent surface of the realist text.

This dyadic quality of the discourse is most palpable in *L'Assommoir* in the contrast between the narrator's metonymic mode and the protagonist's marked tendency to the metaphoric. The parallel but utterly divergent evocations of the huge tenement block clearly illustrate the dualism. On Gervaise's first visit, before her marriage to Coupeau, the house is focalized mainly through the narrator's eyes, although Gervaise is made to share that perception. As in Balzac, Eliot, and Flaubert, it is the metonymic that is preponderant, as one floor after another is rendered through sights and smells during Gervaise's slow climb up to the sixth floor, where Coupeau's sister and brother-in-law live and work. Within the upwardly spiraling movement, the order is that of juxtaposition. Simile is relatively sparse: "les portes uniformes, à la file comme des portes de prison ou de couvent"[21] ("the uniform doors, all in a row like the doors in a prison or a convent"). At the top Gervaise leans over the balustrade and looks down, "se hasardant là comme au bord d'un gouffre" (2: 423; "venturing there as to the edge of an abyss"). By contrast, the echoing reprise in the penultimate chapter, which reiterates that climb, does so from Gervaise's viewpoint and in indirect discourse. There are only two similes: "tandis que Lantier et Virginie, à gauche, faisaient un ronron, comme des chats qui ne dorment pas et qui ont chaud, les yeux fermés" (2: 778; "while to the left, Lantier and Virginia made a purring sound, like cats who are not asleep and who are warm, their eyes shut"); and at the portals, "elle entrait là-dedans, comme dans son deuil" (2: 778; "she went in there, as into her mourning"). Otherwise, it is an outburst of connotative metaphoricity: the entrance is "une gueule ouverte" (2: 778; "a gaping jaw"); the tenement blocks are "ces grandes gueuses de maisons ouvrières" (2: 778; "those hulking beggarwomen of working people's housing"). Following on the theme of her mourning, metaphors of death and decay proliferate: the building is "cette carcasse de caserne" (2: 778; "this carcass of a barrack"); the courtyard strikes Gervaise as "un vrai cimetière" (2: 778; "a veritable cemetery"), "l'ensevelissement de tout un village" (2: 778; "the burial place of a whole village"), and a "ruine" (2, 778). This complex of ideas is completed and summarized in the black effluent emanating from the dyeshop, which is in such stark contrast both to the white of the snow on the ground and to the pleasant light blue or pink that Gervaise recalls from earlier, more hopeful days. The recurrent dye, in its changing color is a striking symbolical metaphor in L'Assommoir to mark the stages of Gervaise's rise and fall.

A similar oscillation between the metonymic and the metaphoric is discernible in Buddenbrooks. Here, too, the metonymic discourse emanates from the narrator, while the metaphoric originates in the protagonists. The fluctuation becomes evident in Buddenbrooks, as in the other texts, in the presentation of places, in this case, interiors more than exteriors. Thus the narrative exposition of the "Landschaftszimmer" in chapter 1 (1: 8–9) is decidedly metonymic in its orderly progression from object to object in language devoid of decorative figuration. The outstanding feature of this room is the wallpaper on which expansive landscapes (hence its name) depict in delicate shades idyllic eighteenth-century scenes of cheerful viniculturists, industrious farmers, and shepherdesses be-decked in ribbons holding immaculate lambs in their laps beside mirroring waters or exchanging kisses with tender shepherds. The suspension points at the end of the description invite readers to meditate on the interpretation of this anachronistic, artificial pastoral whose messages of work, fruitfulness, and lov-ing-kindness are the embodiment of the Buddenbrooks' wish image of the world. In the images on the wallpaper the denotative has a pronounced connota-tive undercurrent. More obviously than in *Le Père Goriot* or *Middlemarch*, this repre-sentation within the fiction incorporates a model central to the novel.

The protagonists' perceptions of their houses in *Buddenbrooks* are, on the other hand, primarily metaphorical. When Tom proposes to put the family home on the market after his mother's death, Tony protests in anguish that she would lose the only "sicheren Hafen" (1: 601; "safe harbor") to which she had known she could always return after her marital misadventures. Tom, however, envisages the house in commercial terms as "totes Kapital" (1: 602; "dead capital"), and remains adamant that it must be sold. He also realizes that for the nouveaux riches Hagenströms, who make the highest offer, the acquisition of the Bud-denbrook house means "die historische Weihe, sozusagen das Legitime" (1: 617; "the historical consecration, the legitimation, as it were") of their upstart wealth. The building, initially portrayed metonymically by the narrator, turns into a metaphor in the protagonists' consciousness through the course of the action.

In the use of metonymy and metaphor, as in the handling of historicity, Henry James is at the opposite end of the spectrum (and of the century) to Balzac. *The Bostonians* is scant on metonymy and rich in connotative metaphor. Metaphors of place in particular abound: the Tarrants' spartan home is called "this sandy surface" that "had been irrigated, in moderation, by another source" (59), that is, by Olive Chancellor's check in return for Verena's companionship. Verena herself, from the comfort of Charles Street, looks back on the little house in Cambridge as "a penal settlement," "a desert of sordid misery" (142). When Olive urges her not "to give up everything and draw the curtains to pass one's life in an artificial atmosphere, with rose-coloured lamps" (128), she also expresses her thoughts in a metaphor of place. Such metaphors persist: Verena, embarking on her education, "traversed the fields of literature with her characteristic light-ness of step" (144), and on her return from Europe is deemed to have "an open mind, it's as wide as the sea!" (185). In wooing Verena, Basil insists "how much brighter and fairer and sweeter the garden of life would be for you, . . . you would find grass, trees and flowers that would make you think you were in Eden" (219).

In a wider sense, too, the entire plot of The Bostonians is metaphoric: it turns on the question of the protagonists' ability to position themselves into their proper places. The feminist strand of that plot is encapsulated in the vivid metaphor Verena uses in one of her speeches: that women "should get out of their boxes" (262). All the characters, male as well as female, are somehow captive in "boxes" of one sort or another. Basil Ransom's "box" is his Southerness; over and over again he is described as "the young Mississippian" (13, 14, 16, 51, 130, 172, 196, 203, 213, 222, etc.) or "the young Southerner" (31, 71, 163, 164, 174, 207, 210, 220, 261, etc.). If Basil is the archetypal Southerner, Olive is the Northerner, specifically the Bostonian, and "in the highest degree a New England type" (197). On his first ceremonial visit to her home in Charles Street, Boston, her drawing room gives Basil "an idea of the natural energy of Northerners" (12); its "organised privacy," stiffly festooned curtains, shelves of cultural objects, want of much upholstery, in short, "the general character of the place struck him as Bostonian" (11). The room, as perceived by the Southerner, is a metaphor for Northern values and lifestyle. Such local metaphorization is expanded to embrace the whole fiction in the tensions between North and South, Boston and New York, the United States and Europe, so that the ideological confrontations underlying the plot are articulated in terms of geographic location. In The Bostonians "an inquiring young Southerner" and "a bright New England girl" (261) engage in a quest for their literal and figurative place in society.

The literal and the figurative, the denotative and the connotative, the metonymic and the metaphoric: these are the binary pairs through which realism explores the possibilities for combining words in such a way as to create what Butor calls "un stable fantasme" ("a stable illusion"). Its strange power of making absent objects present, of "haunting" readers emanates from the subtle instrumentation of the dualistic capacities of language so as to fuse the disparate ideals of truthfulness and pretense. To engage with the configuration of the text is to see how the pretense is implemented into a stable yet intricate illusion.

For the realist does uphold the stability of the encompassing illusion despite occasional breaks in its smooth surface. The enframing devices are not relegated solely to the margins of the fiction; they also comprise, as was shown in chapter

3, sporadic injunctions to readers and dialogues between the narrator and hypothetical readers. However, such interlocutions are calculated to buttress the overall illusion, not to undermine it, as in *Tristram Shandy, Jacques le fataliste et son maître*, and their postmodern progeny. While the limitations of narratorial omniscience and with it the boundaries of the illusion are adumbrated, its essential integrity is never impugned, although the difficulties, indeed the precariousness of the enterprise is hinted. But the fundamental realist impulse is to stabilize the illusion, to keep it intact and to elude suspicions about its authenticity. In this context the narrator's resolute seriousness is of crucial importance in inspiring and maintaining trust. Here again the practices of realism are in sharp contrast to the playful whimsicality of self-conscious narrators who mischievously delight in the relentless deconstruction of illusion.

The posture of the realist narrator rests on confidence in the aptitude of language as a medium to convey meaning. The torturing awareness of the gap between world and word does not become a central issue until the late nineteenth and twentieth centuries in the wake of the insights of Mallarmé and Hofsmannthal. Earlier theoreticians of language tended to take a sanguine and pragmatic approach. John Locke, in his *Essay Concerning Human Understanding* of 1690 already realized that disputes and "errors are generally about the signification of words rather than about the nature of things."[22] Locke comments on the "very unsteady and uncertain significations" (part 3, chap. 10, 4) attached to words, which in turn give rise to "doubt, obscurity, or equivocation" (part 3, chap. 6, 40). But Locke's response is to seek the remedial solution to an ill for which he believes a corrective to exist. The realists' position corresponds to that adopted by Locke. They were not blind to the problem of finding the appropriate vehicles for creating and maintaining the illusion. Eliot's meditation on how to draw a real unexaggerated lion, Flaubert's obsessive pursuit of the *mot juste*, Balzac's verbal prolixity: each in its own way testifies to the struggle involved in the realist endeavor. Yet the very energy invested in that struggle points to the underlying belief in the potential for a successful resolution. In a corollary gesture of faith, readers are projected who command an intelligence and imagination equal to that of the narrator, and who will thus be capable of constructing the words and thereby participating in the illusion.

To read a realist fiction is, therefore, to engage in a performative act. It is a cooperative venture transacted in the medium of the text by narrator and readers functioning in a consensual entente. The narrator initiates, directs, and prompts the delineation and unfolding of the fictional world, which readers grasp through the denotative and connotative aspects of language as well as through metaphor. All is indeed true here, but at the same time all is pretense. The very format of the guiding principle "*All is true*," doubly foregrounded by its appearance in italics and in a foreign language, alludes to its literariness and projects an implied pretense. Truthfulness is posited as the overarching convention of realism; it is not, however, a literal truthfulness, in the sense of a faithful imitation of a prior reality, but rather "the air of reality," the verbal and textual production of an impression of truth. The form of the claim that "*all is true*" in its configuration on the page amounts to a simultaneous proclamation of a creed and an oblique avowal of its stylized nature. All is true within the frame of pretense evoked by the narration. The presentation of place and the projection of its realness to readers exemplifies the problematic duality of realism as it at once asserts its simple artlessness yet turns out to devolve from a complex artfulness.

8

The Enactment of Place

ॐ

A place for everything, and everything in its place.—Samuel Smiles

ॐ What, then, is the ultimate point of this rhetoric of place? What is its role in the economy of the fiction? To claim that place *is* action in realist fiction is perhaps something of an overstatement; not by very much, however. For one of the most distinctive features of this mode of writing is not just the particularity of place already recognized by Ian Watt in the opening chapter of *The Rise of the Novel*, but its absolute centrality to the conduct of the plot. The locale of the action has a significance different in kind from its earlier role as a merely decorative setting or even as the local color favored by the romantics as a means to create an individuated, often exotic scene. In realism place becomes intrinsic to and functional in the action, to a degree where it forms, arguably, one of its mainsprings.

The increasing importance of place through the nineteenth century is an offshoot of larger patterns of thought developing simultaneously in various domains. Philosophy and sociology take their cue from the sciences to foster the ascendancy of determinism, the biologically inspired perception of human life as conditioned by certain internal and external factors. The two fundamental forces, designated today by the blanket terms, "nature" and "nurture," were identified as heredity and environment. Of these two, heredity is obviously more cumbersome to incorporate into a plot since it requires, ideally, the lengthy time span of several generations,[1] although it can be portrayed, albeit more scantily, through the technique of the gradual disclosure of the past, as in Ibsen's *Ghosts*. Heredity was also likely to remain secondary to environment as a motivational impulse because its laws were still relatively little understood. When the Austrian monk, Gregor Mendel (1822–84) published in 1866 his breakthrough findings, the outcome of experiments with the hybridization of the culinary pea, it was in the *Verhandlungen* (*Transactions*) of the obscure Brno scientific society, so that his proofs of the recurrence of patterns of dominant and recessive features as directly dependent on genes were not widely disseminated until the early twentieth century.

If the workings of heredity remained primarily within the province of scientists, the impact of environment was more readily open to observation by novelists. This is where the stimulus derived from the sciences proved most momentous, for it endowed place with a wholly new force and position in the theater of life and literature. Description of setting is, of course, one of the old established conventions of narration. But what had previously been a subsidiary component is transformed by the realists into an essential fulcrum, largely as a consequence of their adoption of the concept of determinism. This was facilitated by the free interchange between the two cultures in the nineteenth century when men (and some women) of letters took a keen interest in the striking advances then being made in the sciences. Balzac's dedication of *Le Père Goriot* "Au grand et illustre Geoffroy Saint-Hilaire comme un témoignage d'admiration de ses travaux et de son génie"[2] ("To the great and illustrious Geoffrey Saint-Hilaire as a testimony of admiration for his works and his genius") is a clear expression of his high regard for this forerunner of Darwin. George Eliot, who moved in free-thinking circles in London, enjoyed friendships with Charles Bray, author of *The Philosophy of Necessity* (1841), and with the rationalist philosopher, Herbert Spencer (1820–1903), who believed that all organic development is a change from homogeneity to heterogeneity. The most ardent advocate for the importation of the sciences into literature was Zola. Claude Bernard's *Introduction à l'étude de la médecine expérimentale* (1865) forms the model for his treatise *Le Roman expérimental* (1880), in which he envisages the novelist as a social scientist engaged in the experimental dissection of the mechanisms of society in a manner parallel to the physician's study of the human body. He sought out specific information from scientific works such as the two-volume *Traité philosophique et physiologique de l'hérédité naturelle dans les états de santé et de maladie du système nerveux, avec l'application méthodique des lois de la procréation au traitement général des affections dont elle est le principe* (1842–50; *Philosophical and Physiological*

Treatise on Natural Heredity in the Healthy and the Diseased Nervous System, Together with the Consistent Application of the Laws of Procreation to the General Treatment of the States Engendered by It) by Dr. Prosper Lucas, and Dr. Valentin Magnan's *De l'alcoolisme, des diverses formes du délire alcoolique et de leur traitement* (1875; *On Alcoholism, On Various Forms of Alcoholic Delirium and Their Treatment*). But it was a literary critic, the philosophical materialist Hippolyte Taine, who, in a series of essays published in the 1860s, emphasized the primacy of "le milieu" in the configuration of the inherited molecule into its mature format. Taine's concept of "le milieu" as the paramount bridge linking the sciences, the social sciences, and literature is a cornerstone of later nineteenth-century thought.

Taine's theories obviously devolve from Darwin, the chief exponent of the crucial influence of environment in shaping the existence of all living things. *On the Origins of Species By Means of Natural Selection, or the Preservation of Favoured Races in the Struggle for Life* (1859) was instrumental in focusing attention on the notion of environment through its demonstration that the individual's and the race's prospects for survival stand in immediate relation to the organism's capacity to adapt to its surroundings.[3] Darwin's conviction that everything is interconnected, even if the connections may at times not be apparent, provides the basis for the constant imbrication of place, persona, and plot in realist fiction. What is more, in Darwin's account of evolution, environment is the decisive trigger of action insofar as it impels individuals to change—or condemns them to extinction if the necessary process cannot be accomplished. The Darwinian precept thus comprises both ambitious upward growth and retrogressive decline, the twin possibilities of nineteenth-century narrative plots. And while these two directions are antithetical, they are nonetheless held together by the common thread of environment as the vital agency in each scenario.

Place therefore assumes supreme importance in realist fiction because it is so intimately implicated in both the formation of personality and the course of events, as has already been suggested in chapter 6. It amounts to far more than an insistently acknowledged background, or an omnipresent context for the action. Background and foreground come to constitute a single powerful entity when locale is not a passive, static situation but an active, dynamic set of circumstances. The interaction between the perceiving, feeling, reflecting self of the protagonists on the one hand and the consensus of their particular material and social world on the other is the ever reiterated and ever changing matter of realist narrative. That interaction may lead to conflict, accommodation, or defeat, depending on the respective strength of the individual and the authority of the prevailing social system. In this respect the plot of realism can be sharply differentiated from that of romanticism where the hero turns his back on an uncongenial, uncomprehending, possibly corrupt society in order to develop his inner self in some preferred idyllic backwoods. That is the pattern delineated in Goethe's *Werther* (1774), and reiterated in a series of variants such as Chateaubriand's *René* (1805) and Foscolo's *Ultime Lettere di Jacopo Ortis* (1802/1816). The protagonists—no longer "heroes"—of realist fiction are, on the contrary, constrained to confront and compromise with their social cadre. The generally painful negotiations between individual idealism and the reigning mentality are the archetypal theme of realism. And that reigning mentality is concretely embodied in place as a physical locale is invested with moral dimensions to such an extent that it becomes, as it were, almost a dramatis persona in its own right.

This conjunction of place and action grows more and more pronounced in the course of the century. In *Eugénie Grandet* (1833), it is as yet relatively slight, although it is well to recall that Balzac structured his *Comédie humaine* according to the place of the action. *Eugénie Grandet* was assigned to the "Scènes de la vie de province." The appearance and atmosphere of Saumur are evoked with considerable detail in the narratorial description with which the novel opens, but then, once the action begins on Eugénie's birthday in November 1819, it seems as if the place were forgotten. Having carefully set the scene, Balzac appears to have done with it and to relegate it to the margins of the plot. Yet the contrast between the provinces and Paris is an important subtext. It first surfaces in the glaring discrepancy between the extreme austerity of the Grandet household and the frivolous luxury of Charles's personal possessions, which dazzle Eugénie and make her aware of the existence of lifestyles radically other than the only one she had hitherto known. In her pathetic efforts to offer Charles a less spartan breakfast and to improve her own appearance, Eugénie begins to make a rudimentary attempt to move beyond her environmental norms, inspired by her attraction to her cousin. Her provincialism is too deeply ingrained to enable her singlehandedly to rise above it. She has been shaped by her milieu and is trapped in it. She would actually make a much richer catch for the fortune-hunting Charles than the Mlle. d'Aubrion whom he eventually marries. However, Mlle. d'Aubrion, artfully manipulated by her mother into clothes and gestures that conceal her shortcomings, has the superficial grace that allures the shallow Charles. He is blinded to Eugénie's potential by her provincialism. To read *Eugénie Grandet* in this light, is, admittedly, to push interpretation somewhat. But this reading serves at least to suggest that the place of the action is more germane to the plot than it may initially seem.

The tension between the glamour of the capital and the dreariness of the provinces is a prominent theme in *Madame Bovary* (1857). Again it is a woman who is the prisoner of an environment that she despises, although she is ironically, in her very limitations, herself a product of it, as the tawdriness of her aspirations reveals. But while a man has the prerogative of a certain freedom of movement, shown in *Eugénie Grandet* by Charles's expedition to the Indies, and in *Madame Bovary* by Rodolphe's and Léon's departure, a woman was supposed to remain meekly within the domestic sphere, fulfilling the expectation of subjection and passivity. So environment had a more immediate and far more restrictive impact on women. Their very malleability and vulnerability to social pressures makes them into the consummate protagonists of realist fiction, shaped by forces beyond their control. Emma rebels against the system and feels contempt for her obligations as household manager and even as mother. Her yearning to transcend the role her gender has imposed on her finds expression in terms of place. Her perusal of Parisian magazines, for example, like her earlier reading of romances in the convent, acts as the springboard for the images she projects. The move from Tostes to Yonville does little to alleviate her boredom. As an acknowledgment of the possibly deleterious effect of place, it carries a certain ironic charge in that Charles sees the issue medically in terms of climate, while Emma has been drinking vinegar and feigning ill health to precipitate a change of location.

For Emma believes locale is the key to happiness. She is convinced that those of her former schoolfellows who live in larger towns must be happier because they can go to theaters and enjoy pleasures denied to her. Inevitably, in her daydreams, Paris is cast as the incarnation of her longings, the locus of desire:

Paris, plus vaste que l'Océan, miroitait donc aux yeux d'Emma dans une atmosphère vermeille. . . . Dans les cabinets de restaurants où l'on soupe après minuit riait, à la clarté des bougies, la foule bigarrée des gens de lettres et des actrices. C'était une existence au-dessus des autres, entre ciel et terre, dans les orages, quelque chose de sublime. Quant au reste du monde, il était perdu, sans place précise, et comme n'existant pas. (62)

Paris, vaster than the ocean, was reflected in Emma's eyes in a rosy mist . . . . In the private rooms of restaurants, where dinner is taken after midnight in the glow of candlelight, a motley crowd of writers and actresses was laughing. It was an existence superior to others, poised between earth and heaven, amidst tempests, something sublime. As for the rest of the world, it was lost, without an exact place, as if it did not really exist.

In this passage, the idealization of the other has as its corollary a rejection of the actual to the point of annihilation. Again, the metaphor is one of place: the rest of the world is "sans place précise" ("without an exact place") because Emma cannot accommodate it in her imagination, and so voids it of reality. Her acute consciousness of the disparity between her own mediocre life and her fantasies, not only of Paris but of all sorts of outlandish scenarios, becomes ever more acute and intolerable. She thinks that her honeymoon would have been more satisfying had it been spent in the mountains or by a lagoon because remote, exotic, in short inaccessible places are, to her mind, more conducive to happiness. Yet her inescapable realm is the world of Yonville, whose womanly norm is the homely Mme. Homais with her concern for her brood of children, whose intellectual heights are the pharmacist's hyperbolic monologues, whose religion is incarnated in the pedestrian, earth-bound Bournisien, and whose festivities are the banal agricultural fair. The town is metaphorically as well as literally a dead end: its main street leads only into a cemetery. Its preoccupation with the mundane is symbolized in the pervasive smell of preserves being made at the end of summer. This place is not the backcloth to Emma's existence but its very fabric. The fact that she is fixed forever in this drab backwater while longing for excitement is a constant source of frustration to her. Her actions are motivated by the urge to break out of the narrowness of Yonville emotionally and, if possible, physically. The place is the cipher for her discontent, and its insistent, intrusive presence the goad to her flights of fancy and her impetuous exploits. Emma's scenario is, however, undermined by the strong current of irony in Madame Bovary. As the workings of her romantic temperament are fully exposed to readers' view, it becomes apparent that she would most likely have been equally restless and dissatisfied elsewhere, perhaps even in Paris. Emma is using place as her favorite scapegoat for rationalizing her state of mind; similarly, its function in the economy of the novel as a whole is that of a metonymic equivalent to her mistaken assumptions. Yonville is, for sure, deadly dreary, but so in the long run are Emma's fantasies. What unites them is the element of cliché. Flaubert's handling of place is much more complex than Balzac's. Yonville is intrinsic to the plot of Madame Bovary precisely through its meretriciousness.

That place is plot is denoted in Middlemarch (1872) by its salient position as the novel's title. The twin stories of Dorothea and Lydgate are conjoined by their common locale and time. The repetition of a like fate universalizes the restrictiveness of this environment for here it is not only a woman who suffers the thwarting of her aspirations but also a man. Every character in *Middlemarch* has, in one way or another, to accept the second best, learning to live in the middle marches of human existence. Place is manifest here less in its physical substantiality than as a mentality that exerts its consensual pressure on all who fall within its orbit. Middlemarch is essentially conservative in the widest sense, wary of change, antagonistic to outsiders, doggedly clinging to its routines, prejudices, and beliefs. That such a place should be suspicious of a strong-minded woman with progressive plans for cottages to house the villagers is probably no surprise. But it is even more hostile to Lydgate, a newcomer with advanced and, incidentally, enlightened medical ideas. He campaigns for the new hospital to have an isolation area to deal with the cholera then crossing Europe. Having trained in Paris, the mecca of medical research at that period, he uses a stethoscope, a new-fangled instrument. One of the upcoming breed of well-educated, general practitioners, Lydgate stands out against the town's five other medical men through his knowledge, his diagnostic acumen, and his shrewd professional judgment.[4] Yet he is a wretched failure in Middlemarch because he fails to take its mentality into account. The transactions between Lydgate and Middlemarch are fraught with misreadings on both sides: he does not grasp the role of politics in hospital appointments, he cannot see how his nonconformist practices alienate his patients, and he does not realize the extent to which his innovative methods are perceived as an affront to the established hierarchy. The Middlemarchers, for their part, at one and the same time credit him with a capacity for miraculous cures,[5] and fear that he will kill (or at least let die) hospital patients in order to procure bodies for his tissue research. Both Dorothea and Lydgate are ultimately vanquished by Middlemarch, insofar as both are driven into more conventional lives. In her second marriage Dorothea assumes the orthodox Victorian role for a woman of her station, becoming a mother, and only secondarily and tangentially Will's helpmate. Lydgate, too, has to tread the beaten path: in London and at fashionable watering places he treats wealthy patients for gout, a disease on which he writes a treatise before his early death. In both their lives Middlemarch has its way.

Like *Middlemarch*, *L'Assommoir* (1877) bears in its title the name of the locale that overshadows the entire novel. "L'assommoir" is a slang term for the drinking dive that corrupts workers with its villanous brew. It is the focal point of the district, luring men from work by providing them with a cheap but noxious temporary release from their misery. Its power stems from the eerie, illicit, distilling machine in the small courtyard at the back:

L'alambic, avec ses récipients de forme étrange, ses enroulements sans fin de tuyaux, gardait une mine sombre; pas une fumée ne s'échappait; à peine entendait-on un souffle intérieure, un ronflement souterrain; c'était comme une besogne de nuit faite en plein jour par un travailleur morne, puissant et muet.[6]

The still, with its weirdly shaped receptacles and endless coils of piping, looked dour and forbidding; no steam was coming out of it; hardly an inner breathing or a subterranean rumbling was audible; it was like some black midnight deed being done in broad daylight by a morose, powerful, and mute worker.

The threat emanating from the still personified as a silent, malicious destroyer is a repetition and reinforcement of the menace represented by the city, which is anthropomorphized in the opening pages as a monster swallowing up the workers as they arrive in the morning: "[L]a cohue s'engouffrait dans Paris, où elle se noyait, continuellement" (2: 376; "The crowd was engulfed into Paris, where it drowned endlessly"), or, even more graphically: "Paris, qui, un à un, les dévorait, par la rue béante du Faubourg-Poissonniers" (2: 378; "Paris, which devoured them one by one into the gaping Poissonniers street"). The metaphor of being swallowed up recurs toward the end of Gervaise's life when she sees the entry to the slum tenement where she has lived as gaping jaws:

La maison était toute sombre. Elle entra là-dedans, comme dans son deuil. A cette heure de nuit, le porche, béant et délabré, semblait une gueule ouverte. Dire que jadis elle avait ambitionné un coin de cette carcasse de caserne! Ses oreilles étaient donc bouchées, qu'elle n'entendait pas à cette époque la sacrée musique de désespoir qui ronflait derrière les murs! Depuis le jour où elle y avait fichu les pieds, elle s'était mise à dégringoler. Oui, ça devait porter malheur d'être ainsi les uns sur les autres, dans ces grandes gueuses de maisons ouvrières; on y attraperait le choléra de la misère. . . . Dans la cour, elle se crut au milieu d'un vrai cimetière; la neige faisait par terre un carré pâle: les hautes façades montaient, d'un gris livide, sans une lumière, pareilles à des pans de ruine; et pas un soupir, l'ensevelissement de tout un village raidi de froid et de faim. (2: 778)

The house was pitch dark. She entered as though into mourning for herself. At this hour of the night the gaping, tumbledown porch seemed jaws opening up to swallow her. To think that so long ago she had aspired to live in a corner of this great bare barrack. Her ears must have been stopped so that she couldn't hear the awful hymn of despair being sung behind those walls! From the very first day that she had set foot in the place she had been going downhill. It must bring ill luck to be piled up one on top of another in these miserable beggars of working-class tenements; you would catch the cholera of penury in them. . . . In the courtyard she thought herself in the middle of a veritable cemetery; the snow made a pale square on the ground: the high walls rose up, a livid gray, without a shimmer of light, like fragments of a ruin; and not a sigh, the burial of an entire village stiffened by cold and hunger.

The sinister, degrading influence emanating from the rampant squalor and brutality in the house is brought out in a series of episodes: the eviction of tenants for arrears of rent; the meanness of the miserly Lorilleux who hang a blanket over their door when they cook a rabbit to keep their succulent morsel secret so as not to have to share it; the abuse and eventual beating to death of the eight-year-old Lalie by her drunken father; and finally, Gervaise's own end as a bad smell under a stairway, as if she had indeed been consumed by the devouring building.

These incidents reveal the nefarious impact of environment, the underlying theme of L'Assommoir. Zola argues in his preface that "mes personnages ne sont pas mauvais; ils ne sont qu'ignorants et gâtés par le milieu de rude besogne où ils vivent" (2: 374; "my characters are not evil, only ignorant and spoiled by the environment of harsh labor and penury in which they live"). The presentation of the environment as an active despoiler is therefore a central facet of the novel. Gervaise herself, though by no means a reflective character, senses that "la mauvaise société, . . . c'était comme un coup d'assommoir, ça vous applatissait une femme en moins de rien" (2: 417; "bad company, . . . is like a blow from a bludgeon, it cracks your skull, it knocks a woman flat into less than nothing"). Here the various meanings of "assommoir" are cleverly layered: it is a bludgeon; technically, it denotes the instrument with which animals are stunned before slaughter. And in slang it is the drinking dive. In one word Zola draws together the destructive factors of this environment: the liquor, the promiscuity in the sexual innuendo contained in the reference to knocking a woman flat, and the numbing of moral sensibility in the blow struck before death. The overwhelming, unavoidable malignancy of the slum is already foreshadowed at the close of the first chapter when Gervaise, looking out of the window, is "prise d'une épouvante sourde, comme si sa vie, désormais, allait se tenir là, entre un abattoir et un hôpital" (2: 403; "seized by a dull horror, as if her life from now on would be held there, between a slaughterhouse and a hospital"). The force of this phrase devolves not only from the sites of dying that flank Gervaise, but also from the grammatical construction that emphasizes her passivity. It is not she who will conduct her life; "tenir" ("held") suggests immobility, powerlessness, imprisonment, in short, the stranglehold that this milieu has on her.

The harm wrought by the slum is further underscored by a subtext of *L'Assommoir*: the contrast between city and country. The dichotomy between Paris and the provinces, a frequent motif in nineteenth-century French fiction, is here invested with inverted signification; whereas the capital is generally the place to make one's career and one's fortune, in *L'Assommoir* it is cast as the locus of degradation and downfall. So at the outset, when Gervaise is newly arrived from Plassans, her southern hometown, she has a kind of energy and buoyancy as she does her best to clean up the filthy room at the decrepit Hôtel Boncoeur, her first quarters in Paris. One of her early hopes is to be able one day to retire to the country, a hope that returns in ironic guise as she recalls it near the end of her life and concludes: "Eh bien, elle y allait, à la campagne. Elle voulait son coin de verdure au Père-Lachaise" (2: 779; "Oh well, she'd get there, to the country. She wanted her patch of green in the Père-Lachaise cemetery"). The conception of the country as a redeeming escape is suggested too in the scene where Goujet asks Gervaise to run away with him. Their conversation takes place on a piece of waste ground between a sawmill and a button factory, where there is a strip of open land with some patches of grass burnt brown, a goat tied to a stake, and a dead tree crumbling in the sun. In what seems like a parody of a bucolic idyll, Gervaise exclaims, "[O]n se croirait à la campagne" (2: 614; "You might think you were in the country"). To her, even this desolate oasis is a respite from the turmoil of the slum, and she leaves "gaie et reposée" (2: 617; "cheerful and relaxed") carrying a basket of dandelions. The restorative qualities of the country are explicitly brought out when Coupeau, after he has begun to fall prey to alcohol, gets a job at Etampes:

[E]t là, il fit près de trois mois, sans se soûler, guéri un moment par l'air de campagne. On ne se doute pas combien ça désaltère les pochards, de quitter l'air de Paris, où il y a dans les rues une vraie fumée d'eau-de-vie et de vin. (2: 673)

And there he was for nearly three months without getting drunk, cured for a while by the country air. People don't realize how refreshed drunkards are simply by getting away from the air of Paris, where the streets are terribly polluted by fumes of spirits and wine.

Although the language of that last sentence uses colloquialisms that would be natural to Gervaise, it also doubles as a narratorial comment on the situation. On his return, Coupeau "était frais comme une rose" (2: 673; "was fresh as a rose"), and had a substantial sum of money, enough to pay off some pressing debts. This interlude in Coupeau's descent is clearly designed to back Zola's fundamental hypothesis that it is the environment that ruins the characters, and that it is, therefore, the primary agent of the action in L'Assommoir.

The Bostonians (1886) is the third of my texts to carry an element of place in its title. The main axis of the plot is the lingering conflict between North and South in the post–Civil War era, which is enacted in the rivalry between Olive Chancellor and Basil Ransom for the favors of Verena Tarrant. The relative social position of various protagonists is also structured by frequent references to place. Subsidiary to the North/South dichotomy is the one between Boston and New York, each of which is endowed with its own aura. The competition between the two cities for leadership of the feminist movement figures in the metropolitan "Wednesday Club" which is described as "New York trying to be Boston" (211). The ambivalent relationship between them is seen from both sides. On the one hand, New York socialites are rather scathing that Verena is brought in to speak: "you must be pretty desperate, when you have got to go to Boston for entertainment" (204). On the other hand, Olive "was not insensible to the pleasure of appearing in a distinguished New York circle as a representative woman, an important Bostonian" (234). But the switch of location, when she visits New York with Verena, leads to a reduction of her authority, for she is on alien ground, and eventually the two women flee in near panic. That Henry Burrage, Verena's first suitor, is a wealthy New Yorker is another complication that strengthens the image of New York as worldly temptation as against the more austere idealism of Boston. An additional counterpoint is created by the background silhouette of Europe on the horizon. Characters are categorized as to whether they have or have not been there. Mrs. Luna, Olive's sister, is immediately introduced as having just returned from Europe; she is shocked that Basil Ransom has not "been anywhere" (4). Olive, though she hates Europe, takes Verena on a tour, partly to remove her from Ransom's influence, and partly to elevate her socially, for the trip to Europe is a distinct cachet in this hierarchical, not to say snobbish, clique.

Following the exposition of the plot in Boston and its development in New York, its resolution is prepared at Marmion on Cape Cod, a locale within the sphere of Boston, yet also apart from it. Ransom has heard that the "Cape was the Italy, so to speak, of Massachusetts; it had been described to him as the drowsy Cape, the languid Cape, the Cape not of storms, but of eternal peace" (283). The interlude on the Cape brings not only a temporary lowering of the tension, but also a realignment of power. Removed from Boston, Olive again forfeits some of her prestige, as she had done in New York. Ransom, on the other hand, finds himself if not exactly on home soil, at least on territory with a more familiar atmosphere, once he recognizes for himself "the southern quality of this pastoral land" (319). So he is empowered by the change of place. The veranda of Olive's summer residence "suggested to him a land of dreams, a country in a picture" (294–95). These terms of tranquillity come to the fore again in the locale where Basil and Verena meet:

They wandered along the waterside to a rocky, shrub-covered point, which made a walk of just the right duration. Here all the homely languor of the region, the mild, fragrant Cape-quality, the sweetness of white sands, quiet waters, low promontories where there were paths among the barberries and tidal pools gleamed in the sunset — here all the spirit of a ripe summer-afternoon seemed to hang in the air. There were wood-walks too; they sometimes followed bosky uplands, where accident had grouped the trees with odd effects of 'style,' and where in grassy intervals and fragrant nooks of rest they came upon sudden patches of Arcady. (314)

Here, the pastoral undertones, the soothing, almost lulling insinuations of this locus amoenus pave the way for the novel's romance closure.

The importance of place in the action is reinforced by its presence as a reiterated source of metaphors in The Bostonians. Verena's mother hopes that "the dry places of her life would, perhaps, be plentifully watered" (59), and indeed "this sandy surface had been irrigated, in moderation" (59) by Dr. Tarrant's income from a wealthy lady patient. Still, Verena "had traversed a desert of sordid misery" (142) before Olive moves her into her own more comfortable home. At times Basil is said to "feel like a man in an open boat, at sea, who should just have parted with his last rag of canvas" (154). The nautical image recurs when Olive's mind is deemed, ironically, "as wide as the sea!" (185). Verena's campaign speech also hinges on a metaphor of place:

Good gentlemen all, if I could make you believe how much brighter and fairer and sweeter the garden of life would be for you, if you would only let us help you keep it in order! You would like so much better to walk there, and you would find grass and trees and flowers that would make you think you were in Eden. (219)

Finally, when Basil decides to try to stop Verena's performance at the Music Hall, he envisages his intervention as preventing "the girl's jump into the abyss" (352), and he cares little for the disturbance he will cause "since he certainly was not going to subside into his place" (352). The quest for each character's appropriate place in relation to the network of social conventions thus coalesces into a metaphoric intertext that echoes the major theme of *The Bostonians*.

Regionalism is almost as central to *Buddenbrooks* (1901) as to *The Bostonians*, and here again a contrast is drawn between north and south. Tony's marriage to Permaneder collapses because she is unable to understand, let alone accept the standards of behavior customary in Munich. Bavaria is a foreign land to her, as indeed it was before the unification of Germany in 1870; it has its own currency, its own idiom, its own cuisine, and its own code of morality. What strikes Tony as disgustingly offensive in her easygoing husband's flirtatious exchanges with the maid is hardly a peccadillo in his eyes, and certainly no grounds for divorce. Their relationship is a tragecomedy of misapprehensions. However, its outcome is already predictable on Permaneder's first visit to her family when he appears as a literally outlandish figure, something of a clown, good-natured for sure, yet a complete puzzle to the proper northern Buddenbrooks. Significantly, they readily embrace Bendix Grünlich as a son-in-law because he is from neighboring Hamburg and has, on the surface, manners like their own. Since his style is similar to theirs, they harbor no suspicions as to his motives, even when he presses his suit with undue urgency—in order to avert imminent bankruptcy. Only Tony has a strong revulsion to him, and it is instinctive rather than rational.

The failure of Tony's marriage to Permaneder through her inability to adapt shows how deeply rooted she is, like all the Buddenbrooks, in her native milieu. As in *Middlemarch*, the unnamed city is the mind's own place, a mentality, a certain stance rather than merely a geographic site. It becomes a motivating force in the fiction, circumscribing the characters' lives, no matter whether they submit or rebel. It functions as a moral, indeed an ethical imperative. Tony acquiesces by marrying Grünlich contrary to her inclinations for the sake of fulfilling her obligations to the family and the firm. Thomas, the doubter and waverer, makes a compromise by giving up the lower-class girl in the flowershop for a financially and socially brilliant match with Gerda, who is, however, more devoted to music than to bearing successors to carry on the family's business tradition. Like Grünlich, Gerda is willingly received into the family, despite her artistic preoccupations, primarily on account of her large dowry. But it is well to recall also that she comes from Amsterdam, another major northern center of trade that has certain cultural affinities with Lübeck. Thomas remains outwardly faithful to the expectations imposed on him by his position as head of the family and the firm. But his exaggeratedly meticulous exterior is no more than a surface disguise for his inner defection from the Buddenbrook creed, which culminates in his discovery of and spiritual conversion to Schopenhauer and his precipitous death. His younger brother, Christian, tries to solve his difficulties by absence, spending much of his life abroad in England and South America, anywhere other than in his hometown. He endeavors to elude the burden of his heritage, yet does so only to his own cost, like Thomas. At the end of the lineage, Hanno opts to contract out of the family model totally by fleeing into the aesthetic pleasures of musical improvisation and into an easeful death.

Place in *Buddenbrooks* therefore represents a coherent system of values to which the individual must subjugate his or her desires. Failure to do so results in sure disaster, although compliance carries no assurance of a successful, let alone happy life. The north German Protestant work ethic is dour to the point of cruelty, casting out and destroying nonconformists. The strength of this communal ethos is emphasized in the references to the doings of the "first families" that punctuate the narrative. This motif has mostly been seen either as an expression of the extreme class consciousness of this society, or as a cryptocomic undercutting through the irony of repetition. But it can also be read seriously as a constant reminder of the frame of expectations within which the Buddenbrooks operate. Their lives are shaped by duty to their caste, and that duty can be fulfilled satisfactorily only by wholehearted allegiance to the dominant tenets. The attempt to get away purely with appearances that clothe an underlying breach of loyalty leads ultimately to the breakdown of the individual and the family.

The interactions between place and persona become ever more symbiotic in the course of the nineteenth century. Eugénie Grandet, though a product of her environment, remains a curiously static figure, unchanging through the ten years of the novel's action, silhouetted against her background as an isolated entity. Emma Bovary, by contrast, deliberately seeks to divorce herself from her milieu, and is unable to do so in part because it is, despite her waywardness and resistance, ingrained in her, as her trite, clichéd fantasies reveal. Thereafter, *what* happens is inseparable from *where* it happens. While Eugénie's and Emma's narratives could be played out in other locations without fundamental alteration of their tales, this is not the case with *Middlemarch*, *L'Assommoir*, *The Bostonians*, or *Buddenbrooks*. In each of these later nineteenth-century novels, the plot derives its driving energy from the site where it occurs, so that action is inextricably dependent on place. For this reason particularity of place is critical to realist writing to an extent and in a way that it is not either before and rarely after.

The vivid and lasting sense of place that emanates from realist fiction is therefore elicited more through enactment than through description. In the determining role that it plays in the fate of the protagonists, place becomes a vicarious reality for readers. We feel constrained by the enveloping gloom of the Grandet house; we are irked by the triviality of Yonville-l'Abbaye; we hear the censorious gossip in Middlemarch; we can virtually smell the Parisian slums in *L'Assommoir*; and we are made to acknowledge the restrictive pressure of the controlling conventions in *Buddenbrooks*. No single phrase can fully capture the function of place in these narratives; at times it is personified, at others it is anthropomorphized, often it is extended into metaphor, always it is decisive in the unfolding of the plot.

In this respect the handling of place in nineteenth-century fiction is very much in consonance with the original meaning of mimesis:

The term "mimesis" derives from Greek *mimos*, a mime, play or actor therein, and seems to have originally meant the mimicking of an animal or person . . . through facial expression, speech, song, dance, or some amalgam of these.[7]

Essentially this amounts not to the copying, with which mimesis later became associated and even equated, but to a reenactment. When the object of such reenactment is itself an action (such as a dance, facial expression, or gesture), the process is more direct than when the mimesis is to be realized in the written word of the novel. For this entails a transfer into a medium of a quite different kind. The public performance involved in mimicking a dance, facial expression, and so on, has to be translated into a verbal texture for private reading. Moreover, verbal art has an innately dual character: it is physical in its shape and length, as is apparent in the disposition of the elements of a poem on the printed page; and it is symbolical in its meanings, which themselves range from the denotative to the connotative. So in verbal mimesis, *poiesis*, making and shaping is more deeply and intrinsically implicated than in the mimesis of a dance or gesture because of the need to translate into another domain.

This basic problem inherent in attempting mimesis in language accounts in part at least for the manifold complications that have beset a concept that "has so stubbornly haunted our civilization."[8] It is, fortunately, not my task here to trace its vicissitudes through the centuries.[9] In the sense of "imitation," however diversely interpreted, it was central to the neoclassical perception of the creative process. But its high prestige from the Renaissance onward was reversed by the romantics, who vehemently rejected the whole idea of imitation[10] in favor of the visionary powers of the imagination. "Originality," "creation," and "genius" had superseded "mimesis" and "imitation" by the beginning of the nineteenth century as the key words of aesthetic theory.

But the creative imagination was more apt for drawing a griffin than "a real unexaggerated lion," to return to George Eliot's example. The realists' problem was how to endow the verbal image of known objects and scenes with life-liveliness, without the obvious inflation ("the longer the claws and the larger the wings") appropriate to a fabulous creature such as the griffin. In grounding their theoretical position in the assertion that "*all is true*," they seem to be trapping themselves in a doctrine of literalist mimesis. Yet, such a reading of realism overlooks the intertext of that phrase in its allusion to the subtitle of Shake-speare's *Henry VIII*, which hints, albeit obliquely and stealthily, at the *poiesis* quintessential to the fashioning of a work of art. The realists walk a tightrope as they overtly profess to be giving a true representation of life as it is lived on "the dusty streets and the common green fields." Their heavy emphasis on truthfulness comes to appear as almost a decoy to distract readers from the artistic processes involved in the weaving of the textual web. For the narratives are representations, products, and as such they must be shaped by the eye and mind of the writer. Baudelaire's ideal, "Je veux représenter les choses telles qu'elles sont, ou bien qu'elles seraient, en supposant que je n'existe pas"[11] ("I want to represent things as they are, or rather as they would be, on the supposition that I do not exist") is impossible to implement. The enframing, indeed transforming "I" (and eye) is an ever present filter in the form either of the perceiving narrator or of the experiencing protagonists.

So the realists resort to manipulating their tightrope act as far as possible by concealment. They conceal *poiesis*, and they do so by pretense, more specifically by a pretense of mimesis. They downplay and suppress the physicality of language, eschewing, for instance, such devices as alliteration and onomatopeia in order to cultivate a style that will seem transparent. Nonetheless, the artistic patterning, as I have tried to show, though hidden, is discernible in the design of such formal features as the frame, the narratorial voice, the uses of history, the games with names, the elision of viewpoint, and the slippage from the denotative to the connotative and from metonymy to metaphor. If the ends of realist fiction claim to be mimetic, its means not only "need not be so,"[12] but in fact cannot be other than poetic (in the widest sense), because realist writing is no less an aesthetic artifact than romantic writing or other modes, and it has its own conventions, of which the major one is the concealment of those very conventions in a pretense of simplicity. *Poeisis* is in realism masked as mimesis.

Hence the "truth" affirmed by the realists as their creed has to be understood "as something which shows itself or *appears*. In this context mimesis can be translated as 'presentation' or 'making present.' "[13] That "making present" of place is manifest in what I designate its enactment: its forcefulness in the text as a propelling factor in the action. In assigning this function to place, the realists prove to be faithful to the initial Greek meaning of mimesis as performance. In these novels place is performed and enacted more than described. The extent to which these performances can be deemed "true" is a matter for social historians. The issue for literary critics is plausibility, and that leads straight back to pretense:

[I]n the context of the *Poetics* [of Aristotle] the term [mimesis] can best be translated as *simulation*. The poets simulate other *technai* and the success of their enterprise does not depend on how 'truthful' they are . . . but on how skillfully they are able to construct their semblance of truth.[14]

The realists' spectacular success by this criterion is evident in the legibility for readers today of the places and the lives they represent in that purportedly plain artlessness that turns out, on rereading, to be a screen for a complex, inventive, self-conscious artistry.

Notes

৵৹

Preface

1. "Le Roman et la poésie," 8.
2. *Correspondance*, 2: 483.
3. *Gesammelte Werke*, 9:80
4. *S/Z*, 17; English translation, 11.

1. Truth to Tell

1. Balzac, *La Comédie humaine*, 2:848.
2. Brombert, *The Hidden Reader*, 21. I am grateful to Ken Rivers and Maryann Weber, members of my 1987 National Endowment for the Humanities Summer Seminar for College Teachers, for putting me onto the right track on this.
3. *Adam Bede*, 171.
4. "Realism in Art: Recent German Fiction," 273.
5. *Correspondance*, 2: 238.
6. *The Art of Fiction and Other Essays*, 12.
7. "Le Roman," *Pierre et Jean*, 14.
8. White, *Metahistory*, 46.
9. *Reading Realism in Stendhal*, 27–28.
10. Hobson, *The Object of Art*, 81.
11. Ibid., 304.
12. *Our Mutual Friend*, 24.
13. "Le Naturalisme au théâtre," 140. The formula also occurs earlier in Zola's career in his art criticism, *Salon de 1863*, with the word "création" in place of "nature."

14. Prendergast, *The Order of Mimesis*, 59.

15. *Art and Illusion*, 6.

16. See Zavarzadeh, *The Mythopoeic Reality*, and Foley, *Telling the Truth*.

17. *Wahrheit und ästhetische Wahrheit*, see especially 138.

18. *Poetics of Reading*, 15–16.

19. *The Gates of Horn*, 26.

20. *The Rise of the Novel*, 9–34.

21. *Les Origines du roman et le roman des origines*, 20; English translation, 7.

22. Swales, " 'Neglecting the Weight of the Elephant . . . ': German Prose Fiction and European Realism," 884.

23. Todorov, "Reading as Construction," 77.

24. "Uber den Realismus in der Kunst," 373–91; English translation, 38–46.

25. Williams, *The Monster in the Mirror*, 257.

26. Devitt, *Realism and Truth*, 11.

27. "The Concept of Realism in Literary Scholarship," 251–53.

28. "Grundsälzliches zum literarischen Realismus," 103.

29. "The Realistic Fallacy," 94–98.

30. Jameson, *Marxism and Form*, 25.

31. *Studies in European Realism*, 49–50.

32. "Balzac's *Les Paysans*: A Disparate Text," 258–98.

33. Marhofer, "*Le Curé de Tours*: A Study in Topography," 99.

34. Frye, "Myth, Fiction, and Displacement," 29.

35. *Bouvard et Pécuchet*, 395.

36. *The Monster in the Mirror*, 3. This statement reiterates Wellek's judgement, cited earlier.

37. Tallis, *In Defence of Realism*, 195.

38. Iser, "Representation: A Performative Act," 217.

39. Smethhurst, "Balzac and Realism," 73.

40. "Ecrire, verbe intransitif?" 30; English translation, 166.

41. Barthes, *S/Z*, 61; English translation, 55.

42. Ibid., 65; English translation, 61.

43. Barthes, "L'Effet de réel," 11–17.

44. Barthes, *Le Degré zéro de l'écriture*, 62–63; English translation, 85.

45. Barthes, *S/Z*, 48; English translation, 41.

46. Todorov, "The Notion of Literature," 8.

47. "Standard Language and Poetic Language," 22–23.

48. See Furst, "Re-reading Realist Fiction."

49. For a fuller survey of the development of critical attitudes to realism see my introduction to *Realism*.

50. Ermarth, *Realism and Consensus in the English Novel*, xiii.

51. *Reading Realism in Stendhal*, 21 and 4 respectively.

52. *Modes of Modernist Writing*, 97.

53. See Furst, "Realism and Its 'Code of Accreditation.' "

54. Stern, *On Realism*, 52.

55. "The Logic of Realism: A Hegelian Approach," 226.

56. Irwin, *Picturing*, 136–37.

57. *Poetry* (1921); *The Complete Poems*, 267.

58. "The Possibility of a Theory of the Novel," 72.

59. Boyd, *The Reflexive Novel*, 92.

60. A parallel awareness of the slipperiness of facts underlies certain of the newer approaches to history, initiated by White's *Metahistory* and exemplified most recently by Simon Schama's *Dead Certainties (Unwarranted Speculations)*.

61. Jefferson, *Reading Realism in Stendhal*, xii.

62. Gombrich, *Art and Illusion*, 49.

63. Macherey, *A Theory of Literary Production*, 64.

2. Let's Pretend . . .

1. Macherey, *A Theory of Literary Production*, 64.

2. *Biographia Literaria*, 2:6.

3. "Appreciating Fictions: Suspending Disbelief or Pretending Belief?" 1–18.

4. "L'Effet de réel," 88.

5. Robert, *Les Origines du roman et le roman des origines*, 73; English translation, 37.

6. *Fictional Worlds*, 46–47.

7. Walton, "How Remote Are Fictional Worlds from the Real World?" 19.

8. Ibid., 20

9. Walton, "Appreciating Fictions: Suspending Disbelief or Pretending Belief?" 3.

10. "How Remote are Fictional Worlds?" 16.

11. Walton, *Mimesis as Make-Believe*, 42.

12. "Points of View in Narrative and Depictive Representation," 54.

13. Ibid., 49.

14. Gombrich, *Art and Illusion*, 6.

15. *Narrative Crossings*, xii.

16. *In Defence of Realism*, 74–75.

17. Pavel, *Fictional Worlds*, 143.

18. Fish, "How To Do Things with Austin and Searle: Speech Act Theory and Literary Criticism," 1022.

19. *Fictional Worlds*, 12.

20. *The Order of Mimesis*, 26.

21. *Mimesis as Make-Believe*, 270.

22. Ibid., 199.

23. Ibid., 6.

24. *The Logic of Literature*, 111.

25. *On the Margins of Discourse*, 47.

26. *Una pietra sopra*, 310–23; English translation, 101–21.

27. *Fictional Worlds*, 63.

28. "Fictionality and Fields of Reference," 243.

29. *Fictional Worlds*, 138.

30. "Representation: A Performative Act," 219.

31. Devitt, *Realism and Truth,* 12–13.

32. *On the Margins of Discourse,* 25.

33. "The Theory of Objects," 86.

34. "Realism Reconsidered," 239.

35. Meinong, "The Theory of Objects," 81.

36. The example is Walton's in "How Remote are Fictional Worlds?" 17.

37. Ibid., 12.

38. Pavel, *Fictional Worlds,* 71.

39. Walton, "Appreciating Fictions: Suspending Disbelief or Pretending Belief?" 6.

40. *Actual Minds, Possible Worlds,* 95.

41. *Poétique de la prose,* 94; English translation, 83.

42. The full title is *Die Philosophie als-ob: System der theoretischen, praktischen und religiösen Fiktionen der Menschheit auf Grund eines idealistischen Positivismus.*

43. Todorov, "The Notion of Literature," 7.

44. Jenkins, "Realism and the Novel Form," 8.

45. Steinmetz, "Der vergessene Leser," 130.

46. See Gombrich, *Art and Illusion,* 206.

47. "Recherches sur la technique du roman," 89.

48. "The Methodology of Nonexistence," 649.

49. *Fictional Worlds,* 29.

50. Levin, *The Semantics of Metaphor,* 116.

51. Ibid., 130.

52. Ibid., 129.

53. Ricoeur, *La Métaphore vive.* 290; English translation, 278.

54. Smith, *On the Margins of Discourse,* ix.

55. *The Language That Makes George Eliot,* 1.

56. *Balzac, James, and the Realist Novel,* 136.

57. *The Language of Fiction,* 11.

58. *The Truest Poetry,* 221.

59. *Les Origines du roman et le roman des origines,* 14; *Origins of the Novel,* 5.

60. "Don Quixote, Ulysses, and the Idea of Realism," 214.

3. Framing the Fiction

1. S/Z, 61; English translation, 54. I am indebted to Deborah Harter for drawing my attention to this passage.

2. "The Parergon," 26.

3. Preface to *The Portrait of A Lady,* 6.

4. Carlisle, *The Sense of Audience,* 8.

5. "Der vergessene Leser," 113.

6. *Forms of Life,* 2.

7. See Marcel Bouteron, "Balzac et *La Comédie humaine,*" *La Comédie humaine,* 1: ix–xxxi.

8. *La Comédie humaine*, 4: 334–35. This passage, too, was pointed out to me by Deborah Harter, to whom I here express my gratitude.

9. For further discussion of this issue see my article "Rereading *Buddenbrooks*."

10. *The Ethics of Reading*, 80.

11. *Middlemarch*, 25.

12. *Fictions of Romantic Irony*, 69–72.

13. Turner, "Social Dramas and Stories about Them," 167.

14. *The Approach to Fiction*, 55.

15. See Mizruhi, *The Power of Historical Knowledge*, 179.

16. Walton, *Mimesis as Make-Believe*, 360.

17. Gombrich, *Art and Illusion*, 16.

18. Prendergast, *The Order of Mimesis*, 102.

19. *The Modes of Modernist Writing*, 40.

20. *Correspondance*, 2: 691.

21. Lucente, *The Narrative of Realism and Myth*, 11.

22. See Ermarth, *Realism and Consensus*, 65–85.

23. Fowler, *Linguistics and the Novel*, 95.

24. *Buddenbrooks*, 596–639.

25. *Madame Bovary*, 11.

26. See chapter 6, "Landscapes of Consciousness."

27. Brown, "The Logic of Realism: A Hegelian Approach," 230.

28. Lerch, "Die stilistische Bedeutung des Imperfektums in der Rede ('style indirect libre')," 488.

29. Demetz, *Formen des Realismus: Theodore Fontane*, 121.

30. Barthes, *Le Degré zéro de l'écriture*, 29; English translation, 33.

31. Dangelzer, *La Description du milieu dans le roman français de Balzac à Zola*, 25.

32. "Frontières du récit," 61.

33. Stowe, *Balzac, James, and the Realistic Novel*, 4.

34. Brooks, *The Melodramatic Imagination*, 126.

35. Hamon, *Le Descriptif*, 65.

36. Sartre, *Qu'est-ce que la littérature?* 172–73.

37. Kiely, "The Limits of Dialogue in *Middlemarch*," 104.

38. Williams, "The Knowable Community in George Eliot's Novels," 258.

39. See Thomas, *Reading "Middlemarch"*, 85–94.

40. *The Bostonians*, 154.

41. Koelb, *Inventions of Reading*, 21.

42. See *Through the Lens of the Reader*, 1–4.

43. Koelb, *Inventions of Reading*, 23.

44. Beddow, *The Fiction of Humanity*, 5.

45. *Reader-Response Criticism*, 201–32.

46. Cf. Ermarth, *Realism and Consensus*.

47. Lanser, *The Narrative Act*, 113.

48. *Structuralist Poetics*, 192.

49. Bruner, *Actual Minds, Possible Worlds*, 9.

50. *Art and Illusion*, 208.

51. Smith, "The Reader as Part of the Fiction: *Middlemarch*," 188.

52. *Adam Bede*, 171.

53. *The Art of George Eliot*, 81.

54. *S/Z*, 10; English translation, 4.

55. English translation, 20.

56. Gaillard, "The Great Illusion of Realism," 760.

57. *Thomas Mann: The Uses of Tradition*, 61.

58. See McCarthy, *Balzac and His Reader*.

59. The term was coined by Maryann Weber, to whom I am indebted for first drawing my attention to this feature of Balzac's narration.

60. "Toward a Theory of the Engaging Narrator," 811. Warhol directs her argument toward gender differentiation, maintaining that it is primarily women narrators (Eliot, Gaskell, Stowe) who favor such a stance. My readings suggest, on the contrary, that engagement is by no means gender-segregated.

61. Stierle, "The Reading of Fictional Texts," 91.

62. See chapter 6, "Landscapes of Consciousness," for further comment on the houses.

63. "Le Descriptif," 224.

64. Irwin, *Picturing*, 6.

65. Levin, *The Gates of Horn*, 127.

66. See, for example, Carlisle, *The Sense of an Audience*; McCarthy, *Balzac and His Reader*; Prendergast, *The Order of Mimesis*; Spady, "The Dynamics of Reader Response in *Middlemarch*"; Stierle, "The Reading of Fictional Texts"; Thomas, *Reading "Middlemarch"*.

67. See Smith, *On the Margins of Discourse*, 28.

4. Not So Long Ago

1. Ong, "The Writer's Audience Is Always a Fiction," 15.

2. Bakhtin, *The Dialogic Imagination*, 84.

3. *The Order of Mimesis*, 235.

4. *Poetics*, 32.

5. *Between History and Literature*, 232.

6. "L'Effet de réel," 87; English translation, 15.

7. *Between History and Literature*, 237–56.

8. *Actual Minds, Possible Worlds*, 43.

9. Butor, "Philosophie d'ameublement," 96.

10. *Mimesis*, 403.

11. Gearhart, *The Open Boundary of History and Fiction*, 8.

12. "Avant-Propos" to *La Comédie humaine*, 1: 7.

13. Auerbach, *Mimesis*, 3–4.

14. Beer, *Romance*, 5.

15. Welty, "Place in Fiction," 58.

16. Eliot, *Daniel Deronda*, 121.

17. Eliot, *Adam Bede*, 171.

18. Balzac, *La Comédie humaine*, 4: 464.

19. This does not mean to imply that the presence of a precise date is either confined to, or proof of, realism. Dates may, instead, be used as a misleading indicator of mode, for instance before a transition into the fantastic, as in some of Isak Dinesen's stories.

20. Hamburger, *Die Logik der Dichtung*; English translation, 110–11.

21. Hamon, *Le Descriptif*, 66.

22. Pike in *The Image of the City in Literature* (13) notes that Flaubert, Dickens, Balzac, and Hugo typically create the Paris or London of a period considerably before the actual time of writing. By displacing the city backward in time, he suggests, they insure metaphorization: the city is thus presented simultaneously as "reality" and located in the realm of the imaginary.

23. See Citron, *Le Poésie de Paris dans la littérature française de Rousseau à Baudelaire*; Raser, *Guide to Balzac's Paris*; Minder, *Paris in der neueren französischen Literatur 1770–1890*; Max, *Les Métamorphoses de la grande ville dans les "Rougon-Macquart;"* Kranowski, *Paris dans les romans de Zola*; Bancquart, *Images littéraires de Paris 'fin-de-siècle'*; Lotz, "L'Image iréelle, bizarre et mythique de Paris chez Balzac et Baudelaire"; Timms and Kelley, eds., *Unreal City*, especially Peter Collier, "Nineteenth Century Paris: Vision and Nightmare"; also the section "Lübeck" in Matter, ed., *Die Literatur über Thomas Mann*, 338–44; Moulden and von Wilpert, eds., *Buddenbrooks-Handbuch*, 11–40; and Block, *Naturalistic Triptych*.

24. See Weimann, "History, Appropriation, and the Uses of Representation in Modern Narrative," 181–85.

25. Lodge, *The Modes of Modernist Writing*, 24.

26. For an assessment of Balzac as a social historian, see Pradalié, *Balzac historien*.

27. Butor, "Philosophie de l'ameublement," 54.

28. *Middlemarch*, 177.

29. Kitchel, ed., *Quarry for "Middlemarch."*

30. Haight, ed., *The George Eliot Letters*, 5: 139.

31. "History by Indirection: The Era of Reform in *Middlemarch*."

32. For a fine overview of the historical situation see Ridley, *Mann: Buddenbrooks*, 10–19; also Moulden and Wilpert, eds., *Buddenbrooks-Handbuch*, 31–35, for a chronological table of the happenings in the Buddenbrook family.

33. *Buddenbrooks*, 179.

34. *Poetics of Reading*, 33–34.

35. *Aspects of the Novel*, 6.

36. *Metahistory*, 3, footnote.

37. *Inventions of Reading*, xi.

5. The Game of the Name

An early, much briefer version of this chapter was presented at the meeting of the International Comparative Literature Association in Munich in August 1988.

1. "Place in Fiction," 59.

2. Preface reprinted in *The Art of the Novel*, 8.

3. *Realism and the Drama of Reference*, 72.

4. *Le Discours du roman*, 194.

5. *The Role of Place in Literature*, 29.

6. See the comments of J. Hillis Miller on the continuing prevalence of mimetic readings of Dickens's *Sketches by Boz* as a representation of London in "The Fiction of Realism."

7. Pavel, *Fictional Worlds*, 73.

8. *Realism and Revolution*, 86.

9. See Zoran, "Towards a Theory of Space in Narrative," 309ff.

10. "Un Discours contraint," 426.

11. "Structure and Style in the Greater Romantic Lyric," 556.

12. "The Rhetoric of Temporality," 207.

13. Mozet, *La Ville de province dans l'oeuvre de Balzac*, 5.

14. "Place in Fiction," 59.

15. *The Rise of the Novel*, 17–18.

16. "Place in Fiction," 62.

17. Walton, *Mimesis as Make-Believe*, 24.

18. Ibid., 42.

19. *Le Descriptif*, 53.

20. *The Art of the Novel*, 35.

21. *Les Origines du roman et le roman des origines*, 20; English translation, 8.

22. Welty, "Place in Fiction," 59.

23. Gelley, "Setting and a Sense of World in the Novel," 193.

24. Butor, "Balzac et la réalité," 88.

25. Downing, "A Famous Boarding-House," 141.

26. "Un Discours contraint," 426.

27. Ibid., 426.

28. Flaubert, *Madame Bovary*, 73.

29. "Explaining Literary Phenomena," 23–24.

30. Harshav, "Fictionality and Fields of Reference," 243.

31. *Fictional Worlds*, 37.

32. For a more detailed discussion see " 'Paris Change!': Perception and Narration" in Furst, *Through the Lens of the Reader*, 27–38.

33. Harshav, "Fictionality and Fields of Reference," 236.

34. Letter to Louis Bouilhet, 25 May 1855. *Correspondance*, 2: 575.

35. See Gombrich, *Art and Illusion*, 221.

36. Wimmers, *Poetics of Reading*, 80–81.

37. Kitchel, ed., *Quarry for "Middlemarch"*, 45.

38. Macherey, *A Theory of Literary Production*, 173.

39. *The Road to Xanadu*, 360ff.

40. "The Logical Status of Fictional Discourse," 332.

41. *On the Margins of Discourse*, 72.

42. "Castration, Speech Acts, and the Realist Difference," 156.

43. *Mimesis as Make-Believe*, 329.

44. Published by Fischer-Taschenbuch in 1983.

45. "Poetry," *The Complete Poems*, 267.

46. "Realism, or, In Praise of Lying: Some Nineteenth-Century Novels."

47. *Metahistory*, 3, footnote.

6. Landscapes of Consciousness

1. Balzac, *La Comédie humaine*, 4: 549.

2. *Wirklichkeit und Illusion*, 310.

3. "Zum Begriff des Realismus für die erzählende Dichtung des 19. Jahrhunderts," 230.

4. Suleiman and Crosman, eds., *The Reader in the Text*, 72.

5. Todorov's article appears in a translation from the French, and does not seem to have been published in the original language. It is therefore not possible to establish exactly what word Todorov used at this point. The translation may in itself be a distortion.

6. Bruner, *Actual Minds, Possible Worlds*, 14.

7. Avni, *The Resistance to Reference*, 45.

8. Kanes, "Langage balzacien: Splendeurs et misères de la représentation," 289.

9. "L'Effet de réel," 88–89; English translation, 17.

10. "Reading as Construction," 73.

11. McKay, *Narration and Discourse in American Realist Fiction*, 36.

12. Dorrit Cohn's phrase, "transparent minds" is an apt key to the mechanics of indirect discourse.

13. Lanser, *The Narrative Act*, 205.

14. "Don Quixote, Ulysses, and the Idea of Realism," 201.

15. *La Comédie humaine*, 2: 480.

16. "Don Quixote, Ulysses, and the Idea of Realism," 200.

17. Lubbock, *The Craft of Fiction*, 220.

18. *Studies in European Realism*, 58.

19. James, *The Bostonians*, 143.

20. The " 'tender' " in quotation marks is surely a citation of Verena's opinion, and therefore a further sign of the narrator's critical detachment from her naive view.

21. Flaubert, *Madame Bovary*, 73.

22. Zola, *Les Rougon-Macquart*, 2: 376.

23. Mann, *Buddenbrooks*, 119.

24. Müller, "Realismus als Provokation," 20.

25. "Philosophie de l'ameublement," 54–56.

26. "Narrate or Describe?" 117–18.

27. "The Fiction of Realism," 98.

28. "De la description," 235.

29. Bachelard, *La Poétique de l'espace*, 26.

30. Eliot, *Middlemarch*, 99.

31. See Swann, "*Middlemarch*: Realism and Symbolic Form," especially 290ff. for other examples of symbolic form in *Middlemarch*.

32. *Gesammelte Werke*, 9: 376–98.

33. "Place in Fiction," 58.

34. *The Image of the City in Modern Literature*, 71.

35. Auerbach, *Mimesis*, 472.

36. Gelley, "Setting and a Sense of World in the Novel," 187.

37. Williams, *The Monster in the Mirror*, 261.

38. See Furst, "Autumn: An Exemplary Case of Paradigm Shift." In *Romantic Lyric Poetry*, ed. Elinor Shaffer (forthcoming).

39. *Werke*, 8: 91.

40. "Human Nature, Social Orders, and Nineteenth-Century Systems of Explanation," 30.

41. Petrey, "Castration, Speech Acts, and the Realist Difference," 155.

42. See Furst, *L'Assommoir: A Working Woman's Life*, especially 105–6.

43. *Actual Minds, Possible Worlds*, 49.

44. Frye, "Myth, Fiction, and Displacement," 26. See also Stierle's notion of the *Relevanzfigur* discussed in chapter 3.

45. Porter, "Flaubert and the Difficulty of Reading," 371.

46. Butor, in "Philosophie de l'ameublement" (51–60), has pointed to Balzac's marked preference for old, well-used objects which endow his figures with a history.

47. For further discussion of metonymy / metaphor see chapter 7.

48. Debray-Genette, "La Pierre descriptive," 298.

49. Zola, *Thérèse Raquin*, 15.

50. *Realism and Consensus*, 67.

51. Schor, "Fiction as Interpretation / Interpretation as Fiction," 168–69.

52. Smith, "Reading as Part of Fiction," 19.

53. Lodge, *After Bakhtin*, 49.

54. Bell, *The Sentiment of Reality*, 191.

55. *Mimesis as Make-Believe*, 273.

56. Ibid., 240–89, is entitled "Psychological Participation."

57. "How Remote Are Fictional Worlds from Real Worlds?" 22.

58. Avni, *The Resistance to Reference*, 46. Avni suggests that this phrase must have been written on the blackboard by Saussure because students' notebooks, from which his *Cours de linguistique générale* was reconstructed, invariably capitalize "fait."

7. Figuring the Pretense

1. "Langage balzacien," 293.

2. *La Comédie humaine*, 3: 481.

3. *Linguistics and the Novel*, 67

4. For example, Petrey, "Castration, Speech Acts, and the Realist Difference"; Lucente, *The Narrative of Realism and Myth*, 145ff; and particularly Miller, "The Fiction of Realism," which will be more fully discussed later in this chapter.

5. "Un Discours contraint," 434.

6. "Standard Language and Poetic Language," 19.

7. See Jenkins, *The Monster in the Mirror*, 8.

8. "La Littérature et l'espace," 47.

9. Linguistics and the Novel, 75–76.

10. "Le Pierre descriptive," 293.

11. Letter to Henry Céard, 22 March 1885; Correspondance, 5: 249.

12. Culler, Structuralist Poetics, 197.

13. She can be equated with the "personne immobile" (La Comédie humaine, 3: 480; "motionless figure") in the first paragraph whom a passing stranger might glimpse behind a window. This could be Eugénie, but the figure's attributes are so generalized ("le regard pâle et froid" ["a pale, cold stare"], "la figure à demi monastique" ["the half monastic face"]), that it is impossible to tell.

14. Schor, "Details and Realism," 7.

15. The Image of the City, 33.

16. The term "typhus" was used generically in the nineteenth century to designate many kinds of enteric fever before a clear distinction was made between what is nowadays called typhus and typhoid fever.

17. "Closing Statement: Linguistics and Poetics," 358.

18. "Closing Statement," 375.

19. The Modes of Modernist Writing (73–124) expounds and explicates the ramifications and complexities of Jakobson's theory with admirable clarity.

20. For a parallel finding see Genette, "Métonymie chez Proust, ou la naissance du récit," which shows a similar "birth" of a totalizing metaphoric narration out of metonymy in A la recherche du temps perdu.

21. Zola, Les Rougon-Macquart, 2: 423.

22. Essay Concerning Human Understanding, part 3: chap. 10, 14.

8. The Enactment of Place

1. The generational approach finds cogent expression in the family novel. Its leading example is Zola's cycle, Les Rougon-Macquart, which traces the legitimate and illegitimate branches of a family through five generations. Midway in the project Zola drew up a family tree to illustrate the manifestations of heredity in various members of the family. Buddenbrooks is constructed on a similar principle, although Mann takes heredity rather less literally and more metaphorically than Zola.

2. Saint-Hilaire (1772–1844), an eminent zoologist, was a precursor of the doctrine of descent in the guise of "transformism."

3. Among the host of discussions of the implications of Darwinism the one that is most concerned with literature is Beer's Darwin's Plots.

4. See Furst, " 'Struggling for Medical Reform in Middlemarch.' "

5. When he correctly recognizes Nancy Nash's complaint as cramps, not the tumor Dr. Minchin had diagnosed, he is held, on her spontaneous recovery, to have the ability to cure cancers.

6. Les Rougon-Macquart, 2: 411.

7. Encyclopedia of Poetry and Poetics, 1039.

8. Spariosu, *Mimesis in Contemporary Theory,* i.

9. See *Encyclopedia of Poetry and Poetics,* 575–79, and 1037–43. Curiously, this reference work omits coverage of realism, moving from "Classic and Romantic" to "Saussure and Pierce."

10. Edward Young, in his influential *Conjectures on Original Composition* (1759), dismisses imitation as a "meddling ape."

11. "Du gouvernement de l'imagination," 284.

12. *Encyclopedia of Poetry and Poetics,* 1038.

13. Spariosu, *Mimesis in Contemporary Theory,* xi.

14. Ibid., viii.

Bibliography

❦

Primary Sources

Aristotle. *Poetics*. Trans. Gerald Else. Ann Arbor: University of Michigan Press, 1967.

Balzac, Honoré de. *La Comédie humaine*. 10 vols. Ed. Marcel Bouteron. 1948. Reprint, Paris: Gallimard, 1976.

———. *La Cousine Bette*. Vol. 6: 135–524 of *La Comédie humaine*.

———. *Eugénie Grandet*. Vol. 3: 480–649 of *La Comédie humaine*.

———. *Illusions perdues*. Vol. 4: 464–1056 of *La Comédie humaine*.

———. *Le Père Goriot*. Vol. 2: 847–1085 of *La Comédie humaine*.

Baudelaire, Charles. "Du gouvernement de l'imagination." *Curiosités esthétiques*. Paris: Conard, 1923.

Coleridge, Samuel Taylor. *Biographia Literaria*. 2 vols. Ed. James Engell and Walter Jackson Bate. Princeton: Princeton University Press, 1983.

———. "Kubla Khan: Or, A Vision in a Dream. A Fragment." *Poems and Prose*. Ed. Kathleen Raine. Harmondsworth: Penguin, 1957.

Dickens, Charles. *Our Mutual Friend*. New York: New American Library, 1980.

Duranty, Edmond. *Réalisme*. Ed. Jules Assézar. Paris: L'Arche du livre, 1970.

Eliot, George. *Adam Bede*. London: Dent, 1966.

———. *Daniel Deronda*. Harmondsworth: Penguin, 1967.

———. *The George Eliot Letters*. 7 vols. Ed. Gordon S. Haight. New Haven: Yale University Press, 1954–55.

———. *Middlemarch*. Harmondsworth: Penguin, 1965.

Flaubert, Gustave. *Bouvard et Pécuchet*. Ed. Albert Cento. Paris: Nizan, 1964.

———. *Correspondance*. 3 vols. Ed. Jean Bruneau. Paris: Gallimard, 1973–91.

———. *Madame Bovary*. Ed. Edouard Maynial. Paris: Garnier, 1947. Trans. Paul de Man. New York: Norton, 1965.

Goethe, Johann Wolfgang von. *Die Leiden des jungen Werthers*. Vol. 8: 15–142 of *Werke*. 15 vols. Ed. Karl Heinemann. Leipzig: Bibliographisches Institut, n.d.

Hoffmann, Ernst Theodor Amadeus. *Der goldene Topf*. Ed. F. W. Mainland. Oxford: Blackwell, 1947.

James, Henry. *The Art of Fiction and Other Essays*. New York: Oxford University Press, 1948.

——. *The Art of the Novel*. New York: Scribner's, 1934.

——. *The Bostonians*. New York: New American Library, 1974.

——. *The Europeans*. Harmondsworth: Penguin, 1964.

——. *The Portrait of a Lady*. Ed. Leon Edel. Boston: Houghton Mifflin, 1963.

——. *Washington Square*. New York: Bantam, 1959.

Lewes, George. "Realism in Art: Recent German Fiction." *Westminster Review* 70 (1858): 488–518.

Locke, John. *Essay Concerning Human Understanding*. Ed. Alexander Campbell Fraser. Oxford: Clarendon Press, 1894.

Mann, Thomas. *Buddenbrooks*. Vol. 1: 5–783 of *Gesammelte Werke*.

——. *Gesammelte Werke*. 13 vols. Frankfurt: Fischer, 1960–74.

——. *Lübeck als geistige Lebensform*. Vol. 11: 376–98 of *Gesammelte Werke*.

Maupassant, Guy de. "Le Roman." Preface to *Pierre et Jean*, 5–28. Paris: Albin, 1968.

Moore, Marianne. *The Complete Poems*. New York: Macmillan/Viking, (1967) 1981.

Nietzsche, Friedrich. *Gesammelte Werke*. Munich: Musarion, 1919–25.

Rousseau, Jean-Jacques. *Les Rêveries du promeneur solitaire*. Paris: Garnier Flammarion, 1964.

Zola, Emile. *L'Assommoir*. Vol. 2: 371–796 of *Les Rougon-Macquart*.

——. *Correspondance*. 8 vols. Ed. H. H. Bakker. Montreal: Presses de l'Université de Montréal, 1978–92.

——. "De la description." 231–36 of *Le Roman expérimental*.

——. "Le Naturalisme au théâtre." 139–76 of *Le Roman expérimental*.

——. *Le Roman expérimental*. Paris: Garnier-Flammarion, 1971.

——. *Les Rougon-Macquart*. 5 vols. Ed. Henri Mittérand. Paris: Gallimard, 1960–67.

——. *Thérèse Raquin*. Paris: Fasquelle, 1968.

Secondary Sources

Abrams, M. H. "Structure and Style in the Greater Romantic Lyric." In *From Sensibility to Romanticism: Essays Presented to F. A. Pottle*, 527–60, ed. F. W. Hillis and Harold Bloom. New York: Oxford University Press, 1965.

Auerbach, Erich. *Mimesis*. Trans. Willard R. Trask. Princeton: Princeton University Press, 1953.

Aust, Hugo. *Literatur des Realismus*. Stuttgart: Metzler, 1977.

Avni, Ora. *The Resistance to Reference: Linguistics, Philosophy, and the Literary Text*. Baltimore: Johns Hopkins University Press, 1990.

Bachelard, Gaston. *La Poétique de l'espace*. Paris: Presses universitaires de France, 1957.

Bakhtin, M. M. "The Bildungsroman and Its Significance in the History of Realism (Toward a Historical Typology of the Novel)." In *Speech Genres and Other Late Essays*, 10–59, trans. Vern W. McGee, ed. Caryl Emerson and Michael Holquist. Austin: University of Texas Press, 1986.

——. *The Dialogic Imagination.* Trans. Caryl Emerson and Michael Holquist. Austin: University of Texas Press, 1981.

Bancquart, Marie-Claire. *Images littéraires de Paris 'fin-de-siècle'.* Paris: Éditions de la différence, 1979.

Barthes, Roland. "Ecrire, verbe intransitif?" In *Le Bruissement de la langue,* 14–31. Paris: Seuil, 1984. "To Write: An Intransitive Verb?" In *The Structuralists,* 155–67, ed. Richard DeGeorge and Fernande DeGeorge. Garden City, N.Y.: Doubleday, 1972.

——. *Le Degré zéro de l'écriture.* Paris: Editions du Seuil, 1953. *Writing Degree Zero,* trans. Annette Lavers and Colin Smith. New York: Hill & Wang, 1968.

——. "L'Effet de réel." *Communications* 11 (1968): 84–89. "The Reality Effect." In *French Literary Theory Today,* 11–17, trans. R. Carter, ed. Tzvetan Todorov. Cambridge: Cambridge University Press, 1982.

——. *S/Z.* Paris: Editions du Seuil, 1970. Trans. Richard Howard. New York: Hill & Wang, 1974.

Beaty, Jerome. "History by Indirection: The Era of Reform in *Middlemarch.*" *Victorian Studies* 1 (1957–58): 173–79. Reprinted in *Middlemarch,* 700–706, ed. Bert G. Hornback. New York: Norton, 1977.

——. *"Middlemarch": From Notebook to Novel.* Urbana: University of Illinois Press, 1960.

Beddow, Michael. *The Fiction of Humanity.* Cambridge: Cambridge University Press, 1982.

Beer, Gillian. *Darwin's Plots: Evolutionary Narrative in Darwin, George Eliot, and Nineteenth Century Fiction.* London: Routledge & Kegan Paul, 1983.

——. *Romance.* London: Methuen; New York: Barnes & Noble, 1970.

Belgrand, Anne. "Espace clos, espace ouvert dans *L'Assommoir.*" In *Espaces romanesques,* 5–14, ed. Michel Crouzet. Paris: Presses universitaires de France, 1982.

Bell, Michael. *The Sentiment of Reality.* London: Allen & Unwin, 1983.

Block, Haskell M. *Naturalistic Triptych: The Real and the Fictive in Zola, Mann, and Dreiser.* New York: Random House, 1970.

Bouteron, Marcel. "Balzac et La Comédie humaine." In *La Comédie humaine,* 1: ix–xxxi. Paris: Gallimard, 1976.

Boyd, Michael. *The Reflexive Novel: Fiction As Critique.* London: Associated University Presses, 1983.

Boyle, Nicholas, and Martin Swales, eds. *Realism in European Literature: Essays in Honour of J. P. Stern.* Cambridge: Cambridge University Press, 1986.

Brinkmann, Richard. *Wirklichkeit und Illusion.* Tübingen: Niemeyer, 1957.

——. "Zum Begriff des Realismus für die erzählende Dichtung des 19. Jahrhunderts." In *Begriffsbestimmung des literarischen Realismus,* 222–35, ed. Richard Brinkmann. Darmstadt: Wissenschaftliche Buchgesellschaft, 1969.

Brodsky, Claudia J. *The Imposition of Form: Studies in Narrative Representation and Knowledge.* Princeton: Princeton University Press, 1987.

Brombert, Victor. *The Hidden Reader.* Cambridge, Mass.: Harvard University Press, 1988.

Brooks, Peter. *The Melodramatic Imagination: Balzac, James, Melodrama, and the Modes of Excess.* New Haven: Yale University Press, 1976.

Brown, Marshall. "The Logic of Realism: A Hegelian Approach." *PMLA* 96, no. 2 (1981): 224–41.

Bruner, Jerome. *Actual Minds, Possible Worlds.* Cambridge, Mass.: Harvard University Press, 1986.

Butor, Michel. "Balzac et la réalité." 79–93 of *Répertoire I*.

———. "Philosophie de l'ameublement." 51–60 of *Répertoire II*.

———. "Recherches sur la technique du roman." 88–99 of *Répertoire II*.

———. *Répertoire I*. Paris: Editions de minuit, 1960.

———. *Répertoire II*. Paris: Editions de minuit, 1964.

———. "Le Roman et la poésie." 7–26 of *Répertoire I*.

Calvino, Italo. "I Livelli della realtà in letteratura." In *Una pietra sopra*, 310–23. Torino: Einaudi, 1980. In *The Uses of Literature*, 101–21, trans. Patrick Creagh. New York: Harcourt Brace Jovanovich, 1982.

Carlisle, Janice. *The Sense of Audience*. Athens: University of Georgia Press, 1981.

Carroll, David. "Mimesis Reconsidered." *Diacritics* 5 (1975): 5–12.

Chambers, Ross. "Describing Description." In *Meaning and Meaningfulness*, 90–121, French Forum 15. Lexington, Ky.: French Forum, 1979.

Citron, Pierre. *La Poésie de Paris dans la littérature française de Rousseau à Baudelaire*. 2 vols. Paris: Editions de minuit, 1961.

Coates, Paul. *The Realist Fantasy: Fiction and Reality Since "Clarissa"*. New York: St. Martin's, 1983.

Cohn, Dorrit. *Transparent Minds*. Princeton: Princeton University Press, 1978.

Collier, Peter. "Nineteenth Century Paris: Vision and Nightmare." In *Unreal City: Urban Experience in Modern European Literature*, 24–44, ed. Edward Timms and David Kelley. Manchester: Manchester University Press, 1985.

Culler, Jonathan. *Structuralist Poetics*. Ithaca: Cornell University Press, 1975.

Dangelzer, Joan Y. *La Description du milieu dans le roman français de Balzac à Zola*. Paris: Presses modernes, 1938.

Dargan, Joan. *Balzac and the Drama of Perspective: The Narrator in Selected Works of "La Comédie humaine."* French Forum 60. Lexington, Ky: French Forum, 1985.

Debray-Genette, Raymonde. "La Pierre descriptive." *Poétique* 43 (1980): 293–304.

de Man, Paul. "The Rhetoric of Temporality." In *Interpretation*, 173–209, ed. Charles Singleton. Baltimore: Johns Hopkins University Press, 1969.

Demetz, Peter. *Formen des Realismus: Theodor Fontane*. Munich: Hanser, 1964.

———. "Zur Definition des Realismus." *Literatur und Kritik* 16, no. 1 (1977): 333–45.

Derrida, Jacques. "The Parergon." *October* 9 (1979): 3–40.

Devitt, Michael. *Realism and Truth*. Princeton: Princeton University Press, 1984.

Doody, Terence. "*Don Quixote, Ulysses*, and the Idea of Realism." *Novel* 12, no. 3 (1979): 197–214.

Downing, George E. "A Famous Boarding-House." In *Studies in Balzac's Realism*, 136–50, ed. Preston Dargan and W. L. Crain. 1932. Reprint, Chicago: University of Chicago Press, 1967.

Ermarth, Elizabeth Deeds. *Realism and Consensus in the English Novel*. Princeton: Princeton University Press, 1983.

———. "Realism, Perspective, and the Novel." *Critical Inquiry* 7, no. 3 (1981): 499–520.

Fish, Stanley. "How To Do Things with Austin and Searle: Speech Act Theory and Literary Criticism." *Modern Language Notes* 91, no. 5 (1976): 983–1025.

Foley, Barbara. *Telling the Truth: The Theory and Practice of Documentary Fiction*. Ithaca: Cornell University Press, 1986.

Forster, E. M. *Aspects of the Novel*. London: Arnold; New York: Harcourt, Brace & World, 1927.

Fowler, Roger. *Linguistics and the Novel*. London: Methuen, 1977.

Freedman, Ralph. "The Possibility of a Theory of the Novel." In *The Disciplines of Criticism*, 57–77, ed. Peter Demetz, Thomas Greene, and Lowry Nelson Jr. New Haven: Yale University Press, 1968.

Fried, Michael. "Representing Representation." In *Allegory and Representation*, 94–127, ed. Stephen J. Greenblatt. Baltimore: Johns Hopkins University Press, 1981.

Frye, Northrop. *Anatomy of Criticism*. 1957. Reprint, New York: Atheneum Press, 1969.

———. "Myth, Fiction, and Displacement." In *Fables of Identity*, 21–38. New York: Harcourt, Brace & World, 1963.

Furst, Lilian R. *L'Assommoir: A Working Woman's Life*. Boston: Twayne, 1990.

———. *Fictions of Romantic Irony*. London: Macmillan; Cambridge, Mass.: Harvard University Press, 1984.

———. Introduction to *Realism*, 1–23. London: Longman, 1992.

———. *Realism: An Anthology of Critical Texts*. London: Longman, 1992.

———. "Realism and Its 'Code of Accreditation.'" *Comparative Literature Studies* 25, no. 2 (1988): 1–26.

———. "Rereading Buddenbrooks." *German Life & Letters* 44, no. 4 (1991): 317–29.

———. "Re-reading Realist Fiction." In *Sensus Communis*, 11–22, ed. Peter Boerner, János Riesz, and Bernhard Scholz. Tübingen: Gunter Narr, 1986.

———. "'Struggling for Medical Reform in Middlemarch.'" *Nineteenth-Century Literature* 48, no. 3 (1993): 341–61.

———. *Through the Lens of the Reader: Explorations of European Narrative*. Albany: State University of New York Press, 1992.

Gaillard, Françoise. "The Great Illusion of Realism." *Poetics Today* 5, no. 4 (1984): 753–66.

Gearhart, Suzanne. *The Open Boundary of History and Fiction*. Princeton: Princeton University Press, 1984.

Gelley, Alexander. *Narrative Crossings: Theory and Pragmatics of Prose Fiction*. Baltimore: Johns Hopkins University Press, 1987.

———. "The Represented World: Toward a Phenomenological Theory of Description in the Novel." *Journal of Aesthetics and Art Criticism* 37 (1979): 415–22.

———. "Setting and a Sense of World in the Novel." *Yale Review* 62 (1973): 186–201.

Genette, Gérard. *Figures II*. Paris: Editions du Seuil, 1969.

———. "Frontières du récit." 49–69 of *Figures II*.

———. "La Littérature et l'espace." 43–48 of *Figures II*.

———. "Métonymie chez Proust, ou la naissance du récit." *Poétique* 2 (1970): 156–73.

Gombrich, E. H. *Art and Illusion*. Princeton: Princeton University Press, 1960.

Goodman, Nelson. *Of Mind and Other Matters*. Cambridge, Mass.: Harvard University Press, 1984.

———. *Ways of World Making*. 1934. Reprint, Indianapolis: Hackett Publishing, 1978.

Gossman, Lionel. *Between History and Literature*. Cambridge, Mass.: Harvard University Press, 1990.

Graver, Suzanne. *George Eliot and Community: A Study in Social Theory and Fictional Form*. Berkeley: University of California Press, 1984.

Hamburger, Käthe. *Die Logik der Dichtung*. Stuttgart: Klett, 1957. *The Logic of Literature*, trans. Marilyn J. Rese. Bloomington: Indiana University Press, 1973.

———. *Wahrheit und ästhetische Wahrheit*. Stuttgart: Klett & Cotta, 1979.

Hamon, Philippe. *Le Descriptif: Introduction à l'analyse du descriptif*. Paris: Hachette, 1981.

——. "Un Discours contraint." *Poétique* 16 (1973): 411–45. Partial translation by Lilian R. Furst and Seán Hand, in *Realism*, 166–85, ed. Lilian R. Furst. London: Longman, 1992.

Hardy, Barbara. Introduction to *Daniel Deronda*, 7–30. Harmondsworth: Penguin, 1967.

Harshav (Hrushovski), Benjamin. "Fictionality and Fields of Reference." *Poetics Today* 5, no. 2 (1984): 227–51.

Harvey, W. J. *The Art of George Eliot*. London: Chatto & Windus, 1961.

Heller, Erich. "The Realistic Fallacy." In *The Artist's Journey Into the Interior and Other Essays*, 87–98. New York/London: Harcourt, Brace Jovanovich, 1959.

Hewitt, Douglas. *The Approach to Fiction*. London: Longman, 1972.

Hobson, Marian. *The Object of Art: The Theory of Illusion in Eighteenth Century France*. Cambridge: Cambridge University Press, 1982.

Höfner, Eckhard. *Literatur und Realität: Aspekte des Realismusbegriffs in der französischen Literatur des 19. Jahrhunderts*. Heidelberg: Carl Winter, 1980.

Holub, Robert. *Reflections on Realism: Paradox, Norm, and Ideology in Nineteenth-Century German Prose*. Detroit: Wayne State University Press, 1991.

Howell, Robert. "Fictional Objects: How They Are and How They Aren't." *Poetics* 8, nos. 1/2 (1979): 129–77.

Irwin, Michael. *Picturing: Description and Illusion in the Nineteenth Century Novel*. London: Allen & Unwin, 1979.

Iser, Wolfgang. "Feigning in Fiction." In *The Identity of the Literary Text*, 204–28, ed. Mario J. Valdés and Owen Miller. Toronto: University of Toronto Press, 1985. First published as "Akte des Fingierens. Oder: Was ist das Fiktive im fiktionalen Text?" In *Funktionen des Fiktiven. Poetik und Hermeneutik* 10 (1983): 121–53.

——. "Representation: A Performative Act." In *The Aims of Representation*, 217–32, ed. Murray Krieger. New York: Columbia University Press, 1987.

Jakobson, Roman. "Closing Statement: Linguistics and Poetics." In *Style in Language*, 350–77, ed. Thomas A. Sebeok. Cambridge: MIT Press, 1960.

——. *The Fundamentals of Language*. The Hague: Mouton, 1956.

——. "Über den Realismus in der Kunst." In *Texte der russischen Formalisten*, 373–91, ed. Jurij Striedter. Munich: Fink, 1969. "On Realism in Art." In *Readings in Russian Poetics*, 38–46, ed. Ladislaw Matejka and Krystyna Pomorska. Cambridge: MIT Press, 1978.

Jameson, Fredric. *Marxism and Form*. Princeton: Princeton University Press, 1971.

Jean, Raymond. *La Littérature et le réel*. Paris: Albin Michel, 1965.

Jefferson, Ann. *Reading Realism in Stendhal*. Cambridge: Cambridge University Press, 1988.

Jenkins, Cecil. "Realism and the Novel Form." In *The Monster in the Mirror*, 1–15, ed. D. A. Williams. London: Oxford University Press, 1978.

Kadish, Doris Y. "Landscape, Ideology, and Plot in Balzac's Les Chouans." *Nineteenth-Century French Studies* 12, no. 4, and 13, no. 1 (1984): 43–57.

Kanes, Martin. "Langage balzacien: Splendeurs et misères de la représentation." In *Balzac: l'invention du roman*, 281–94, ed. Claude Duchet and Jacques Neefs. Paris: Belfonds, 1982.

Kiely, Robert. "The Limits of Dialogue in Middlemarch." In *The Worlds of Victorian Fiction*, 103–23, ed. Jerome H. Buckley. Cambridge, Mass.: Harvard University Press, 1975.

Kitchel, Anna Theresa, ed. Quarry for "Middlemarch." Cambridge: Cambridge University Press; Berkeley: University of California Press, 1938.

Klotz, Volker. Die erzählte Stadt. Munich: Hanser, 1969.

Knoepflmacher, Ulrich. George Eliot's Early Novels: The Limits of Realism. Berkeley: University of California Press, 1968.

Koelb, Clayton. Inventions of Reading: Rhetoric and the Literary Imagination. Ithaca: Cornell University Press, 1988.

Kohl, Stephan. Realismus: Theorie und Geschichte. Munich: Fink, 1977.

Köpeczi, Béla, and Peter Juházs. Littérature et réalité. Budapest: Akadémiai Kiadó, 1966.

Kranowski, Nathan. Paris dans les romans de Zola. Paris: Presses universitaires de France, 1968.

Krieger, Murray, ed. The Aims of Representation: Subject / Text / History. New York: Columbia University Press, 1987.

Lanser, Susan S. The Narrative Act: Point of View in Prose Fiction. Princeton: Princeton University Press, 1981.

Lauer, Reinhard. Europäischer Realismus. Wiesbaden: Athenaion, 1980.

Lerch, Eugen. "Die stilistische Bedeutung des Imperfektums in der Rede ('style indirect libre')." Germanisch-Romanische Monatsschrift 6 (1914): 470–89.

Lerner, Laurence. The Truest Poetry. London: Hamilton, 1960.

Levin, Harry T. The Gates of Horn: A Study of Five French Realists. New York: Oxford University Press, 1963.

Levin, Samuel R. The Semantics of Metaphor. Baltimore: Johns Hopkins University Press, 1977.

Levine, George. The Realistic Imagination: English Fiction from Frankenstein to Lady Chatterley. Chicago: University of Chicago Press, 1981.

——. "Realism, or, In Praise of Lying: Some Nineteenth-Century Novels," College English 31 (1970): 355–65.

——. "Realism Reconsidered." In The Theory of the Novel, 233–56, ed. John Halperin. New York: Oxford University Press, 1974.

Lewis, Thomas Edward. The Novel and the Referent: Essays in the Semiotics and Ideology of Nineteenth-Century Novelistic Realism. Ann Arbor, Mich.: University Microfilms International, 1978.

Lodge, David. The Language of Fiction. London: Routledge & Kegan Paul; New York: Columbia University Press, 1966.

——. "Middlemarch and the Idea of the Classic Realist Text." In After Bakhtin: Essays on Fiction and Criticism, 45–56, London: Routledge, 1990.

——. The Modes of Modernist Writing. Ithaca: Cornell University Press, 1977.

Lotz, Hans-Joachim. Die Genese des Realismus in der französischen Literaturästhetik. Heidelberg: Carl Winter, 1984.

——. "L'Image iréelle, bizarre et mythique de Paris chez Balzac et Baudelaire." In Paris au XIXè siècle, 93–106. Lyons: Presses universitaires, 1984.

Lowes, John Livingstone. The Road to Xanadu. Boston: Houghton Mifflin, 1927.

Lubbock, Percy. The Craft of Fiction. 1926. Reprint, London: Jonathan Cape, 1954.

Lucente, Gregory. The Narrative of Realism and Myth: Verga, Lawrence, Faulkner, Pavese. Baltimore: Johns Hopkins University Press, 1981.

Lukács, György. "Auf der Suche nach dem Bürger." In Thomas Mann, 9–48. Berlin: Aufbau, 1949.

———. "Narrate or Describe?" In *Writer and Critic*, 110–48, trans. Arthur Kahn. London: Merlin, 1970; New York: Grosset & Dunlap, 1974.

———. *Studies in European Realism*. Trans. Edith Bone. London: Hillway, 1950.

Lutwack, Leonard. *The Role of Place in Literature*. Syracuse: Syracuse University Press, 1984.

Macherey, Pierre. "Balzac's *Les Paysans*: A Disparate Text." In *A Theory of Literary Production*, 258–98, trans. Geoffrey Wall. London: Routledge & Kegan Paul, 1978.

Mann, Karen. *The Language That Makes George Eliot*. Baltimore: Johns Hopkins University Press, 1983.

Marcus, Steven. "Human Nature, Social Orders, and Nineteenth-Century Systems of Explanation: Starting with George Eliot." *Salmagundi* 26 (1975): 20–42.

Marhofer, Esther. "*Le Curé de Tours*: A Study in Topography." In *Studies in Balzac's Realism*, 91–120, ed. W. Preston Dargan and W. L. Crain. 1932. Reprint, Chicago: University of Chicago Press, 1967.

Matter, Harry, ed. *Die Literatur über Thomas Mann: Eine Bibliographie*, especially "Lübeck," 338–44. Berlin: Aufbau, 1972.

Max, Stefan. *Les Métamorphoses de la grande ville dans les "Rougon-Macquart."* Paris: Nizet, 1966.

McCarthy, Mary Susan. *Balzac and His Reader: A Study in the Creation of Meaning*. Columbia: University of Missouri Press, 1982.

McKay, Janet Holmgren. *Narration and Discourse in American Realist Fiction*. Philadelphia: University of Pennsylvania Press, 1982.

Meinong, Alexis. "The Theory of Objects." In *Realism and the Background of Phenomenology*, 76–117, ed. Roderick Chisholm. Glencoe, IL.: Free Press, 1960. First published in *Untersuchungen zur Gegenstandstheorie und Psychologie*. Leipzig, 1904.

Miller, David. *Narrative and Its Discontents*. Princeton: Princeton University Press, 1981.

Miller, J. Hillis. *The Ethics of Reading*. New York: Columbia University Press, 1987.

———. "The Fiction of Realism: *Sketches by Boz, Oliver Twist*, and Cruikshank's Illustrations." In *Dickens Centennial Essays*, 85–153, ed. Ada Nisbet and Blake Nevius. Berkeley: University of California Press, 1971.

———. "Optic and Semiotic in *Middlemarch*." In *The Worlds of Victorian Fiction*, 125–45, ed. Jerome H. Buckley. Cambridge, Mass.: Harvard University Press, 1975.

Minder, Robert. *Paris in der neueren französischen Literatur 1770–1890*. Wiesbaden: Steiner, 1965.

Mittérand, Henri. "Fonction narratif et fonction mimétique: Les personnages de *Germinal*." *Poétique* 16 (1973): 477–90.

———. "Le Lieu et le sens: L'espace parisien dans *Ferragus* de Balzac." In *Le Discours du roman*, 189–212. Paris: Presses universitaires de France, 1980.

Mizruhi, Susan L. *The Power of Historical Knowledge: Narrating the Past in Hawthorne, James, and Dreiser*. Princeton: Princeton University Press, 1988.

Morgan, Janet. "The Meanings of *Vraisemblance* in French Classical Theory." *Modern Language Review* 81, no. 2 (1986): 293–304.

Moulden, Ken, and Gero von Wilpert, eds. *Buddenbrooks-Handbuch*. Stuttgart: Alfred Körner, 1988.

Mozet, Nicole. *La Ville de province dans l'oeuvre de Balzac*. Paris: SEDES / CDU, 1982.

Mukarovsky, Jan. "Standard Language and Poetic Language." In *A Prague School Reader on Aesthetics, Literary Structure, and Style*, 17–30, ed. Paul L. Garvin. Washington, D.C.: Georgetown University Press, 1964.

Müller, Klaus-Detlef. "Realismus als Provokation." In *Bürgerlicher Realismus*, 1–25. Königstein: Athenäum, 1971.

Nelson, Brian. "Realism: Model or Mirage?" *Romance Studies* 1 (1972): 1–17.

Nochlin, Linda. *Realism*. Harmondsworth: Penguin, 1971.

Ong, Walter J. "The Writer's Audience Is Always a Fiction." *PMLA* 90, no. 1 (1975): 9–21.

Parsons, Terence. "The Methodology of Nonexistence." *Journal of Philosophy* 76, no. 11 (1979): 649–62.

Pavel, Thomas. *Fictional Worlds*. Cambridge, Mass.: Harvard University Press, 1986.

Peckham, Morse. "Is the Problem of Literary Realism a Pseudo-Problem?" *Critique: Studies in Modern Fiction* 12 (1970): 95–112.

Petrey, Sandy. "Castration, Speech Acts, and the Realist Difference: S/Z versus *Sarrasine*." *PMLA* 102, no. 2 (1987): 153–65.

———. *Realism and Revolution*. Ithaca: Cornell University Press, 1988.

Pike, Burton. *The Image of the City in Modern Literature*. Princeton: Princeton University Press, 1981.

Porter, Dennis. "Flaubert and the Difficulty of Reading." *Nineteenth-Century French Studies* 12, no. 3 (1984): 366–78.

Pradalié, Georges. *Balzac historien*. Paris: Presses universitaires de France, 1955.

Pratt, John Clark, and Victor A. Neufeldt, eds. *George Eliot's "Middlemarch" Notebooks: A Transcription*. Berkeley: University of California Press, 1979.

Preminger, Alex, ed., with Frank Warnke and O. B. Hardison. *Encyclopedia of Poetry and Poetics*. Princeton: Princeton University Press, 1965.

Prendergast, Christopher. *Balzac: Fiction and Melodrama*. London: Edward Arnold; New York: Meier & Holmes, 1978.

———. *The Order of Mimesis*. Cambridge: Cambridge University Press, 1986.

Price, Martin. *Forms of Life: Character and Moral Imagination in the Novel*. New Haven: Yale University Press, 1983.

Pugh, Anthony C. "Reflecting on Realism." *Romance Studies* 1 (1972): 112–30.

Putnam, Hilary. "Is There a Fact of the Matter about Fiction?" *Poetics Today* 4, no. 1 (1983): 77–81.

Raser, George B. *Guide to Balzac's Paris*. Choisy-le-Roi: Imprimerie de France, 1964.

"Realism: A Symposium." *Monatshefte* 59, no. 2 (1967): 97–130.

Reed, T. J. *Thomas Mann: The Uses of Tradition*. Oxford: Clarendon Press, 1974.

Ricoeur, Paul. *La Métaphore vive*. Paris: Editions de minuit, 1975. *The Rule of Metaphor: Multidisciplinary Studies in the Creation of Meaning in Language*. Trans. Robert Czerny, with Kathleen McLaughlin and John Costello, S. J. Toronto: University of Toronto Press, 1977.

Ridley, Hugh. *Mann: Buddenbrooks*. Cambridge: Cambridge University Press, 1987.

Riffaterre, Michael. "Explaining Literary Phenomena." In *Text Production*, 1–25. New York: Columbia University Press, 1983.

———. *Fictional Truth*. Baltimore: Johns Hopkins University Press, 1990.

Rignall, John. *Realist Fiction and the Strolling Spectator*. London: Routledge, 1992.

Ritchie, J.M. "The Ambivalence of 'Realism' in German Literature 1830–1880." *Orbis Litterarum* 15 (1961): 200–17.

Robert, Marthe. *Les Origines du roman et le roman des origines*. Paris: Grasset, 1972. *Origins of the Novel*. Trans. Sacha Rabinovitch. Bloomington: Indiana University Press, 1980.

Romano, John. *Dickens and Reality*. New York: Columbia University Press, 1978.

Royer, Jean. "Lübecker Gotik und Lübercker Strassenbild als Leitmotiv in *Buddenbrooks*." *Nordelbingen* 33 (1964): 136–50.

Sagave, Pierre-Paul. "Zur Geschichtlichkeit von Thomas Manns Jugendroman: Bürgerliches Klassenbewusstsein und kapitalistische Praxis in *Buddenbrooks*." In *Literaturwissenschaft und Geschichtsphilosophie: Festschrift für Wilhelm Emrich*, 436–52. Berlin: Aufbau, 1975.

Sartre, Jean-Paul. *Qu'est-ce que la littérature?* Paris: Gallimard, 1945.

Schama, Simon. *Dead Certainties (Unwarranted Speculations)*. New York: Knopf, 1991.

Schor, Naomi. "Details and Realism." *Poetics Today* 5, no. 4 (1984): 701–10.

——. "Fiction as Interpretation / Interpretation as Fiction." In *The Reader in the Text*, 165–82, ed. Susan R. Suleiman and Inge Crosman. Princeton: Princeton University Press, 1980.

Schwarz, Egon. "Grundsätzliches zum literarischen Realismus." *Monakshefte* 59, no. 2 (1967): 100–106.

Searle, John R. "The Logical Status of Fictional Discourse." *New Literary History* 6, no. 2 (1975): 319–32.

Smethhurst, Colin. "Balzac and Realism." *Romance Studies* 1 (1972): 64–76.

Smith, Barbara Herrnstein. *On the Margins of Discourse*. Chicago: University of Chicago Press, 1978.

Smith, Jane S. "The Reader as Part of the Fiction: *Middlemarch*." *Texas Studies in Literature* 19 (1977): 188–203.

Spady, Carole Howe. "The Dynamics of Reader Response in *Middlemarch*." *Rackham Literary Studies* 9 (1978): 64–75.

Spariosu, Mihai, ed. *Mimesis in Contemporary Theory: An Interdisciplinary Approach*. Philadelphia: John Benjamins Publishing, 1984.

Steele, H. Meili. *Realism and the Drama of Reference: Strategies of Representation in Balzac, Flaubert, and James*. University Park: Pennsylvania State University Press, 1988.

Steinmetz, Horst. "Der vergessene Leser: Provokatorische Bemerkungen zum Realismusproblem." In *Dichter und Leser*, 113–33, ed. Ferdinand von Ingen. Groningen: Wolters-Noordhoff, 1972.

Stern, J. P. *On Realism*. London: Routledge & Kegan Paul, 1973.

Stierle, Karlheinz. "The Reading of Fictional Texts." In *The Reader in the Text*, 83–105, ed. Susan R. Suleiman and Inge Crosman. Princeton: Princeton University Press, 1980.

Stowe, William. *Balzac, James, and the Realist Novel*. Princeton: Princeton University Press, 1983.

Suleiman, Susan R., and Inge Crosman, eds. *The Reader in the Text*. Princeton: Princeton University Press, 1980.

Swales, Martin. " 'Neglecting the Weight of the Elephant . . . ': German Prose Fiction and European Realism." *Modern Language Review* 83, no. 4 (1988): 882–94.

——. *Thomas Mann: A Study*. London: Heinemann; Totowa, N.J.: Rowman & Littlefield, 1980.

Swann, Brian. "*Middlemarch*: Realism and Symbolic Form." *English Literary History* 39 (1972): 279–308.

"A Symposium on Realism." *Comparative Literature* 3, no. 3 (1951): 193–285.

Tallis, Raymond. *In Defence of Realism*. London: Arnold, 1988.

Tau, Max. *Der assoziative Faktor in der Landschafts- und Ortsdarstellung Theodor Fontanes*. Oldenburg: Schulze & Schwarz, 1928.

Thomas, Jennie. *Reading "Middlemarch."* Ann Arbor, Mich.: UMI Research Press, 1987.

Timms, Edward, and David Kelley, eds. *Unreal City: Urban Experience in Modern European Literature.* Manchester: Manchester University Press, 1985.

Todorov, Tzvetan. "The Notion of Literature." *New Literary History* 5, no. 1 (1973): 5–16.

——. *La Poétique de la prose.* Paris: Editions du Seuil, 1971. Trans. Richard Howard. Ithaca: Cornell University Press, 1977.

——. "Reading as Construction." In *The Reader in the Text,* 67–82, ed. Susan R. Suleiman and Inge Crosman. Princeton: Princeton University Press, 1980.

Tompkins, Jane P. "The Reader in History: The Changing Shape of Literary Response." In *Reader-Response Criticism,* 201–32, ed. Jane P. Tompkins. Baltimore: Johns Hopkins University Press, 1980.

Turner, Victor. "Social Dramas and Stories about Them." *Critical Inquiry* 7, no. 1 (1980): 141–68.

Vaihinger, Hans. *Die Philosophie als-ob: System der theoretischen, praktischen und religiösen Fiktionen der Menschheit auf Grund eines idealistischen Positivismus.* Leipzig: Meiner, 1911.

Van Inwagen, Peter. "Creatures of Fiction." *American Philosophical Quarterly* 14, no. 4 (1977): 299–309.

Walton, Kendall L. "Appreciating Fictions: Suspending Disbelief or Pretending Belief?" *Dispositio* 5, no. 13 (1981): 1–18.

——. "How Remote are Fictional Worlds from the Real World?" *Journal of Aesthetics and Art Criticism* 38, no. 1 (1978): 11–23.

——. *Mimesis as Make-Believe.* Cambridge, Mass.: Harvard University Press, 1990.

——. "Points of View in Narrative and Depictive Representation." *Noûs* 10, no. 1 (1976): 49–61.

Warhol, Robyn R. "Toward a Theory of the Engaging Narrator: Earnest Interventions in Gaskell, Stowe, and Eliot." *PMLA* 101, no. 5 (1986): 811–18.

Watt, Ian. *The Rise of the Novel.* Berkeley: University of California Press, 1957.

Weimann, Robert. "History, Appropriation, and the Uses of Representation in Modern Narrative." In *The Aims of Representation: Subject / Text / History,* 175–215, ed. Murray Krieger. New York: Columbia University Press, 1987.

Weisgerber, Jean. *L'espace romanesque.* Lausanne: Editions l'age d'homme, 1978.

Wellek, René. "The Concept of Realism in Literary Scholarship." In *Concepts of Criticism,* 222–55, ed. Stephen J. Nichols Jr. New Haven: Yale University Press, 1963.

Welty, Eudora. "Place in Fiction." *South Atlantic Quarterly* 55 (1956): 57–72.

White, Hayden. *Metahistory.* Baltimore: Johns Hopkins University Press, 1973.

Williams, D. A., ed. *The Monster in the Mirror.* London: Oxford University Press, 1978.

Williams, Raymond. *The Country and the City.* London: Chatto & Windus; New York: Oxford University Press, 1973.

——. "The Knowable Community in George Eliot's Novels." *Novel* 2, no. 3 (1969): 255–68.

Wimmers, Inge Crosman. *Poetics of Reading.* Princeton: Princeton University Press, 1988.

Young, Edward. *Conjectures on Original Composition.* New York: Stechert, 1917.

Zavarzadeh, Mas'ud. *The Mythopoeic Reality: The Postwar American Nonfiction Novel.* Urbana: University of Illinois Press, 1976.

Zoran, Gabriel. "Towards a Theory of Space in Narrative." *Poetics Today* 5, no. 2 (1984): 309–35.

Index

Index

Lilian R. Furst is Marcel Bataillon Professor of Comparative Literature at the University of North Carolina, Chapel Hill. Her recent books include *Fictions of Romantic Irony* (1984), *L'Assommoir: A Working Woman's Life* (1990), *Through the Lens of the Reader: Explorations of European Narrative* (1992), *Realism* (1992), and, with Desider Furst, an autobiography in two voices, *Home Is Somewhere Else* (1994).